ISLAM AND IMPERIALISM IN SENEGAL

Hoover Institution Publications

ISLAM AND IMPERIALISM
IN SENEGAL

Sine-Saloum, 1847–1914

————————◆————————

MARTIN A. KLEIN

Published for the
Hoover Institution on War, Revolution and Peace
by Stanford University Press, Stanford, California, 1968

Stanford University Press
Stanford, California
© 1968 by the Board of Trustees of the
Leland Stanford Junior University
Printed in the United States of America
L.C. 67-26527

To the N'Gom family of Kaolack
who opened many doors
and made the experience of Senegal
a rewarding one

PREFACE

THE RECENT GROWTH of interest in African history has produced few works dealing with the transition from traditional authority to the colonial system. Most historians have preferred to deal either with periods in which African states controlled their own destinies or with the development of modern nationalism. Many have also preferred to deal with large areas and broad questions, with the whole continent or a large part of it. As a result, they make too many generalizations that are not supported by sound research on limited areas and restricted time periods. This study, by contrast, concentrates on one complex of states during a period of transition.

The Serer states are interesting for several reasons. They are a meeting ground of three worlds—the worlds of the European Catholic, the pagan African, and the Moslem African. The people of the Serer states, along with the Wolof people and the Poular-speaking peoples, constitute a very close and interrelated group. The Serer are especially interesting because of their resistance to change, or rather because of the direction change has taken with them. Their traditional culture and religion have been very resilient, resisting for a long time both Moslem and Catholic missionary efforts. Furthermore, though the Serer have adapted to a cash-crop and market economy, they have been less dependent on the market, and thus less liable to debt than their neighbors.

My decision to concentrate on political units and not on a cultural entity was dictated both by the nature of the archives and by my central concern with the structure of power. The states involved are Sine and Saloum, two 400-year-old Serer states, and the neighboring Moslem Wolof state founded by Ma Bâ in Rip in 1861. After 1887, the date of the French conquest, this study is concerned with the *cercle* of Sine-Saloum and the *cercle* of Nioro (which were combined in 1904). It thus discusses three traditional states, two administrative units, and five ethnic groups speaking four different languages.

My account begins in 1847 with the earliest French gunboat visits to the Saloum River. A year later, the first Catholic missionaries arrived at Joal, on the coast of Sine. In 1849, a French navy lieutenant signed commercial treaties with Sine and Saloum; they were the last equal treaties between French and African rulers. An active trade in peanuts had already begun, and it led to French invasions of Sine and Saloum in 1859 and 1861, and to new treaties less favorable to the Serer states. In 1887, after a generation in which the Serer states were pressed both by French imperialists and by Moslem revolutionaries, a lightning campaign established French authority in the area.

The victory of 1887 was the end of one process and the beginning of another. In 1887, the French writ did not extend far. To make its authority effective, the colonial regime had to come to terms with both the traditional elites and the rising Moslem elites. Direct administration involved not so much the elimination of the chiefs as the destruction of their authority in areas where the French chose to make policy. Traditional political institutions were exploited rather than abolished, and the traditional state was transformed into a modern bureaucratic structure. The colonial administration co-opted the old elites into its governmental bureaucracy, and unwittingly consigned many of their traditional functions to the Moslem elites. As a result, even though Islam and the Moslem elites were defeated in 1887, they played a dominant role in the processes of integration that succeeded a generation of war and revolution.

This study is based primarily on written sources—documents found in archives in Paris, London, Dakar, and Bathurst. Except for letters sent by African chiefs, these documents were written by outsiders, many of whom were unsympathetic to the cultures they described, and lacked a real understanding of the people involved. Trying to piece together a complete picture from these accounts, I became painfully aware of the problem that always faces the historian who deals with an alien culture. He can participate in the culture he describes only by a vigorous extension of his imagination.

I have supplemented the documents with a study of the oral traditions. The web of tradition in the Serer states is a very complex one, for not only does every state have its unique traditions, but so too does every family and every village. I used three types of informants. The first, the traditional historians and praise-sayers (*griots*), were of limited value, though the best among them, those motivated by high standards of professional integrity, were valuable sources. Traditionally paid to say what the patron wants to hear, many griots are mercenary; moreover, their distortions are not always predictable. The second group, members of chiefly lineages with an interest in family history, were much more valuable. Comparing the griots' traditions with the royal traditions allowed me to correct distortions and form a reasonably accurate picture of pre-colonial Serer society. Aged peasants in rural villages comprised the third group, which was potentially as valuable as the second. Generally these men knew particular versions of the traditions surrounding the origin of their states and their villages, as well as traditions associated with nearby villages. They were difficult to work with because, though hospitable, they were often reluctant to talk freely with a stranger. When this barrier was surmounted, it was generally because they knew and trusted my interpreter.

Although oral traditions can be distorted, the distortions are not necessarily greater than those in written documents. Much oral history is confirmed by written sources, and I have reason to believe that, in at least one case, a tradition was more accurate than a report submitted by a French army officer. Even when it is accurate, however, the oral tradition may not give us what we want to know. Traditions are important as a source of property rights and status, but one cannot expect traditions to provide sociological analysis, except occasionally between the lines. The

father of Léopold Sédar Senghor was a peasant who became a
wealthy trader, and yet among the sons of his neighbors he is
remembered only for being "ngol," the possessor of many cattle.
Nevertheless, for all its limitations, the oral tradition is often the
only source we have.

I would like to thank the many people who not only have made
this study possible, but also have made it a rewarding and often
exciting experience. First thanks go to Professors S. William Hal-
perin and Lloyd A. Fallers of the University of Chicago, who
supervised this work in its original form as a doctoral dissertation, and Professor Jan Vansina of the University of Wisconsin,
who stimulated me both as a teacher and as a scholar. Professor
Vansina's book, *Oral Tradition*, was especially helpful.

A number of scholars in France and in Senegal also helped me;
they include Dr. G. Debien, Dr. Abdoulaye Ly, Dr. Paul Pelissier, M. Vincent Monteil, now director of the Institut Fonda-
mental d'Afrique Noire (I.F.A.N.), M. Pathé Diagne, Governor
Hubert Deschamps, and M. Roger Pasquier. I must also specially
mention M. Samba N'Diaye of I.F.A.N. and Father Henri Gravrand of Fatick, both of whom are engaged in important research
on the Serer and who gave freely of their time and knowledge.

It is not possible to thank all the Senegalese who were generous
with their hospitality and their knowledge. For their unsolicited
aid I am greatly indebted to M. Khar N'Doffène Diouf, Al Hajj
Ibrahima Niasse, and Dr. Mamadu Bâ of Kaolack. In addition,
Abdou Boury Bâ, *chef d'arrondissement* at Birkelane, and Bur
Sine Mahecor Diouf gave freely from their great knowledge of
the oral tradition. My other informants are listed in the Bibliography—all were generous and helpful. I am grateful to M. Pierre
Basse, who took me to the M'Bissel area where Sine was born,
and to M. Papa N'Diogou Senghor for a very rewarding after-
noon at the Senghor family homestead in Djilas. In the Gambia,
I would like to thank Abdoulaye A. N'Jai and Peter Cavay of
Yundum College and Malik Secka of Bathurst. Particularly I
thank the family to whom this book is dedicated; the home of
M. Alboury N'Gom in Kaolack was my base for many trips, and

his sons, Babacar, Boubakar, Doudou, and Habib, were invaluable guides, interpreters, and friends.

Professor Vansina, M. Monteil, M. Pasquier, G. Wesley Johnson, Peter Duignan, Lewis Gann, Ernst Benjamin, and Alan Hoben gave helpful criticism of earlier versions. My most severe and most helpful critic has been my wife, who braved many a hot dusty Senegalese road while we searched for griots and who waged a mighty war on clichés during the writing of the book.

The research and the writing were done on grants from the Foreign Area Training Program and the Hoover Institution. I am responsible for all translations, all ideas, and any errors.

M. A. K.

CONTENTS

ILLUSTRATIONS

AFRICAN RULERS
AND FRENCH OFFICIALS

RULERS OF SINE AND SALOUM, 1825 TO THE PRESENT

Sine

Ama Diouf Faye	c. 1825–53	Dialigui Sira Diouf	1885–86
Coumba N'Doffène Diouf	1853–71	Niokhorbaye Diouf	1886–87
Sanoumon Faye	1871–78	M'Backé Deb N'Diaye	1887–98
Semou Mack Diouf	1878–82	Coumba N'Doffène	
Amadi Baro Diouf	1882–84	Diouf	1898–1924
M'Backé Kodou N'Diaye		Mahecor Diouf	1924–
(M'Backé Mack)	1884–85		

Saloum

Ballé N'Dougou N'Dao	1825–53	Semou Djimit Diouf	1894–98
Bala Adam N'Diaye	1853–56	N'Déné Diémou N'Dao	1898–1901
Coumba N'Dama M'Bodj	1856–59	N'Déné Diogop Diouf	1901–11
Samba Laobé Fall	1859–64	Semou N'Gouye Diouf	1911–13
Fakha Fall	1864–71	Gori Diouf	1913–19
Niahoul M'Bodj	1871–74	Mahava Tioro Diouf	1919–35
Sadiouka M'Bodj	1874–79	Fodé N'Gouye Diouf	1935–
Guédel M'Bodj	1879–94		

ADMINISTRATORS OF SINE–SALOUM, 1887–1909

Librecht d'Albreca	1887	Victor Valantin	
E. A. Martin	1887–88	(interim)	1898
Lucien Rabourdin	1888	Georges Poulet	1898–99
J. Génébre	1888–90	Victor Valantin	
Ernest Noirot	1890–96	(interim)	1899–1900
Abdoulaye Diaw		Victor Allys	1900–1901
(interim)	1896	Amédée Charles Lefil-	
Hippolyte Alsace	1896–98	liâtre	1901–9

GOVERNORS OF SENEGAL AND GOVERNORS-GENERAL OF FRENCH WEST AFRICA, 1850–1915

Governors[a]			
Auguste Protet	1850–54	René Servatius	1882–83
Louis L. C. Faidherbe	1854–61	A. Seignac-Lesseps	1884–86
J. B. Jauréguibéry	1861–63	Genouille	1886–88
Louis L. C. Faidherbe	1863–65	Léon Emile Clément-	
J. M. E. Pinet-Laprade	1865–69	Thomas	1888–90
François Xavier Valière	1869–76	Henri de Lamothe	1890–95
Louis Brière de l'Isle	1876–81		
Louis Ferdinand		Governors-General[b]	
De Lanneau	1881	E. Chaudié	1895–1900
Henri Philibert Canard	1881–82	Noël Ballay	1900–1902
Aristide Vallon	1882	Ernest Roume	1902–8
		William Ponty	1908–15

[a] This list does not include the names of interim Governors.

[b] In 1895, when the Federation was formed, the title "Governor of Senegal" was superseded by the title "Governor-General of French West Africa." The Governor-General ruled Senegal directly and supervised the other territories until, in 1904, Lieutenant Governors with authority to govern directly were appointed for each of the territories. Camille Guy was the first such Lieutenant Governor for Senegal.

ISLAM AND IMPERIALISM IN SENEGAL

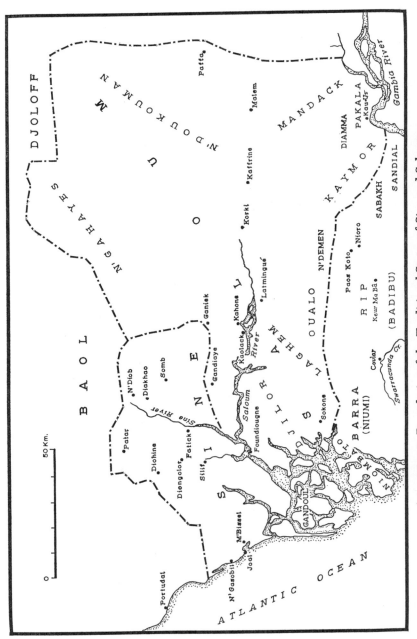

Approximate Boundaries of the Traditional States of Sine and Saloum

THE LAND AND THE PEOPLE

An ASPHALT ROAD connects Dakar with the rich peanut-producing lands of Sine-Saloum. Every December, about a month after the end of the rains, this highway suddenly turns into a bustling trade artery as a long line of trailer trucks starts moving the year's harvest to the ports of Kaolack and Dakar; the fast, heavy trucks contrast with the slow-moving donkeys carrying the peanuts to the market towns where the trucks take over.

Just east of Dakar the road runs through a brown and barren sandy stretch that makes Cape Verde's name seem very inappropriate. It passes factories and an oil refinery, and goes through Rufisque, once the capital of the peanut trade. It is now a quieter city, and its wide main street is barren and shadowless. From Rufisque the road moves into rural Senegal—first, into a scenic area of rolling hills dotted with straw-hutted peasant villages and plentiful, carefully maintained trees. Then it descends into the open flatness that is more typical of Senegal. This is Sine.

When I first drove through, it was late May, less than a month before the rains, and Sine looked dry, brown, and inhospitable. The peasants toiled diligently in the hot sun, clearing the soil, leaving extensive fields brushless and open, awaiting the rains. With the first rains, Sine's hard, unfriendly appearance gave way to a lush green growth, in places reminiscent of the American Middle West. In less than three months, the millet was over ten feet high, and no place could have looked more fertile than Sine, where most of the land is cultivated.

Throughout the summer, the peasants are constantly in the fields. When the planting is done, the weeding begins; it continues almost until it is time to harvest. With the end of the rains in November, green gives way to brown quicker than the peasants can bring in their crops. The peanuts are sold, and the solid straw granaries are repaired and made ready to receive the millet crop. The weather becomes cool and dry. This is the time of festivities, the time for marriages and circumcision ceremonies. It is also the beginning of the waiting time.

The Senegalese peasants have long been prisoners of the seasonal cycle. Every June, as the humidity builds up and the granaries empty, they carefully prepare their fields and wait. If the rain does not come—and nature is very fickle—then hunger will be their lot the following year. Senegal straddles several climatic zones. Only the Senegal River saves northern Senegal from the complete aridity of the desert. Dakar averages about 21 inches of rain a year; Kaolack, less than 40 miles further south, gets over 30; and Bathurst gets 42, all of this in the four months between late June and early November.[1] If the peasant could count on this much rain, he would be fortunate. But in some years, he receives too much; in others, the humidity builds up, and nothing happens until late July or August.[a]

And yet Senegal has long been a land of peasants, dependent on the land for their livelihood. The only exceptions are the peoples of the coastal areas, who combine fishing with farming, and the Fulbe herdsmen found in all parts of Senegal. Of the peasants in the area, the Serer alone have developed an intensive form of agriculture. One does not find in Serer areas the shifting cultivation common elsewhere in Africa. The Serer, especially those of Sine, do not move, and the visitor does not see fields that have been returned to bush to restore their fertility. Instead, the Serer early developed a two-field system; one field was devoted to millet, and the other was left fallow and used to pasture cattle. With the development of the peanut trade, peanuts were planted third in the rotation.

[1] Numbers refer to Notes (pp. 243–59), primarily citations of sources. Footnotes are designated by letters.

[a] R. Rousseau, "Les Pluies au Sénégal 1887 à 1927," *Bulletin du Comité d'Etudes Historiques et Scientifiques de l'Afrique Occidentale Française* (hereafter *BCEHS*), XIV (1931), 168. Over a forty-year period, annual rainfall at Kaolack varied from 24 to 48 inches, at Dakar from under 10 to 37 inches.

The Serer peasant carefully protects selected trees, thus giving his lands a park-like appearance, and he systematically manures his fields, staking out his cattle first in one area, then in another. Paul Pelissier has suggested that the Serer peasant's devotion to his land may have developed from the herdsman's devotion to his cattle, for much of the successful peasant's surplus wealth goes into cattle. At the same time, the Serer peasant is proud of his full granaries, and less likely than his neighbors to borrow to feed his family during the "hungry season," the two months before the first millet is ripe. Though he devotes extensive land to peanuts, the Serer peasant has resisted the temptations of monoculture—which placed the Wolof peasants in the hands of moneylenders—and he usually grows enough to feed his family.[2] The Wolof are more liable to debt, and since they do not protect their lands as carefully as the Serer do, their soil often erodes. The Serer have made a better adaptation to economic change because they have changed less. They were able to fit a cash crop into their cycle without radically changing their work patterns.[b]

As the road passes south through Sine, it goes through stretches of completely flat, barren land, land so saline (especially near the ocean and the Saloum River) that farming is impossible. A fast car moves quickly through these stretches, crosses the unmarked border between Sine and Saloum, and within fifteen minutes is in Kaolack, Senegal's second port. Kaolack is dominated by one major activity— the export of peanuts. The city sits near the limit of navigation of the Saloum River, a misnamed inlet of the Atlantic Ocean. Above the city the stream is a narrow trickle; even in the rainy season it does not fill the ample river bed that formed in a wetter age. The economic development of the Kaolack area was long limited by the difficulty oceangoing vessels had in crossing the bar and traversing the passages between the islands in the mouth of the inlet. The

[b] An economist might suggest that the peasant who borrows and who buys much of his food with revenue from the sale of a cash crop is maximizing his own interest. However, most debt is not for productive purposes, and peasants who meet their own food needs seem better off.

channel has been regularly dredged since the turn of the century, and oceangoing vessels can dock here to load peanuts and peanut oil for European markets. Smaller boats can travel up the Sine River, a branch of the Saloum, to Fatick, the economic center of Sine.

The growth of Kaolack has been aided by an artificial frontier that cuts part of Senegal off from the Gambia River, its natural trade outlet. The Gambia is the finest river route to the interior in West Africa; oceangoing vessels sail up it for 150 miles, and smaller boats can go fifty miles further. Several tributaries enter the Gambia from the north. These were important trade arteries in the nineteenth century, when peanuts were moved by donkey, camel, and human labor to factories (trading stations) on water transport routes. Farming naturally tended to be most intensive near these factories.

With the exception of Niombato, a small coastal region that straddles the Senegal-Gambia border, the territory north of the Gambia River has long been largely free of thick undergrowth, and has had no other natural barriers to impede trade or the movement of troops. The land is open, and only the twisted baobab trees break its monotony.

The People

The sandy soils of Senegal have for centuries nutured a variety of peoples, most of them related by language and custom, and a network of states varying in size from a half-dozen villages to several hundred thousand people. A striking characteristic of the area is that its political and cultural geography underwent no radical changes in the four centuries between the arrival of the first Portuguese navigator, Alvise Cadamosto, in 1455, and the French conquest. There had been migrations, dynastic changes, revolutions, and internal structural changes, but the peoples and states noted by Cadamosto and Valentim Fernandes in the fifteenth century were still in approximately the same places as in the nineteenth century.

The major groups still living in Sine-Saloum in the last century were the Serer, the Wolof, the Fulbe, the Toucouleur, and the Mandinka peoples.[c] A 1904 monograph reported the following census figures for the four provinces into which the French had divided the region.[d]

	Sine	W. Saloum	E. Saloum	Nioro	Total
Serer	62,560	13,860	—	170	76,590
Wolof	—	12,322	16,969	12,924	42,215
Fulbe	3,744	7,099	3,834	4,246	18,923
Toucouleur	455	547	1,911	2,899	5,802
Mandinka	139	3,552	1,297	354	5,342
Others	—	108	—	115	223
	66,898	37,488	24,011	20,698	149,095

The population of Saloum was probably substantially larger before the religious wars began in the 1860's.

Confusion about which peoples should be called Serer has continued to the present time, when the classification "Serer and Niominka" is used to refer to a number of groups whose institutions vary radically. The largest of these groups is the Serer-Sine, who live in Sine and Saloum. Two neighboring peoples, the Niominka of the Saloum delta islands, and the Serer-N'Diéghem, who live east of Portudal and M'Bour, speak closely related dialects, but differ from the Serer-Sine in two respects. They have an egalitarian social structure, and have not participated in complex political systems. The Nones of the Thiès area, the N'Doute of southern Cayor, and the Safen of southern Baol speak languages of W. J. Pichl's Cangin group.[3] Nevertheless, for centuries travelers identified all except one of these peoples as the Serer (or "Sereris"). The Serer-Sine were generally identified in travelers' accounts as "Barbacajis" or "Barbesins," that is, people of the Bur Sine. In this study I will use the term Serer to refer only to the Serer-Sine.

The Serer language was very similar to the languages spoken

---

[c] All are Negro peoples very similar to each other in appearance except for the Fulbe, who are light-skinned Negroes.

[d] ARS, 1 G 290. (Archives and the abbreviations used in citing them are listed at the beginning of the Notes, p. 243.) The four provinces of Sine-Saloum were similar in extent to the three traditional states, with Saloum divided in two. (See p. 225n for an account of a later division.) Like most head counts made in Africa, this probably underreports, especially in eastern Saloum and Nioro.

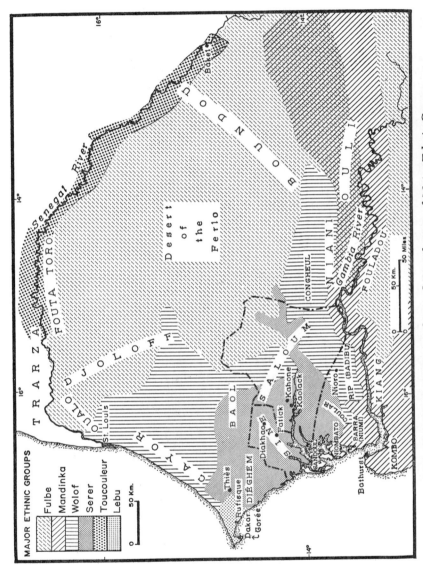

Major Kingdoms of Senegambia and Distribution of Major Ethnic Groups

MAJOR ETHNIC GROUPS

Fulbe
Mandinka
Wolof
Serer
Toucouleur
Lebu

0   50 Km.

Desert
of the
Ferlo

TRARZA

Senegal River

FOUTA TORO

BOUNDOU

DJOLOFF

WALO

OUALO

NIANI

OULI

BOULADOU

CAYOR

BAOL

SINE

SALOUM

CONGHEUL

Gambia River

RIP (BADIBU)

FOULAR

BARRA (NIUMI)

KIANG

KOMBO

St. Louis

Thiès
Rufisque
Dakar
Gorée
DIÉGHEM
Diakhao
Fatick
Kahone
Kaolack
Nioro
GOMBATO

Bathurst

Baket

50 Miles

50 Km.

by the Wolof, Fulbe, Toucouleur, and Mandinka peoples.[e] The customs and institutions of the five were also very much alike, although a commitment to pastoral life was unique to the Fulbe, and the practice of matrilineal inheritance was found only among the Serer. (Some writers have suggested, however, that the Wolof had matrilineal inheritance before the introduction of Moslem law.)[4] All five peoples had roughly parallel social structures, marked by the existence of distinct status groupings of nobles, free peasants, and slave warriors, as well as castes of artisans. The different states were constructed largely on the same model, and were tied to each other by diplomatic and marital alliances.[f] The most important factor dividing the peoples of Senegambia was the differential impact of Islam. In this, the Serer stood out as the one group that had undergone no conversion.

Two series of migrations brought these peoples to their present locations—the first a southward migration of Wolof, Serer, Toucouleur, and Fulbe, the second a movement of the Mandinka along both banks of the Gambia River during the thirteenth and fourteenth centuries.[5] The southward push was a consequence of the movement of Berber tribes into southern Mauritania, and of the appearance there in the eleventh century of the powerful Islamic sect, the Almoravides. It was part of a larger pattern of movement that resulted from the slow desiccation of the Sahara. The Serer states were the result of the merging of these two lines of migration. Serer-speaking migrants

[e] The Toucouleur and Fulbe speak the same language, Poular, which Greenberg classifies along with Serer-Sine and Wolof in the northern subgroup of the Niger-Congo family of languages. Greenberg's assertion that Poular is a West African language is based on its similarity to Serer-Sine. Mandinka is one of Greenberg's Mandingo languages, the second section of the Niger-Congo family. See J. H. Greenberg, "The Classification of Fulani," in *Studies in African Linguistic Classification* (New Haven, 1955), pp. 24–32. See also L. Homburger, "Le Sérère-Peul," *Journal de la Société des Africanistes*, IX (1939), 85–102.

[f] The participation of the Serer in a largely Wolof international system and the fact that Wolof was spoken at the factories have led to a certain confusion about the relations between the two groups. Some writers have assumed that the peasantry was Serer and the elite was Wolof. This was not true. Sine was solidly Serer. Saloum was mixed, but the Wolof were immigrants, not conquerors. See Pathé Diagne, "Les Royaumes Sérères," *Présence Africaine*, No. 54 (1965), pp. 142–72.

from the Senegal river valley had no complex political institutions until they came into contact with a small group of northward-moving Mandinkas. These Mandinka migrants founded several small states, and gradually extended their control over the Serer peoples; in time they took over much of the Serer culture as well as the Serer language. (Professor Pichl has pointed out that the Serer language shows almost no Mandinka influence; the Serer did take over the Wolof "Bur" in preference to "Mad," their own word for king.) The neighboring Serer N'Diéghem and the Niominka escaped being influenced by this merging of traditions. The kings, or Burs, of both Sine and Saloum were chosen from among the *guelowar*, the matrilineage that led the Mandinka migration.[6]

Sine and Saloum were later incorporated within the Djoloff Empire of the Wolof peoples; Saloum may, in fact, have been built up by Djoloff as a buffer state on the frontier of Mali, which occupied the southern part of Senegambia. By the middle of the fifteenth century, Djoloff no longer exercised effective dominion over Sine, and in the sixteenth century the successful revolt of the Wolof state of Cayor broke the Djoloff Empire up into its constituent units. From the time of the Cayor revolt to the middle of the nineteenth century, the balance of power within the Senegambian system was not radically changed. Certain states benefited from the slave trade more than others, but the benefits were not substantial enough to overturn the balance of power.

Social Structure

One of the results of the guelowar conquest and the participation of the Serer in the Senegambian state system was the elaboration of a hierarchical social structure. The Serer can be divided into five major status groups and a number of subgroups.[9]

---

[9] The term "status groups" is being used here to refer to groups with a well-defined common status. Though movement between certain of the groups was possible and all participated in the values and customs of the larger community, each can be said to have had to some degree a distinctive style of life and well-defined rules of behavior. On the term "status group," see the footnote in Max Weber, *The Theory of Social and Economic Organization*, trans. by A. M. Henderson and Talcott Parsons (Glencoe, Ill., 1947), pp. 347–88.

First, there was the nobility, which consisted of actual and potential holders of royal power and their relatives. In Sine and Saloum, only guelowar, members of the matrilineage of the Mandinka conquerors, could become Bur. Guelowar candidates could depend most on relatives who were not themselves contenders, and thus each candidate had around himself a group of trusted relatives.

Second, there were the *tyeddo*, the warriors who largely made up the entourages of the Burs and the other major chiefs. Chosen originally from the slave class and attached directly to the crown, they were called "slaves of the crown." In theory dependent on the Burs, they were, in fact, independent, powerful, and sometimes unruly. Vincent Monteil reports that in Cayor they had the power to choose or depose a Bur, and they exacted in exchange for their support the right to pillage the peasantry at will.[7] In Sine and Saloum, their position was not clearly so independent, but every major chief was to some degree the creature of his entourage. In the case of the Burs, this was a force that usually exceeded five hundred men.[h] Chiefly entourages also included *sourga*, free peasants who took service with powerful chiefs in exchange for maintenance.[8]

In the third and largest status group were the *jambur*, the commoners or free peasants. Higher in status than the tyeddo, they had less power, but they participated in the political system, and their consent was necessary for its operation. A number of major chiefs, including the second most important, the Grand Jaraf, were chosen from their ranks. By and large, they did not take part in fighting unless their villages or their perceived interests were threatened.

[h] Like the term "Serer," the term "tyeddo" has come to have several meanings. The French generally used the term to refer to all members of the power structure. Thus, the first census divided the population of Sine into "tyeddo" and "Serer," the latter word being used to mean peasant. The French made no distinctions between the different groups clustered around the holders of power. Historical circumstances have created a second ambiguity. The tyeddo was the group most resistant to Islam. Therefore, the terms "Moslem" and "tyeddo" were frequently used in opposition to each other, and "tyeddo" has come to mean pagan. I will use the word "tyeddo" to refer either to the "slaves of the crown" as a group or to military forces of the Serer and Wolof states.

There has never been any bar to marriage between people in the three top status groups, though the nobility tended to seek politically desirable marriages. The traditional account of the origin of the Serer states tells of a symbolically important marriage between the sister of the man who led the guelowar migration and a champion Serer wrestler. It is quite probable that within the entourages of Burs, members of the three groups moved quite freely, but they were differentiated by the positions and dignities to which each could aspire.

Fourth came a series of endogamous castes of which the most important was the griot. Caste status was inherited and was attached to an economic activity. Members of the castes of artisans (blacksmiths, jewelers, leatherworkers, weavers, and makers of wooden tools) were often attached to the wealthier and more powerful freeborn lineages. Each of these groups played a strikingly important role in economic life. The griots were the historians, the genealogists, the musicians, and the praise-sayers. Most griots were attached to families, and thus most historical accounts that were passed down from father to son had as their goal the glorification of a patron. The Bur was accompanied when he traveled by a troupe of griots who continually tapped small drums and chanted his praises. When Serer armies went into battle, the griots were there to sing their past triumphs. However, the most rigid of marital taboos was against marriage with griots. They could not be buried in soil, and their corpses were generally placed in the arms of giant baobab trees. At the same time, griots were well rewarded for their work and often became rather wealthy. Furthermore, the talented griot was respected for his accomplishments. The griot as a musician gave pleasure. As a praise-sayer, he was feared and catered to. As a genealogist, he was a source of legitimacy. As a historian, he was the society's collective memory.

Fifth and last were the slaves. Those who were not recruited into tyeddo ranks can be divided into two groups, trade slaves and domestic slaves. The trade slaves had been bought or taken as prisoners of war, and were usually sold before they formed any ties with the owner's family. The domestic slaves were members of an extended family, and were dependents of the head of that family. The slave was given land to farm for himself, but was obligated to work five mornings a week on his master's land. Though the sale of domestic slaves was not unknown, it was unusual. The slave was a member of the community, and he participated in its interrelationships and obligations. Slavery was more a matter of social status than property rights, and it is in this form that it has persisted into modern times.

The social structure of the Wolof, Toucouleur, and Mandinka groups was similar to that of the Serer, and it was possible for people to move from one of these groups to another at the same social level. Freedom of movement was especially valuable to those who contested power unsuccessfully. Frequently, the loser in a power struggle fled to a neighboring state. In some cases, the refugees received sufficient land and privileges to stay in their new homes.

In spite of the guelowar conquest, Toucouleur models seem to have been more important than Mandinka models in elaborating Serer social structure. Many of the status terms are of Poular origin (*badolo, tyeddo*), and stratification was most elaborate and most rigid among the Toucouleur. In fact, the imposition of caste and status-group lines, which do not exist among the Niominkas and the Serer N'Diéghem, seems to have been a late development. In certain fringe areas of Sine, there are no tyeddo, and local people can date within the last century or two the arrivals of members of different caste groups.[9]

The Political System

The two Serer states had many similarities and only a few significant structural differences. In both states, the Bur was the highest political and religious personality. He was the embodiment of state power, and the personification of the ancestors. In addition, he was charged with operating the state and with conciliating those forces beyond the control of man. An early Bur was deposed when "the sun became dark and the earth

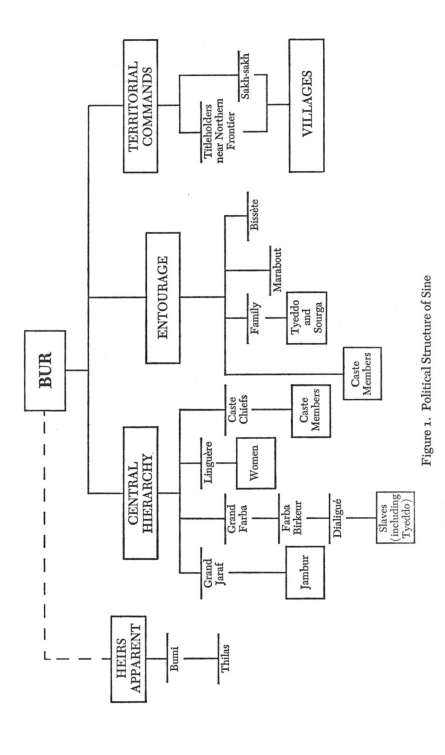

Figure 1. Political Structure of Sine

shook violently."[10] A Bur who reached old age was subject to ritual murder because it was believed he could no longer guarantee that cattle and women would remain fertile.[i]

In theory, the second-ranking chief, the Grand Jaraf, chose the Bur after consultations with the major titleholders, who formed an inner council. According to Diagne, the consent of the Farba, a chief who was chosen from among the tyeddo to speak for the servile classes, was also necessary.[11] The man selected as Bur was then confirmed by an assembly of tyeddo and jambur, which probably included village chiefs and family heads from all parts of the kingdom.

Rules governing the succession were qualified by the claims of de facto power. Since only male guelowar were eligible to become Bur, the birth of each male guelowar was reported to the Grand Jaraf, who was charged with keeping a mental *état civil*. In theory, the oldest male guelowar became Bur. In practice, the guelowar who could amass the most power ascended the throne. Birth, family ties, alliances with neighboring chiefs, and the ability to support a large entourage were all important. Constitutional processes merely confirmed and gave legitimacy to the most powerful. Succession conflicts were resolved speedily with minimal bloodshed, but the inevitability of a succession conflict was the most important weakness of the Serer states; and in the nineteenth century, this weakness created an opportunity for outside intervention.[j]

Just as the Grand Jaraf alone theoretically chose the Bur, so too he alone could order the distinctive drumbeat that meant that the Bur had been deposed. In practice he could give this order only when he had the support of a large part of the community. Deposing a Bur usually caused substantial conflict. The

[i] Henri Gravrand, *Visage africain de l'église* (Paris, 1961), p. 138. It is unlikely that ritual murder took place very often.

[j] The pattern of conflict differed from state to state. In Sine, matrilineal succession pressed candidates to seek support from partilineal relatives. (The Serer determine descent by both the mother's and the father's lines, but matrilineage plays a more important role in Serer life.) The result was that most succession conflicts revolved around three patrilineages. In Saloum, however, two branches of the guelowar matrilineage regularly opposed each other. On no occasion in the nineteenth century was there a confrontation of brothers.

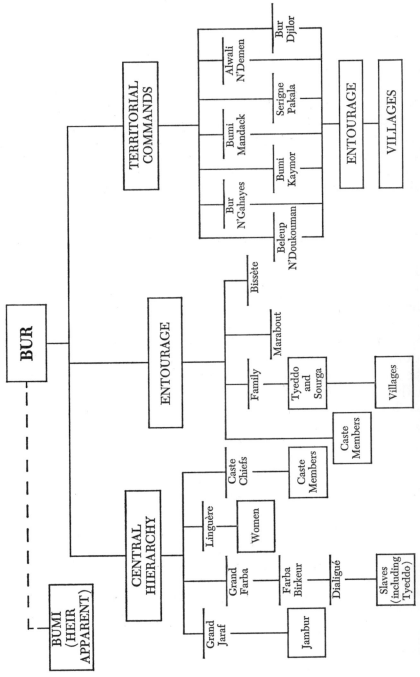

Figure 2. Political Structure of Saloum

Grand Jaraf was chosen by the Bur from among the leading jambur chiefs, but the choice had to be approved by an assembly of jambur. The Grand Jaraf was the chief of the jambur, as well as their judge and their spokesman in royal councils. His authority could be revoked only by the jambur assembly, and thus he was an independent voice in royal councils, a check on royal power. The Grand Jaraf was also the interim ruler after the death of a Bur, and it was he who was given custody of the deceased Bur's horse, saber, and war drums. When a new Bur was chosen, the Grand Jaraf broke the hides of the war drums, and they were subsequently re-covered.

The heir apparent was called the Bumi. He was chosen by the Bur, but there was often little option since powerful members of rival lineages had to be conciliated. The rival was always a potential challenger, and, as such, he was usually kept out of the capital, and in Sine he was assigned to a distant village. In Saloum, the Bumi often held one of a series of major territorial chiefships. The inability of the Bur to keep the Bumi powerless suggests that power, though in theory concentrated absolutely in the Bur, was in practice diffused.

At least two major chiefs, the Grand Farba and the Farba Birkeur, were chosen from among the tyeddo. In early diplomatic contacts with the French, it was always the Grand Farba who accompanied the Bur and seemed to be the second in command. He was also chief of and judge for the slaves. The Farba Birkeur was charged with running the Bur's household and was called the chamberlain in some French accounts. At the time of the conquest, he was also supervising tax collections.

There were other major titles in both states. Each of the castes had a chief who represented it at court, and other important officials held titles related to territorial commands or court functions. The power and responsibilities of these different chiefs were defined partly by tradition, partly by their personal attributes, and partly by their relation to the Bur. Thus, in 1850 the real power in Sine was the Bur's father, who held a relatively unimportant title. Two titles deserve special mention. The Linguère was either the Bur's mother or his sister. As chief of the women, she played an important ritual role and was the judge in certain cases, such as those involving adulterous wives. In order to support a small court, she was given the tax revenues from two or three small villages. At many times in Senegambian history, Linguères were able to exercise real power. There was also at every Senegambian court at least one *marabout,* who prayed for the Bur and handled correspondence. These marabouts, whose ancestors had originally come from other ethnic groups, were gradually assimilated into Serer society, and they were often given titles and villages as rewards for their services. In Saloum, one family that had served as the Burs' marabouts for almost four centuries built up a good-sized area of fourteen villages.

In Sine, the Bur's power rested directly on the villages. (See the chart of Sine's political structure, Figure 1.) In 1891, no territorial chief commanded more than three of Sine's 125 villages. In all villages not under a major titleholder, the Bur was represented by a *sakh-sakh,* who lived in the village and served as both judge and tax collector. Alongside the sakh-sakh was the village *jaraf,* chosen from the patrilineage of the village's founder. The Bur's control over the appointments of most of the major titleholders and all of the sakh-sakh gave him a control over Sine that neighboring rulers did not always have over their states.

Saloum was larger than Sine, and in the eighteenth century much more powerful, but the Bur Saloum's power was far more restricted than the Bur Sine's. (See the chart of Saloum's political structure, Figure 2.) In central Saloum, the Bur's authority rested directly on the villages, though he was not represented within the villages. Taxes were collected by bands of tyeddo. A number of major titleholders ruled villages in this area, but these titles were usually bestowed at will by the Bur. In most cases, the titles were those of the chiefs of small states that had been conquered early in Saloum's history and incorporated within in the Saloum political system.

In addition to this central area, there were five major chiefships over which the Bur Saloum had only partial control. Each commanded from 5,000 to 10,000 people. To the east of the core area there was Djilor, which had been conquered early in Saloum's history. The Bur Saloum could select the Bur Djilor, but his nominee had to be approved by a popular assembly. In the seventeenth and eighteenth centuries, the M'Bodj family succeeded in making Djilor their own, and thereafter the Bur Saloum was forced to make his choice from their ranks. In eastern Saloum, there were four chiefships, all largely settled by Wolof migrants from Djoloff. Each of the four titles passed in the patrilineal line of the founder, and the Bur Saloum had only limited control over the holder.[k] The rules of succession operated to maximize the power of four of these five patrilineages of Wolof origin. Intermarriage with the guelowar gave these powerful lineages many candidates for the Burship. Not surprisingly, more than half of the Burs were members either of the M'Bodj family or of one of the powerful eastern Saloum families. In addition to these major titleholders, there were a number of minor officials, each of whom commanded from two to twelve villages.

At the height of his power, the Bur Saloum had the means to check his underlings. He received revenue from the slave trade and the Saloum saltworks, as well as from Mandinka tributaries. This income made it possible for him to support a large military force. However, with the decline of the slave trade, the Bur's power was diminished, and the inherent weaknesses of the Saloum political system again became evident.

Contrasting Conceptions of Senegalese Society

The scholar studying traditional Senegalese society is faced with two radically different conceptions of how that society operated. For the French of the nineteenth century, the tyeddo were essentially immoral parasites who lived off the labor of the peasantry. In French eyes, the tyeddo were drunkards and

---

[k]These chiefs were the Beleup N'Doukouman, the Bumi Mandack, the Bumi Kaymor, and the Serigne Pakala. The last of the four was not incorporated in the system until the eighteenth century. The title was held by a marabout family, the Cissés, who were the only major titleholders who did not get involved in the competition for the Burship. The two Bumis are not to be confused with the Bumi who was the heir apparent.

thieves, and the state was essentially oppressive. On the other hand, many modern Senegalese view the traditional state as a well-integrated one, in which each of the groups had its rights and obligations, and in which power was dispersed and the individual respected. No one has expressed this conception better than Léopold Sédar Senghor, the Serer-born French poet, who is now President of Senegal. He writes:

> The legislative assembly is composed of high dignitaries, local leaders, and chiefs of clan families. From them comes the wisdom that is rooted in the knowledge of traditions, the experience of life, and consciousness of their responsibilities. . . .
>
> Authority belongs to the king, whose domination is of a spiritual nature. He symbolizes the unity of the kingdom. He is the descendent of the leader of the people, and at the same time he represents them. The king has authority because the people "honor themselves in the person of the king, and honor the king himself and his past"; because the king is elected of the people and by the people through the intermediary of the principal heads of families; because the electors can suspend him or depose him. His power is effective because it rests on authority and is exercised through the mediation of numerous ministers whom the sovereign can neither choose nor send away.[12]

Both the French version and Senghor's reflect certain ideological predispositions. The French sought to justify the conquest on the ground that it freed the peasants from the oppressive tyeddo. Senghor seeks to reassert the dignity of Negro-African cultures, a dignity long denied by Senegal's French proconsuls; ironically Senghor's explanation is couched in the language of European political theory. The reality was more complex than either the French or the African view of it.

The authority of the state depended on both tradition and a preponderance of force; and not surprisingly this force was often used for the aggrandizement of those near the center of power. The tyeddo were proud, assertive, and frequently unruly. It was not unusual for bands of tyeddo to demand gifts from merchants or to raid villages that had already paid their taxes. Though their power was based on their proximity to the central authority, the tyeddo were most assertive in their own behalf when that central authority was weakest. A strong Bur kept the tyeddo in check or directed their energies in his own interest, but during periods of conflict there was less restraint. Upon receiving word that a Bur had died, the merchants, most of whom were Africans from Gorée, usually withdrew from the kingdom until the succession had been clearly resolved.

There was a constant tension between tyeddo and peasants. Faced with demands they considered excessive, the peasants had three possible responses: to pay, to migrate, or to resist. If the demands were not too great or tyeddo power seemed overwhelming, they often paid. Otherwise they resisted or migrated. They were neither unarmed nor passive. Most important, many owned guns. Ernest Noirot, an early Administrator, wrote:

> Although the Serer population owed to the Bur, represented by his lesser chiefs, taxes in kind and fines for misdemeanors, the tyeddo preserved toward them a certain caution in order not to expose themselves to armed conflict. At a moment's notice a cry was uttered, and in a flash of the eye the women and children retreated toward the granaries, while the men, armed with guns and bows, imposed themselves by force of numbers on the tyeddo, who beat a hasty retreat.[18]

The tension between tyeddo and peasants in Sine was undoubtedly mitigated by the presence in the village of the sakh-sakh, who, as the Bur's personal representative, would help protect the peasants from random demands of tyeddo bands. He was a burden to the village in that he had to be supported by the peasants and was able to help assure the Bur's political control over them, but he was vulnerable to peasant reprisals, which could take the form of noncompliance, armed resistance, or witchcraft.[1]

The successful integration of the Serer state has been attested to by its success in weathering the tests of time. Five hundred

---

[1] In the Wolof states, the tension between tyeddo and peasants was undoubtedly a factor speeding up the Islamization of the peasants. Islam was strongest among the jambur, partly because the jambur turned to marabout leadership in their conflicts with the pagan tyeddo.

years of history gave Serer institutions the sanction of tradition, and thereby confirmed frontiers, obligations, and privileges. Everyone had a place in the Serer state, although some had more important places than others. The number of positions available and the rewards open to those seeking them were numerous. An individual operated within the system not as an individual, but rather as a member of a lineage and a status group, and all lineages participated in the system in some way. Until the nineteenth century, the constant struggle of individuals and lineages to improve their positions tended to perpetuate the system because all competing groups accepted its legitimacy.[14] Only in the nineteenth century did a competing source of legitimacy, Islam, offer itself.

In order to better understand the operation of the Serer state, we must examine the way in which it established and maintained its authority. There were four ways a state could extend its authority. It could colonize a lightly settled area as the early guelowar did. It could incorporate existing units and assimilate their leaders as Saloum did with Djilor and the Wolof groups who migrated to eastern Saloum. It could impose taxes by force and thus achieve implicit acceptance of the state's authority; and finally, it could absorb slaves, either as tyeddo or as members of the lowest status group.

In areas where authority was well established, there were regular taxes, which have been discussed by Aujas and Bourgeau. The Bur received one animal from every herd and about one-tenth of the millet crop. A field in every village was worked for the support of the royal household, and there were certain special taxes and prohibitions. The saltworks were a royal monopoly and were granted by the Bur to a royal favorite. At every important trading site he had a representative called the *alcati*, who was a customs official. The alcatis kept much of the customs revenue, not necessarily because they should have, but because a preliterate society had few ways of enforcing accountability. Fines levied for criminal acts went not to the wronged party, but to the state, and they were divided between the Bur and the judge.[15]

The wealth collected from the peasants played an important role in the operation of the state; it was not just the prize. The political power of a Bur, or of any other chief, depended on his ability to support an entourage and to maintain a certain position. It was imperative that he be well dressed, ride fine horses, and have griots to chant his praises. More important, perhaps, was the entourage, the band of warriors who would do the Bur's bidding and who could be trusted in war and on political missions. In building up an entourage, the Bur often looked first to his family; he could usually trust those relatives who were not his rivals. To attract followers and hold their loyalty, the Bur had to possess certain personal qualities—in particular, courage and intelligence. At the same time, the loyal followers had to be rewarded. It was by the distribution of his wealth and the key positions he commanded that the Bur maintained his power. The Burs who did not carefully maintain their entourages and limit the power of potential rivals could be deposed, though the resources of the Bur were such that a competent man could usually maintain himself.

The insecurity of the Bur's position, its elective nature, and the need to conciliate different groups within the society meant that power was in effect collegial. Although the state in theory invested all power in the Bur, it could operate effectively with a weak or figurehead Bur. A number of Burs were quite young, in some cases adolescents, and they obviously represented a coalition of lineages. In general, the society operated best when there was a strong Bur, but even the strongest were limited in the exercise of power by their assembled chiefs.

THE EUROPEAN PRESENCE

The European Powers in Senegambia

THE PEOPLES OF SENEGAMBIA have been in regular contact with Europeans since the middle of the fifteenth century. The first Europeans to visit them were Portuguese ship captains sent out by Prince Henry the Navigator in his effort to outflank North African Islam and tap the West African gold trade directly. For these early explorers, who slowly and cautiously moved their ships along the barren Mauritanian coast, the Senegal River area was the first hint that richer regions lay to the south. Cape Verde, sighted by Diniz Diaz in 1445, took its name not from an excess of verdure, but from the contrast with the parched lands farther north. At the Senegal River, brown gave way to green, and white to black.

By the end of the century, the Portuguese had rounded the Cape of Good Hope and explored much of the coast below the Senegal River. Although the Gold Coast early became the most important center of Portuguese commercial activity, there was also active trade on the Senegal and Gambia rivers. In 1488, a Wolof prince named Bemoym, probably the Bumi Djoloff, visited Portugal, where he was entertained in a manner befitting his royal status, and was converted to Christianity. Before he reached his homeland, Bemoym was killed by the admiral who was supposed to support him in his struggle for power.[1] Portuguese traders moved up both rivers, exchanging cloth and hardware for gold dust, gum arabic, and slaves. The many descendants of these traders and their African wives were important intermediaries in the region's trade long after Portugal lost its power there.

By 1500 Spain and Portugal claimed most of the known world. Their profits soon aroused the interest of other maritime nations, and attracted a flock of interlopers and privateers. By the end of the sixteenth century, the initiative had passed to the northern nations. The smaller and faster ships of English, Dutch, and French privateers harassed the Spanish and the Portuguese, first in West Africa and the Caribbean, then in distant Asian sea lanes. Before long, the north European powers were themselves seeking to monopolize the trade of key areas. West Africa's importance to Europe increased in the seventeenth century as the development of sugar plantations in the West Indies created a demand for slave labor.

In the European powers' struggle for domination of West Africa, Senegambia had a strategic importance, both as the first point where food and water could be obtained and as one of the few areas where sailors could go ashore without fear of malaria. In 1588, the Dutch chose Gorée, a barren and uninhabited island off Cape Verde, as a base. French and British ships operated out of various ports along the coast, but in 1659, the French established themselves on the island of St. Louis in the mouth of the Senegal River. Two years later, the British took James Island in the Gambia River. In 1677, the French fleet seized Gorée; and a year later, the Treaty of Nijmegen confirmed the conquest. Thereafter the struggle was between France and Britain. Though the three island bases regularly changed hands, and though British sea power tended to prevail, Gorée and St. Louis were generally returned to the French in the peaceful settlements. Neither island was a primary objective in the struggle for international dominion. [a]

Each of the three bases became the center for the commercial penetration of a part of the mainland. Operating out of St. Louis, the French developed a commerce in gum with the Moors, and created a series of trading posts along the Senegal River that

[a] Léonce Jore, *Les Etablissements français sur la côte occidentale d'Afrique de 1758 à 1809* (Paris, 1965). After the Seven Years War, Britain took over St. Louis and incorporated it in the colony of Senegambia, but French traders from Gorée evaded British duties, and France regained possession during the American Revolution.

tapped the slave trade of the populous Bambara states of the upper Niger.[2] Trade in gum, which was used by the French textile industry for printing on high-quality cloth, soon became as lucrative as the slave trade in the river area. The English textile industry was concentrating on cheaper products and did not have the same interest in gum. Bambouk, in the upper Senegal river valley, had gold that lured the Portuguese south, and gold, ivory, wax, and hides were traded; but trade in these products did not approach gum or slaves in volume.

On the Gambia River, the British constructed a string of factories, which, like those of the French on the Senegal, tapped the trade as far as the western Sudan. Though the Gambia did not reach the gum-producing areas, it was a better route to the interior than the Senegal, which was navigable only part of the year. The Gambia trade was largely in the hands of Mandinka middlemen, who brought slaves, gold, ivory, and wax down the river. Francis Moore estimated in 1735 that about one hundred Mandinka merchants were regularly involved in the trade and that the English factories bought over two thousand slaves a year from them.[3]

Gorée was primarily a point where ships returning from the more populous Slave Coast could stop for food and water, and if cargoes were not full, for a few extra slaves. French governors were told that Gorée

> has no other purpose than to protect the slave trade, to serve as an emporium for this trade, to offer a place for rest and provisioning to French navigators who wish to trade on the coasts of Africa, and to sell them slaves belonging to inhabitants of this isle.[4]

Petty traders from Gorée conducted most of this trade in slaves and provisions at Rufisque in Cayor, Portudal in Baol, Joal in Sine, and Albreda in Niumi at the mouth of the Gambia.[b]

The factories established at Rufisque, Portudal, and Joal on

[b] The British generally blocked French efforts to move up the Gambia, but when the French were paying good prices, Mandinka traders found their way down to Albreda. There were periods, of course, when Albreda was not competitive, but the French held on in order to keep the door open to the Gambia trade.

the Petite Côte, which stretched from Cape Verde to Saloum, were old ones, dating to early Portuguese visits.[c] When Alexis de St. Lo visited the Petite Côte in 1635, the three factories were all thriving and competitive centers of trade, but from 1679 on, the French sought to close the area to traders from other nations. A resident, or trading company representative, was placed in each of the villages, and he saw that the annual customs payments from the French were made to each of the three rulers, the Bur Sine, the Teigne Baol, and the Damel Cayor. At each of the factories there was also an alcati, who was the ruler's representative. The alcati, who was the highest local authority, handled all tax collections, and was responsible for dealing with foreigners.[d] The factories, both on the rivers and along the coast, usually consisted of a cluster of small, unfortified wood or straw structures; the resident and the traders were dependent on the good will of the alcati and the local people for conditions in which trade could flourish.

Francis Moore describes relations with the alcati at Kau-Ur in the Gambia as follows:

> It is customary, when factories are settled, [that] the Persons belonging to them, under the Charge of the People of the nearest large Town, . . . are obliged to take care of it, and to let none impose upon the White Men, or use them ill. And if anybody is abused, they must apply to the Alcade [alcati], the head Man of the town, and he will see Justice done. . . . This man is, up the River, called Toubab Mansa, which is in English, the White Man's King. But in most parts of the River he is called Alcade, and hath a great power. . . . This Alcade decides all Quarrels, and has the first voice in all Conferences concerning Things belonging to his Town. If a person wants any Thing to be done by a good number of People, the best way is to apply to the Alcade, who will agree with you about

[c] At Joal, much of the trading was done through a community descended from early Portuguese traders. On the Petite Côte in the 1630's, see Alexis de St. Lo, *Relation du voyage du Cap-Verd* (Rouen, 1637).

[d] The term *alcati* comes from the Portuguese *alcade*, which in turn is derived from the Arabic *al-qā'id*. In parts of the Gambia, it is used to designate village chiefs.

it, and order people to dispatch with it; but if a Factor does
not take care to keep in with the Alcade, he will seldom or
never get things done as they ought to be. The Alcade's is a
very beneficial place, for both Company and separate Traders
pay a custom for every slave they buy, sometimes one bar
per head, sometimes not so much, but that is according to the
Place you are at.[5]

During the late eighteenth century, the Petite Côte posts
played a minor role in the slave trade. They rarely provided as
many as fifty slaves apiece each year. The French took fewer than
two thousand slaves a year from Senegambia; the vast majority
of these came from the interior. By 1770, the factory at Rufisque
had been closed, and within a decade, Portudal and Joal followed, though this undoubtedly meant that the trade was being
carried on without a resident.

In spite of Saloum's wealth and power, neither the French
nor the British opened a factory on the Saloum River. Nevertheless, Saloum did a large trade. Long before the eighteenth century, the Bur Saloum had extended his domains to the Gambia
and was gradually pushing up river. He procured slaves in war
or purchased them with salt. (The salt was made from the shal-
low waters of the Saloum River.) Many of the Mandinka traders
brought their slave caravans either to the factory at Kau-Ur or
to Kahone, the capital of Saloum. When the Bur had a large sale
to make, he invited the British to come to his capital. Francis
Moore describes the trade this way:

> Whenever the King of Barsally [the Bur Saloum] wants Goods
> or Brandy, he sends a messenger to our governor at James
> Fort to desire he would send a sloop there with a cargo; this
> News being not at all unwelcome, the Governor acts accord-
> ingly. Against the arrival of the said sloop, the King goes and
> ransacks some of his Enemies Towns, seizing the People, and
> selling them for such commodities as he is in want of, which
> commonly is Brandy or Rum, Gunpowder, Ball, Guns, Pistols,
> and Cutlasses for his Attendants and Soldiers; and Coral and
> Silver for his Wives and Concubines. In case he is not at war

with any neighbouring King, he then falls upon one of his own Towns, which are numerous, and uses them in the very same Manner.[6]

To the French, Saloum's trade seemed a rich plum, and the river was regularly cited in reports from Africa as one of the best undeveloped sites on the coast. The only Governor who actively sought relations with Saloum, however, was the Comte de Repentigny. Repentigny had gone to Africa in 1785 with plans for a more aggressive commercial policy, and he immediately proceeded to negotiate commercial treaties with six African rulers, including those of Baol, Sine, and Saloum. He does not seem to have expected any sizable expansion of trade at Portudal and Joal—for he did not place residents there again—but he had plans for Saloum.

Repentigny made the trip to Saloum himself. Sandéné N'Dao, the Bur, surrounded by an entourage of about four hundred horsemen and a group of chanting griots, received him. The negotiations for the treaty took five days, and were conducted with the major chiefs before a popular assembly. The final draft, written in Arabic and French,[e] provided that Saloum would grant France a monopoly of trade, and that Saloum would cede the island of Kasthiambee to France. The French were permitted to take wood and water and to trade in the interior. Saloum was to give three hostages and was to receive a generous annual subsidy: guns, cloth, whiskey, wool, powder, musket balls, ammunition, 120 bars of iron, four ounces of coral, and four ounces of amber.[7] Of Sandéné, Repentigny wrote:

> Of all the princes I have seen up to this day, he is the only one to whom one can really give the name of King. The order . . . that he has established in Kahone, where he lives, the care and the trouble he takes to arouse the emulation of his subjects and to attract commerce to his states, prove that he has views and projects of aggrandizement. His cavalry is large. All of the horses in his kingdom belong to him. They are only entrusted

[e] The Arabic version was prepared by the marabout at the Bur's court.

to those of his subjects whom he allows to use them. He is surrounded by warlike princes.[1]

The treaties with Baol and Sine were less extensive. They stipulated the customs to be paid, and provided for the reactivation of the posts at Joal and Portudal.

The projected factory in Saloum was never built. Before the French monarchy could find funds for a Saloum resident, Louis XVI was overthrown. With the diversion of French attention to the Revolution at home, and with Great Britain's abolition of the slave trade in 1807, an important era in Senegambian history came to an end.

The slave trade never reached the proportions in Senegal that it did in more populous areas farther along the coast; thus its effect on Senegambian societies was limited. It altered but did not upset the balance of power, nor did it lead to the emergence of a powerful state based on the trade. The absence of a slave-trading empire was due largely to European success in bypassing the coastal states and establishing inland posts; but other factors were also important. First, there was no densely populated hinterland to raid. Population concentrated along the rivers and the coast, mostly because inland areas had limited rainfall and a low water table. Second, there seems to have been a "cultural brake" limiting the commitment of Senegambian states to the trade. At least one French Governor complained that the Wolof rulers did not make war often enough.[9] Few rulers sold their own subjects except as punishment for a crime, though there are some references to the Bur Saloum's raiding his own villages.[9] And yet the slave trade did have some impact.

[1] Repentigny letter, 11 June 1785, ANP, Colonies C6 18; On a visit to Sandéné made several years later, see "R. G. V." [R.-C. Geoffroy de Villeneuve], *L'Afrique, ou histoire, moeurs, usages et coutumes des Africains* (Paris, 1814), III, 140–61. The statement suggests that control of horses may have been an important element in the Bur's power. Though horses were raised in Baol, there were never enough for local needs, and two-thirds of most Senegambian armies traveled on foot. A good horse was worth from six to fourteen slaves. See Raymond Mauny, *Tableau géographique de l'ouest africain au Moyen Age* (Dakar, 1961), pp. 283–86.

[9] Francis Moore, *Travels into the Island Parts of Africa* (London, 1758), pp. 127–28; Villeneuve, IV, 35–36. Moore pictured the Bur Saloum as a very despotic ruler.

First, it stimulated warfare. The Petite Côte factories, for example, encouraged conflicts between the Bur Sine and his neighbors to the north. Prisoners taken in these wars were sold.[10] Second, enslavement replaced fining as the most common criminal penalty. Thus, one French Governor wrote about Cayor:

> When a man has cohabited with a girl and he has had a child by her, he must pay three slaves, and if he lacks the means, he is enslaved himself. Those responsible for fights, constant theft, false accusation are condemned to considerable fines, which they are never able to pay, and then they are imprisoned and sold to the captains of ships.[h]

A third result of the trade was a change in power structure. It increased the power of the rulers and the major chiefs, who distributed most of the income, increased the size of the tyeddo class, and led to tension between tyeddo and peasants. The income went to the rulers and the tyeddo; and the peasants, who received little or no income, were subject to raids by the tyeddo of neighboring kingdoms.[i] Because of his favorable geographic location, close to two rivers and to sources of sea salt, the Bur Saloum was one of those who made the largest profits in the slave trade. He does not seem to have had a monopoly, but he was clearly a large trader. By the eighteenth century, he had extended Saloum's border and was collecting tribute from at least two of his neighbors, Badibu (Rip) and Niumi (Barra). (Rip and Barra are Wolof names for the Mandinka states of Badibu and Niumi.) Moore describes the Bur's power in 1731 thus:

> This king is potent and very bold; His Dominions are large, and divided into several parts, over which he appoints Governors, called Boomeys, who come every year to pay Homage to Him. These Boomeys are very powerful, and do just what

[h] Bibliothèque Nationale, Manuscripts Français No. 12080, p. 13. After the end of the transatlantic trade, enslavement seems to have declined as a criminal penalty.

[i] It is not clear how many peasants were armed with guns before the beginning of the peanut trade. The tyeddo had firearms from the early eighteenth century, and large numbers of peasants were armed in the late eighteenth century. The decline of the slave trade—it did not end until after the conquest—did not necessarily ease tensions between peasant and tyeddo. Many tyeddo simply shifted their efforts to other kinds of harassment.

they please with the People; and altho they are feared, yet
they are beloved. Other Kings generally advise with their
Head People, and scarcely do anything of great Consequence
without consulting them first, but the King of Barsally is so
absolute, that he will not allow any of his people to advise
him, unless it be his Head-Man (and Chief Slave) called
Ferbro, viz. (Master of the Horse) who carried the King's
Sword in a large Silver-Case of a great Weight, and who gives
Order for what things the King wants to have, or to be done,
and in Battle he is the Leader of his men.[11]

Sine did not extend its control over surrounding areas, but the
Bur Sine actively participated in the slave trade and benefited
greatly from it. Le Brasseur wrote in 1776:

When Barbesin [the Bur Sine] has many slaves, he abandons
his house at d'Yongolor to come stay in the village where the
French factory is located. It is then that spirits are in a constant state of fermentation, and the commercial discussions
sometimes cause blood to flow. The French merchants, who
are unable to persuade themselves that a Negro king can
understand the price and quality of goods they bring him,
are wrong about Barbesin, which is often unfortunate for
them. Barbesin is always perfectly aware of the price of Slaves
in the colonies, never considers the captain of a slaver other
than a person who wants to deceive him, and because of this
simple suspicion, for which he has good reason, he demands
merchandise that they refuse to give him, he fixes the price
himself, and the captain is forced to raise his sails and come
to complain to the governor at Gorée in order to avoid losses
involved in a useless stay. . . .[12]

The visits of African rulers to the factories were not welcome.
They were hard bargainers, and were often unruly guests. Moore
refused to sign for goods in the Kau-Ur factory until he had a
promise that the Bur Saloum would not pay him any visits. His
reason was a previous visit:

In the first place he took Possession of Mr. Roberts own Bed,
then having drank Brandy till he was drunk, at the Persuasion

of some of his People, order'd Mr. Roberts to be held, whilst himself took out of his Pocket the Key to his Storehouse, into which he and several of his People went, and took what they pleased; his chief Hank was Brandy, of which there happened to be but one Anchor. He took that out, drank a good deal of it, made himself drunk, and then was put to bed. . . . The King and all his Attendance profess the Mahometan Religion, notwithstanding they drink so much Strong Liquors; and when he is sober, or not quite fuddled, he prays. Some of that persuasion are so strict, that they will sooner die than drink Strong Liquors; but the King is of quite another opinion, for he will sooner die than drink Small when he can get Strong.[j]

The slave trade also contributed to the growth of trading communities, which remained even after abolition of the trade foreclosed their means of earning a living. The most important were St. Louis and Gorée. Both were lively multiracial communities with limited numbers of Frenchmen and many mulatto and Negro artisans, commercial employees, and petty traders. St. Louis had a mulatto mayor in the eighteenth century. Most of the Negroes were slaves, but as artisans and petty traders they were in little danger of being sold and often benefited from the trade themselves. St. Louis was the larger and more prosperous, with 7,000 people; Gorée had 2,500.[13]

There was also an active slave trade on the mainland. Most important to it were the large traders who moved to and from populous areas of the interior with slave caravans and imported European goods. More modest merchants, Africans living around the different factories, combined trade and agriculture. They bought slaves where and when they could, and when they could not, they dealt with simpler products—dried fish, palm wine, and salt made from sea water. It is difficult to get much information about these petty traders. They accumulated wealth only in the form of cattle, and the oral tradition has preserved little but a memory of their numerous cattle.

[j] Moore, pp. 83–85. But Moore did not dislike the Bur. He wrote that "the King himself is a good natur'd Man, and when sober, is unwilling to use any White Man ill, especially those belonging to the Company." Moore, pp. 94–95.

The Abolition of the Slave Trade

British abolition of the slave trade in 1807 permanently altered the relationships between the major groups involved in Senegambian commerce. At that time, Britain controlled Gorée, and the impact of abolition on the Gorean economy was cushioned by the island's role as a naval base and by the availability of cheap manufactured goods, which British industry was producing throughout the period of the Napoleonic wars. Gorée's population grew, and the island became the emporium for the developing legitimate commerce. At the end of the Napoleonic wars, Gorée and St. Louis were returned to the French, and many Goreans followed the British to Bathurst rather than revert to slave status.

Under British pressure, the Restoration government agreed in 1815 to abolish the slave trade, and Julien Schmaltz, the first French Governor, received these explicit instructions: "The slave trade having been abolished, you will see to it that the inhabitants of Gorée do not engage in this traffic."[14] Undoubtedly the Goreans would have resumed the trade illegally, but conditions were no longer favorable. The new British base at Bathurst, founded in 1816, was located at the narrow mouth of the Gambia River, where a cannon could control the river's traffic. The presence of British ships and the difficulty of moving slaves overland for nighttime loading on isolated beaches soon stifled the Senegambian trade.[k] A slave trade continued throughout the century, but the selling took place either at local markets or at markets in the interior. In particular, a large number of slaves from the western Sudan were moved to the Guinea coast, where numerous small inlets facilitated secret traffic. Thus, for

[k] Bathurst traders and British officials continually accused French officers of cooperating with slavers. It seems probable that they much exaggerated the extent of the trade and the complicity of French officials, who had instructions not to permit it. The colonial administration did approve an indentured labor system, however, which virtually amounted to slave labor within the colony. Both the administration and private persons could purchase slaves and then free them on condition of a fixed term of service, which was ten or twelve years in the case of an army enlistment. See François Zuccarelli, "Le régime des engagés à temps au Sénégal (1817–48)," *Cahiers d'Etudes Africaines*, II (1962), 420–62.

the French, the Peace of Vienna brought about the loss of a valuable item of trade in a shrinking colonial domain. Louis XVIII entrusted the administration of this domain to a Bordeaux shipbuilder, Pierre Barthélemy Portal, who created a plan for developing and expanding the French possessions. Instead of having workers transported to plantations in the Caribbean, Portal wanted to establish plantations in Africa, where a potential labor force already existed. Schmaltz was chosen for the Senegal command because he had experience with the Dutch colony of Java. He and his successor, Baron Jacques François Roger, studied Senegal's agricultural possibilities and tried to set up plantations. Their efforts were not successful because the Senegalese trading communities were reluctant to take up agriculture, and such attempts were always subject to petty harassment by neighboring African states. In 1826 Baron Roger resigned, and the plans for agricultural development were given up.[15]

St. Louis pursued the gum trade with increased energy, and thus was able to compensate for the loss of the slave trade. Gorée, however, lacked a single important trade product, and competed bitterly with Bathurst for the trade that existed. Though Paris, under both the Restoration and the July Monarchy, was generally determined to avoid conflict with Great Britain, Gorée and Bathurst were aggressively hostile to each other, and each settlement sent repeated complaints home about its rival's violation of treaty arrangements. The British closed the Gambia to French boats, but France did not have similar power to bar Bathurst traders from the Saloum River and the Petite Côte, though treaties gave France the exclusive right to trade there. The situation was further complicated by two other factors: first, French products could not compete with the large stockpiles of industrial goods built up by the British during the Napoleonic wars, or with American rum and tobacco; and France's war-ravaged merchant marine could not meet colonial needs. Second, France's traditionally protectionist trade policy, the *exclusif*, made it difficult for Gorée traders to deal in non-French products. Schmaltz's instructions had explicitly stated that the purpose of colonies was to favor and extend the mother country's commerce. No exceptions were to be made.[l] Gorée's trade, which had blossomed under the wartime absence of restraint, found itself squeezed by French and British mercantilist policies. Smuggling became widespread. Gorée traders often bartered secretly with captains of American vessels that put into the island for supplies or repairs.[m]

Many French officials there were sensitive to the island's problems. Naval officers at Gorée repeatedly wrote Paris describing the difficulties of the Goreans and suggesting ways to alleviate them. Both the traders and the young officers wanted to promote the island as an emporium for the small but growing legitimate commerce in West Africa. In 1822, in answer to the various protests, Gorée was made an *entrepôt fictif* for "natural products foreign to Europe."[16] This made it possible for products listed as those not made in Europe to pass through the island without being taxed. The result was an immediate increase in Gorée's commerce.[n] The coastal traders continued to plead for help, but the following period seems to have been one of prosperity; Gorean boats moved farther and farther south and established their commercial dominion as far as Sierra Leone.[17] Gorée's commercial expansion was aided by the decline of mercantilist policies. In 1828 the British opened colonial ports to foreign shipping, and the French gradually extended the list of products not taxed at Gorée. In 1852, the island was made a free port.

The desire to develop Gorée's trade led to several explorations of the coastal states, of which the most important was made by Sauvigny, a botanist, in 1822. In his report Sauvigny meticu-

---

[l] François Zuccarelli, "L'entrepôt fictif de Gorée entre 1822 et 1852," *Annales Africaines* (1959), pp. 261–62. The key rules of the *exclusif* were that 1) colonies were to trade exclusively with France, 2) navigation to and from France was reserved to the French merchant marine, and 3) foreign merchants were forbidden to do business in the colonies.

[m] On one occasion, Schmaltz was forced to permit an American ship to unload because he needed its cargo of lumber to repair the roofs of government buildings before the rains began. See George Brooks, "American Legitimate Trade with West Africa 1789–1914," unpublished Ph.D. dissertation, Boston University, 1962, chap. 3. The most important American import from Senegambia was hides for the New England shoe industry.

[n] The most striking proof of the change was the sharp drop in Bathurst's revenues from £4,000 a year to £2,000. Brooks, p. 138.

lously described plant life, commented favorably on Serer work habits, and praised Saloum's political stability. According to Sauvigny, the Bur was an elderly man, respected and obeyed by his subjects, and he regularly collected from each trader duties determined by the size of the trader's boat. The Bur, who had been present at talks with Sauvigny, remembered perfectly the terms of the treaty, and regretted that France never carried them out. Sauvigny noted potential items of trade (hides, wax, rice, and millet) and suggested building a small trading post.[18] Roger wanted to build one, but Paris was not interested in hides and wax, and merely asked for further study.[19]

Sauvigny's report did not indicate any great need for protection, but Gorée traders continually pressed for either a local military post or periodic visits from a "floating post." Their first interest was in keeping out the English. "On this coast, where the commerce has been controlled for time immemorial by the population of Gorée, we are meeting English competition," an 1837 petition from a group of Gorée merchants protested.[20] The merchants also wanted to gain more control over the terms of trade. In particular, they wanted fixed customs fees and protection from occasional exorbitant and unjust demands by the tyeddo.[21]

Many of the Commandants at Gorée did not like the traders. However, traders and military men had similar interests, especially their opposition to the dominance of St. Louis, the residence of the Governor. Most of the officers at Gorée found themselves speaking frequently for the traders. Particularly vigorous was Dagorne, who was Commandant from 1835 to 1843 and was an early exponent of a vigorous imperial policy. Dagorne wrote in 1836:

> The two parts of the colony have such different objectives that they have in common only their submission to the same authority. These two parts have views and interests that are essentially distinct, although not opposed. . . . Since the Governor and the department heads know only St. Louis, because communication difficulties do not permit them to know Gorée and the dependencies, it happens that the needs of Gorée are neither well understood nor even well known in the capital. . . .

The men in the coasting trade, who venture forth with small numbers of Negroes, are timid and do not dare to take a chance in carrying their merchandise to savage peoples if an efficient and nearby protection does not assure them complete security. . . .

It is not an African utopia that I wish to establish here: Africa offers no Eldorados; but work and perseverance can find here abundant resources. . . . Time and persistence are necessary, and we need at the head of the colonial government a man who wants to remain here for some time and who knows more of the colony than St. Louis and the Senegal River.[22]

Dagorne was one of a group of nationalistic and imperialistic naval officers who wanted a more aggressive policy on the West African coast. The most important of these was Edouard Bouët-Willaumez, whose exploration of the coast in 1838 led to the establishment of a number of fortified factories.[23] Toward 1840 the demand for vegetable oils in France was increasing, and certain Bordeaux and Marseille commercial interests began to support the naval imperialists. Though François Guizot, the prime minister, was generally careful not to threaten British interests, he elaborated a policy of seeking fortified stations, where the navy could provision its ships and French merchants could trade with security.[24] Starting in the Casamance in 1838, the French set up fortified factories in the Rivières du Sud (now Guinea), along the Ivory Coast, and in Gabon. No post was set up in the Saloum River, though numerous officers recommended establishing either a permanent post or regular visits from French gunboats.[25]

The factories in the palm oil area were not very successful. The French had placed a garrison there to protect a growing trade in palm oil, but they found that the cost of the garrison was not justified. The palm oil trade did not rise to expectations because French demand for the product was limited. The much more extensive British market for palm oil was dependent in large part on a growing soap industry, but the French consumer refused to buy yellow soap made from palm oil. The French soap industry did not become interested in palm oil until better methods of treatment removed the yellow color.[26] Marseille soap makers did, however, find another vegetable oil that could be mixed with olive oil to make the blue marble soap for which Marseille was known. This was peanut oil, and it made Gorée's fortune. The first order for peanuts was placed in the Gambia in 1833, and in 1841 a small purchase was made in Senegal. A little over a thousand kilos (about a ton) was shipped to Marseille. In 1845 it was 187,000 kilos (about 205 tons), and in 1854, almost five million kilos (about 5,500 tons).[o] Portuguese slave traders had taken the peanut from America to West Africa in the sixteenth century; and peanuts had subsequently been grown in small amounts in many areas, but had never been traded. The peanut is ideally suited to Senegal's light sandy soils and is easy to grow.[27] Both Gorée and St. Louis participated in the peanut trade, but most of the benefits went to Gorée. The commerce of the island increased from less than two million francs in 1840 to over ten million in 1859. By 1865 Gorée had surpassed St. Louis in economic importance.

One result of the French consumer's rejection of yellow soap was an increase in Gorée's control over coastal commerce between the Senegal River and Sierra Leone. The British dominated the coastal areas from Sierra Leone southward—throughout the palm oil zone—except for Dahomey, where Victor Regis, a Marseille palm oil merchant, had important interests. The cultivation of peanuts by peasants for market started in areas closest to St. Louis and Gorée, but it spread very quickly to the Rivières du Sud. Even in the Gambia, peanut exports were handled largely by French commercial houses and bought by French industry.[p] As early as 1843, the French five-franc piece (the "dollar") was recognized as legal tender in the Gambia. The French commercial houses took the lead in switching from barter to cash payments, much to the displeasure of British

[o] The British trade in palm oil was both larger and older. Liverpool had been importing it since the 1770's, and by 1851, Britain's annual imports were over 30,000 tons. See Allan McPhee, *The Economic Revolution in British West Africa* (London, 1926), p. 32.

[p] David Gamble, "History of the Groundnut Trade," *Contributions to a Socio-Economic Survey of the Gambia.* (London, 1949), pp. 55–69. In 1860 the Governor complained that he could count in the port of Bathurst "thirty tricolours, six stars and stripes, and but one Union Jack." J. M. Gray, *A History of the Gambia* (Cambridge, 1940), p. 384.

traders and government. The Gambian government had been supported by import duties, but the local preference for coins, used as money and ornaments, forced Bathurst to increase her revenues by imposing an export duty on peanuts.[q]

The peanut trade transformed Senegal from a stagnant relic of the slave trade into a bustling colony. To be sure, other factors stimulated French imperialism, in particular the psychology of France's military proconsuls and the arrival of the first missionaries, but it was the peanut trade that gave French commercial interests an involvement in African policy, and it was the rising volume of trade that induced Paris to listen to the imperialistic proposals of the young officers in Africa. In 1854, a group of Bordeaux merchants requested a Governor willing to stay in Senegal long enough to give French policy some continuity; they suggested for the post Major L. L. C. Faidherbe, a young military engineer who had come to Senegal in 1852.[28] Faidherbe and another engineer, J. M. E. Pinet-Laprade, who became Governor in 1865, laid the foundations of France's African empire; and they did it largely in spite of the skepticism of their government and its reluctance to sanction an aggressive policy.[r]

Recent historical work has played down the importance of economic motives in European imperialism.[29] It is not our purpose here to examine these broad interpretations of imperialism except as they apply to the motives for French policy in Senegambia, and in particular to Sine and Saloum. Even in this limited area, the forces operating to expand the colonial enterprise were complex. They changed from one period to the next and operated differently on different levels of decision making. We can, however, single out four considerations that were important in the expansion and the operation of that empire.

[q] Sir Alan Pim, *The Financial and Economic History of the African Tropical Territories* (Oxford, 1940), pp. 34–35. The five-franc piece was known as the "gourde" in Senegal. It was widely used until World War I.

[r] Faidherbe was Governor from 1854 to 1865, with the exception of a brief interregnum from December 1861 to July 1863, when Jean Jauréguibéry held the office. Pinet-Laprade became Commandant of Gorée in 1859 and Governor of Senegal in 1865. He died in 1869, victim of a cholera epidemic in St. Louis.

First, there was the situation in Europe, probably the most important factor affecting decisions made in Paris. During the first half of the nineteenth century, conflict with England was minimized because France, diplomatically isolated as a result of the Peace of Vienna, was forced to approach England gently. However, European power conflicts persisted, and they later led nations to annex regions imagined rich in order to keep out their European rivals. In general, expansion took place during periods when France was strong and was not faced with immediate European challenges.

Second, there was the military influence. Until 1882, command positions in West Africa were monopolized by the military. Colonial officers tended to be strongly nationalistic, and they smarted at the humiliating defeats of 1814 and 1870. Many of them craved action and enjoyed command. Both the military leaders and their civilian successors enjoyed the exercise of power for its own sake.

Third, there was a bureaucratic interest. From the colonial office in Paris to the lowest command post in Africa, every official had a vested interest in the expansion of the colonial enterprise, or rather, every man could make his importance most evident by promoting that part of the colonial enterprise with which he was concerned. For the peacetime army officer, Africa meant easy victories and more rapid advancement. For the civilian bureaucrat, expansion meant faster advancement, higher pay, and more power.

Fourth, there was the economic motivation. Without profits or the hope of profits, the would-be empire builders would have had a very small constituency. Viewed in terms of the whole French economy, the peanut trade was not statistically important, but it created a group that could be depended on to press certain questions at home. Men like Faidherbe, Pinet-Laprade, and Bouët-Willaumez were not necessarily motivated by economic considerations, but they understood that they could sell the idea of empire to Paris only if they could interest French commerce and pay at least part of their way. In general, the arguments for empire were most convincing when pressed by both military and economic interests. In their correspondence with Paris, Senegal's military proconsuls continually discussed commercial prospects and attempted to justify actions in economic terms. "In Sine and Saloum," Faidherbe wrote, "the interests of commerce are always the first preoccupation."[30] This point of view often had to be impressed on lower-ranking officers less sensitive to commercial considerations. While he was Governor, Pinet-Laprade wrote his post commanders: "The goal that we pursue, you know, is the extension of commerce."[31] Faidherbe was also aware that Paris was reluctant to pay the bills for unremunerative empire-building operations, so he increased both local taxation and the participation of local militias in military campaigns.

A new era in French imperialism was clearly marked by the report made in 1851 by the Commission des Comptoirs et du Commerce des Côtes d'Afrique. The committee included many strong supporters of imperial expansion, among them, Bouët-Willaumez, his brother Auguste Bouët, and Victor Regis. Not surprisingly their report recommended stepping up French activity in Africa. It stated:

> For several years, the commerce in oleaginous materials, peanuts and palm oil has been causing a revolution in the habits of certain parts of these coasts. In giving these countries a new means of exchange, we are encouraging there the importation of our manufactured products, both for the coast and the interior. By giving value to labor, so productive on such fertile land, one does more for the development of civilization and the abolition of the odious traffic in slaves than by any repressive measure.[32]

The report went on to recommend that Gorée receive a separate administration and be made a free port. It also called for more troops in West Africa and more factories.[33] Within several years all of these recommendations were carried out.

The Second Empire, with its desire for military prestige, was more responsive to the idea of expansion than the July Monarchy had been. Although the Empire was never committed to Africa and although Faidherbe's most eloquent dispatches did not arouse Napoleon III's imagination, Paris was willing to authorize an increase in the very small West African garrison and support successful initiatives by the men in Africa as long as the enterprise did not prove too costly.[8] It was, however, the men in Africa, and in particular Faidherbe, who made the key decisions and laid the foundations for an empire. A tall, austere, and somewhat haughty military engineer from Lille, Faidherbe arrived in Senegal in 1852, having served in Guadeloupe and Algeria. A product of France's elite École Polytechnique, Faidherbe was restless in subordinate positions, but he demonstrated brilliance and imagination when freed from restraint. He had a shrewd political sense, a good grasp of military realities, and the ruthlessness and self-confidence necessary for action. Faidherbe's willingness to come to terms with alien cultures was reflected in his patronage of Islam, which drew the ire of the missionaries; this tolerance made it possible for France to rule alien Moslem populations. Although he was a republican, he believed that most of mankind's progress resulted from the creation of great military empires; and although he was an abolitionist, he saw that an imperialist policy dictated that he not threaten the existence of slavery in neighboring African states.

Faidherbe was primarily interested in control of the Senegal river valley and the eventual penetration of the rich lands of the Sudan. It was Pinet-Laprade who founded Dakar in 1857 and directed French expansion in the area from Cape Verde south.[34] He was less imaginative than Faidherbe, but was competent and thorough and a strong supporter of French intervention in mainland affairs. Like most interventionist military officers, he saw himself as an agent of civilization, and believed that French military action was liberating the unhappy peasants from their tyeddo oppressors. Unlike Faidherbe, he was not tempted by dreams of a Sudanese empire, but in his dispatches he pictured a Senegalese colony extending from the Senegal

---

[8] Only in 1860 did the authorized effective strength of French forces in West Africa go above 2,000—and of these, about half were African troops recruited in Senegal.

River to the Saloum River, and advocated control of carefully delimited zones dominating other river routes to the interior.[35]

Faidherbe's first years as Governor did not affect Sine or Saloum, but they gave a sign of things to come. When Faidherbe was given command of Senegal, Gorée was placed under the commander of the West African naval squadron. Five years later, when Gorée and newly founded Dakar (1857) were re-integrated with Senegal, Faidherbe was able to claim that his forces had occupied Oualo, the Wolof state opposite St. Louis, and had ended the tradition of making customs payments to the Moors on the north bank and to the Toucouleur on the south bank of the Senegal River. The Moors had been brought to terms in a three-year war, during which Faidherbe's troops kept the Moors' herds from watering at the river. More important, in 1857 the French fort at Medina succeeded in repelling the Toucouleur conqueror, Al Hajj Umar Tall, who was then forced to direct his efforts toward the interior.[36] In 1859, Faidherbe was ready to turn to new projects.

BRICK CHAPELS AND PAGAN PRINCES

Commerce and Politics in Sine and Saloum

FOR A GENERATION after the French reoccupation of Senegal in 1817, the Gorée traders repeatedly asked France to reactivate old factories and to threaten the use of force to protect commerce from British competition and tyeddo harassment. If nothing else, the traders wanted regular gunboat visits, but the trading done in Saloum did not justify even this. In 1837 a treaty was signed with the Bur Sine regulating customs and setting up procedures for dealing with shipwrecks. The treaty gave France land for a factory, but no factory was ever built on the land.[1] However, as commerce in peanuts and other products increased, the economic justification for intervention was strengthened. After fortified factories were built on the Guinea coast, Saloum was frequently nominated as a likely site for a new trading post. Finally, in 1847, a gunboat visited Saloum, and regular visits were made thereafter.

In March 1849, another French gunboat dropped anchor at Fatick, a village on the Sine River that was becoming commercially important. After brief talks, French officers signed a treaty with the Bur Sine. Ten days later a similar treaty was signed at Kahone with the Bur Saloum. Sine again gave France land for a factory at Joal, and Saloum authorized a factory at Kaolack. The treaties set up schedules for annual subsidies and tariff payments to the African rulers, and the Burs promised to protect French traders and to demand nothing that was not covered by the treaties. Each treaty provided that in case of shipwreck the Bur was to keep one-third of the cargo, and the rest was to be returned to Gorée. Neither treaty gave the French exclusive trade rights, and the Sine treaty explicitly denied the French the right to build a fort.[a] Equally important, neither treaty helped ease difficulties with the tyeddo. Throughout the 1850's the traders intermittently complained of tyeddo demands for "gifts," and of fights that resulted when these gifts were not provided.

Within a year of the two treaties, the French navy was back. In Sine, a naval officer sought the return of some stolen cattle. In Saloum, complaints led the Serer, at French insistence, to punish a man who had molested a trader.[2] The military authorities were taking on a difficult role of arbitrator. As many Commandants well realized, they had no way of checking claims put forth by the traders, who were not all men of integrity; and it is probable that exaggerated claims frequently strained relations with African rulers. In spite of this, the military authorities at Gorée regularly used their influence to force payment of claims.

Sine and Saloum were ideally suited for the rapid expansion of the peanut trade. Farther north, peanuts were moved to coastal factories by camels and donkeys. In Sine and Saloum, the Saloum River's many inlets facilitated cheap transportation by dugout canoes, and trade developed at a number of points, most of them within Saloum. This development brought about a certain amount of political change. The slave trade had strengthened the rulers, the major chiefs, and their entourages. The peanut, however, was a peasant crop, grown at first as a small supplementary crop by subsistence farmers. The income from peanuts was much more widely distributed than the income from the slave trade, and since peasants used their new income to purchase guns from Gorée traders, the peanut trade

---

[a] FOM, Sénégal IV 24 b. Sine was to receive nineteen demijohns of liquor every year, to be divided among thirteen leading officeholders. The much more generous Saloum treaty set up complex tariff schedules that varied according to the location of the factory.

enabled them to defend themselves from tyeddo raids, and thus altered the balance of power.

The rulers, of course, still had an interest in protecting trade, as long as they could keep lesser chiefs from intercepting tax revenues. Strong rulers, like Ballé N'Dougou N'Dao of Saloum, were generally successful in controlling their tyeddo and protecting traders. Ballé, who first came to the throne in 1825, reigned unchallenged after winning a succession conflict. He was respected by the traders, and Kahone seems to have been a safe place to trade while he was alive.[b] Traditionally, the trading season had been limited to the months that followed the end of the rains; when the season was over, the traders burned down their huts, and returned to Gorée. The peanut trade, however, gave rise to the practice of traders advancing goods on credit to subtraders, who remained in business all year long. To prevent petty conflicts of various sorts, Ballé limited the trading season, and insisted that the traders leave, taking their goods with them, when it was over. This policy was later adopted in modified form by the French government.[3]

At the time of Ballé's death in 1853, a conflict that had been building up for many years between two branches of the guelowar lineage suddenly broke out. One branch traced its descent from the princess Kévé Bigué, the other from her sister, Diogop Bigué. Ballé was the fourth consecutive member of the Diogop Bigué lineage to hold the throne. When he died, the inevitable succession struggle took place, and a fifth member of the same line, Bala Adam N'Diaye, prevailed. The French were relieved, because his rival was unpopular with the traders.[4] A French officer visited Bala Adam later that year and received a promise that the 1849 treaty would be followed.[5] However, Bala Adam died in 1856, and this time the succession conflict was not easily resolved. The Kévé Bigué candidate was pushed aside in favor of Coumba N'Dama M'Bodj, but the losers continued to chal-

---

[b] Commandant of Gorée to Governor, January 1853 and 12 Feb. 1853, *ibid.*, ARS 4 B 18. Ballé was so widely respected that, when a French administrator laid out new streets in Kaolack forty years after his death, one was named "Bour Saloum Ballé."

lenge the decision, and in 1859, Coumba N'Dama was killed in a battle with the Kévé Bigué leader, Coumba Dianké Bountung. Once again, a Diogop Bigué candidate was chosen, and once again he had to fight to keep his throne.

In Sine there was also a strong central authority, but in this case, power was held less by the Bur, Ama Diouf Faye, than by his father, the Sandigui N'Diob. The Sandigui emerged from a power conflict in the 1820's as the most influential person in Sine. Ineligible to become Bur, he pushed the candidacy of his guelowar son. After a series of battles, Bur Sine Ama Coumba was defeated. Ama Coumba was still in exile when the missionaries arrived in 1848, and missionary accounts indicate that the Sandigui was in firm control.[6] When the Sandigui died in 1851, many expected the return of Ama Coumba,[7] but Ama Diouf remained in power until his early death in 1853.

When his successor, Coumba N'Doffène Diouf, was elected, the traders in Sine pulled back to Joal expecting a succession struggle.[8] Father Luiset of the Catholic mission predicted that the Bumi, Sanoumon Faye, would defeat Coumba N'Doffène. Luiset considered them both drunkards and had no preference.[9] Coumba N'Doffène's succession was, surprisingly, one of the few to go unchallenged during the nineteenth century. Tradition has it that Coumba N'Doffène and Sanoumon Faye were born at about the same time but that Coumba N'Doffène's birth was reported first to the Grand Jaraf, and thus he became the heir. Coumba N'Doffène was a strong leader whose word was generally accepted by the traders, but as we shall see, at times he had his reasons for giving very limited protection to the traders, and sometimes even less to the missionaries.[10]

The Missionaries

Senegambia had never been a site of major missionary activity. The limited Portuguese effort had little impact, and in earlier years there had been French priests only in St. Louis and Gorée. In the late eighteenth and early nineteenth century, however, there was a resurgence of the missionary impulse, which began first in England, where it was associated with the abolitionist crusade. A number of missions were founded in and around Bathurst in the 1820's.

A similar, Roman Catholic, movement in France began in the 1840's with the work of Father François Marie Paul Libermann, who was a converted Jew.[c] From the first, the job of bringing Christianity to Africa was costly. In 1843, seven missionaries, supported by the Ministry of the Navy and Colonies, were sent to West Africa. Of the seven, five died and one quit before the first year was up. Then, in 1846, Father Benoit Truffet was named Vicar Apostolic of Senegambia and Guinea.[d] Father Truffet's arrival was followed within seven months by his death, an unfortunate loss for the Church. Had he lived, the history of the missions might have taken a very different course. Truffet was convinced of "the absolute necessity of detaching as completely as possible our Church of Africa from any connection with the governments of Europe, who will try to protect it only in order to prepare its chains."[11] Truffet's brief experience in Africa persuaded him that contact with the worst of European civilization had only corrupted the African peoples, who were essentially good and were responsive to the Christian message. "These poor people," he wrote, "have never seen Catholic priests; they have scarcely seen anyone but merchants who are always covetous, often scandalous, always impious."[12] Truffet believed that a truly Christian community could be formed only if it was free of contact with Gorée; he thought this community should depend for security not on French guns, but on the good will of African rulers. His belief was confirmed when a Catholic priest, who had been arrested by the Damel Cayor, was speedily freed as a result of the intercession of the Eliman Cape Verde, a Moslem chief.[13]

[c] Libermann founded the Congregation of the Mission of the Sacred Heart of Mary in 1842. Six years later, it was combined with the older Holy Ghost Fathers, with Libermann as Superior.

[d] J. B. Piolet, *Les Missions Catholiques Françaises au XIXe Siècle* (Paris, 1902), V, 21–35; "Rapport sur l'histoire de la Mission, 1843–60," CSE, 157 A I. Mission activities regularly received French government subsidies, though many Governors either were anticlerical or at least restricted mission activities to avoid offending the Moslems.

In 1848, Monsignor Aloysius Kobès arrived at Gorée to take Truffet's place, and the first missions were founded on the mainland. Dakar, opposite Gorée, was chosen as the center of the mission. Kobès was head of the mission until his death in 1872, and his ideas, often totally opposed to those of Truffet, shaped its history. He had tremendous energy and a vigorous mind. Determined and optimistic, he was quite willing to use his ties with France to accomplish what he sought. In less than fifteen years, he was able to claim over eight thousand Catholics, with communities at St. Louis, Gorée, Joal, and Bathurst (at British request), a seminary, a trade school, separate schools for boys and girls, and a number of books in and about African languages.[e] However, as a result of his policies, Catholicism was limited until very recently to coastal areas and to the periphery of African society. Kobès did not succeed either in forming an African clergy or in penetrating Senegal's largest pagan group, the Serer. Part of the reason for his failure lay in his preference for the large enterprise over the lonely mission station, and for French protection over the less sure shelter of an African ruler's patronage.

Fathers Arragon and Gallais, the first missionaries at Joal, were more like Truffet than was Kobès. Kobès was a manager, a leader; Arragon and Gallais were dedicated men, willing to spend the rest of their days in an African village; but Arragon was sent on to other assignments after just a few months. Gallais stayed, and was an excellent missionary. A simple soul, able to change his mind, he was one of the few early missionaries to take a genuine interest in African society and to seek to incorporate himself in it. He accepted Libermann's much-quoted dictum, "Be Negro with the Negroes," and always dated his letters "Joal, kingdom of Sine."

---

[e] *Mission de la Sénégambie en 1862* (Dakar, 1862), found in CSE, 157 A IV. Some of the eight thousand were already Catholic, or at least considered themselves Catholic. The work of conversion was very slow, and had its first success on the fringes of traditional society or among those in regular contact with Europeans. The first converts at Joal were two old women who died soon after their conversions.

Joal was a trading community that was partly dependent on Sine but to a large degree autonomous, "a Republic of San Marino," Gallais called it.[14] The presence of a community that called itself Portuguese and Catholic made the town especially interesting to the missionaries, though their interest soon turned to shock. Descended from Portuguese traders, the Joal Portuguese were as dark as their Serer neighbors, and were Catholic in name only. Father Arragon, when he visited in 1847, found only two men who could make the sign of the cross. All, he reported, wore *gris-gris* (Moslem charms) and had two or three wives.[15] Gallais considered the Portuguese of Joal "the fruits of crime and libertinage," and was shocked that the religious leader of the community was a heavy drinker who had three wives, numerous concubines, and twenty-four children.[16] Gallais felt that Joal did not provide the best entry into Serer society. He saw that Joal modeled itself on Gorée, with which it had commercial ties.[17] Gallais preferred to work with the simpler folk of the surrounding villages, but the Joal Portuguese opposed a missionary effort that would deprive them of their distinctiveness. Joal residents often told the missionaries that God had meant the Serer to be pagan. The Fathers further alienated the Joal Catholics by trying to reform their way of life. "You can speak to them of a temperate Christianity," Gallais wrote, "but they can scarcely conceive of it; they take you for Mohammedans and say coldly that a Christian should drink."[18] Joal became a source of rumors and of constant agitation against the missionaries.

The mission at Joal was established without anyone's asking the permission of the Bur Sine, but shortly after the arrival of the missionaries, a group of tyeddo came to demand the liquor that all traders paid the Bur. The missionaries explained, as they were to continue explaining for a decade, that they had not come to trade. The visit of the Bur's emissaries persuaded Gallais that a trip to Diakhao, Sine's capital, was necessary. In October 1848, after the alcati of Joal decreed that the mission chapel should be built of straw instead of wood, Gallais made the first of many trips. His report to Libermann was a triumphant one. When he arrived, the tyeddo were lined up in front of huts, every man magnificently dressed, and armed with gun and knife. The Bur and his father greeted Gallais warmly, expressed curiosity about his costume and his person, and willingly granted him permission to build a small wooden chapel.[19]

Toward the end of December the Bur came to Joal. He was mounted on a superb horse, and accompanied by a troupe of griots and over a thousand warriors. The griots continually beat drums and chanted his praises. Gallais was impressed. "The Serer people," he wrote to Father Bessieux, "are a people numerous and powerful and well worth your pastoral solicitude."[20] The day after his arrival, the Bur, the Farba, and the Bur's marabout came to visit the chapel. The Bur questioned Gallais about Christain belief, and the Christian missionary engaged in a brief competition with the marabout over knowledge of Old Testament history. Several days later, the Bur and a group of tyeddo asked to be present at what he called the missionary's salaam.[21]

Ama Diouf and the Sandigui expressed great interest in Christianity, particularly in Christian religious images, in all their conversations with Gallais. Though firmly pagan, the Serer had been subjected to Moslem proselytizing, and had some familiarity with Koranic versions of Old Testament tales and with Moslem religious ideas in an elementary form. In spite of this, the conflict between the two faiths often came down to even more practical questions, in particular, the Moslem prohibition against alcoholic drink and the Catholic opposition to polygamy. When asked his religion, one pagan village chief answered: "We are tyeddo. Our religion is to drink."[22] The Catholics found great interest in religious images, and the Moslems found that gris-gris were their most useful tools. Marabouts in pagan areas made a living by selling gris-gris that contained verses of the Koran. Gallais and his colleagues never realized that the African's interest both in images and in gris-gris was rooted in his perpetual desire to conciliate mysterious forces. The missionaries did not understand the essential pluralism of African traditional belief. On one occasion, Ama Diouf told Gallais that he thought "Issa" [Jesus] was probably the second most important prophet after

Mohammed.[1] He was quite willing to incorporate both of the new religious messages in his inherited pattern of belief, but he, like most of the Serer, was not willing to drop the security of religious eclecticism.

In February 1849, the Bur Sine gave a friendly trader a plot of land at Joal for the missionaries. Later that year, Gallais made another voyage to Diakhao and was treated well. He had free access to the Bur's apartments and was referred to as "the Bur's white marabout."[23] On his return, he wrote, "We are no longer suspect and ambitious strangers, but Serer citizens incorporated in the nation—faithful supporters and friends of the established power, which we recognize as coming from God."[24] At this meeting Gallais had been granted the land Kobès wanted for his school and farm; and in 1850, the mission of N'Gasobil was founded several kilometers north of Joal. However, the Serer rulers did not remain this friendly for long.

The greatest problem facing the missionaries was that Sine feared French military power and saw the missionaries as agents of that power. This fear was exacerbated by the French abolition of slavery in 1848, and by the presence of French gunboats in coastal waters. "Sine trembles and fears the cannon of the terrible M. Bouet," Gallais wrote in 1849.[25] The missionaries were never able to allay this fear, perhaps because the Joal Portuguese played on it in their efforts to get rid of the Fathers. The missionaries were expressly forbidden to build in stone, and Ama Diouf told Gallais he feared that the missionaries would build a fort and bring in cannons during the night.[26]

In this context, the Sandigui's repeated requests that the missionaries settle at Diakhao represented a major opportunity. "Shrewd old Sandidhé [Sandigui] has even invited me to come live with him like his Moor and his other marabouts," Gallais wrote. "He appears to me to be frightened of cannons, of our taking over the whole country, of the abolition of slavery, and twenty other difficulties that have been suggested . . . by the knavish and cunning self-labeled Christians and white men of

[1] According to Vincent Monteil, a Moslem, too, could call "Issa" the second most important prophet, "Allah's own Word and Spirit." Personal communication.

Joal."[27] Undoubtedly Ama Diouf and Sandigui wanted to use the missionaries in the same way they used their marabouts— as secretaries, as advisers, and as sources of magic. But if the missionaries had accepted the offer, they could have penetrated Sine and served as intermediaries between the two alien worlds in the difficult years that followed. Gallais had been interested at one time in moving the mission to the interior,[28] so it seems likely that it was Kobès who rejected the invitation, both because he preferred to use his limited resources for projects along the coast, and because he feared the inroads of disease at an inland station.[g] After 1859 Sine was to remain closed to the Church for over half a century.

Almost from the moment of its establishment in early 1850, the mission at N'Gasobil faced systematic harassment designed to force its evacuation. The local people were forbidden to sell anything to the mission or to send their children to the school. Shortly after a French naval officer interceded to try to bring an end to the harassment, an African employee was kidnapped from N'Gasobil; he was never found. In April, Gallais went to Diakhao, where the Sandigui told him that there had been complaints about the missions and that it would be safer in Fatick, Diakhao, or "any other place which does not depend on the French." He expressed fear that the French would arm the men of N'Diéghem or would debark merchandise without paying the customs, and he refused to accept gifts that Gallais brought with him. Soon after this, the chapel at N'Gasobil was pillaged.[29] Throughout this period and for many years after, the most important factor motivating the policies of the Serer rulers was a desire to preserve their independence. N'Gasobil was probably singled out for harassment because it was isolated and could not be easily surveyed.

[g] In the first fourteen years, 149 missionaries had gone to Senegambia. Though most of these were young men, 49 died at their posts and 46 returned to France, many for health reasons. *Mission de la Sénégambie,* 157 A IV. With time, the missionaries learned to care for themselves better and the death rate declined. Father Lamoise, who arrived at Joal shortly after Gallais's departure in 1852, spent over fifty years on the Petite Côte.

In January 1851, when Monsignor Kobès stopped at Joal on the way back from Gabon, emissaries from the Bur Sine asked passage on his boat. Only after reaching Gorée did Kobès discover that his friendly fellow passengers carried a letter requesting that N'Gasobil be closed.[30] In July 1851, Gallais went to Sine to present his condolences on the death of the Sandigui, and he got confirmation of the Bur's concessions; but soon the harassment began again, and N'Gasobil had to be closed. By this time, two other Petite Côte missions were already closed as a result of pillaging by the tyeddo of the Damel Cayor.

After the departure of Gallais in 1852 and the death of the Sandigui and Ama Diouf, there was no meaningful contact between the missionaries and the Serer rulers. On the Petite Côte, only the Joal mission continued, generally tolerated but occasionally harassed. In 1856, Kobès went to Sine with Father Lamoise of Joal and a French officer. When he presented his complaints to Coumba N'Doffène, the Bur wanted to know why the Fathers had not spoken up earlier. The Farba asked why they had not come either to congratulate Coumba N'Doffène on his accession or to offer condolences on the death of his relatives. The missionaries wanted to build a brick chapel, but this was the one point on which Sine was most sensitive, and the more insistent Kobès and Lamoise became, the more the Serer saw their fears of aggressive French designs confirmed. When Lamoise threatened to build without permission, the Bur told him he would be killed if he did so. The Bur was interested in Catholic teachings, and he invited Lamoise to visit him again, but he was adamant on the question of building in stone.[31]

Throughout the 1850's the missionaries were harassed with requests for gifts, occasional thefts, and threats. Kobès wrote the Commandant at Gorée several times requesting government aid. "Tell the Bur," he wrote, "that the missionaries are not traders and that consequently they do not have to pay duties, that they are occupying a piece of land which the French government by treaty has the right to take for a factory."[32] As early as 1850, one of the missionaries being harassed at N'Gasobil had written in even stronger terms:

The best security is for us to have cannon; that very name will rid anybody here of any thought of aggression! I understand the gravity of such a measure, but after all the expenses we have undergone and the work we have done, I do not believe that we can expose this establishment to the ruin that is probably imminent.[33]

European Intervention

Up to this time, the French apparently did not actively intervene in the affairs of the Serer states. They did not support candidates for office, probably because they lacked the information on which to base a choice of allies. Nor is there any suggestion in the archives that the Gorée traders interfered in any way.[h] However, the case for intervention was building up. Merchants and missionaries were addressing complaints to Gorée, and Gorée regularly sent naval officers to protest to the Burs. In 1856, the French cut off trade on the Saloum River briefly, but this stopped the incidents for only a short time. Intervention was further encouraged by the increase in trade and the conviction that security would bring an even more rapid increase. In 1859, Pinet-Laprade estimated the Saloum trade at 4,000 barrels of millet (used to feed Gorée), 25,000 bushels of peanuts, and 1,000 hides.[34]

Undoubtedly the French wanted to assert their primacy on the Saloum River before the British took a strong stand. The French were able to do this in spite of long-standing British commercial ties with Saloum because the British were reluctant to commit themselves beyond Bathurst.[i] For the French, Senegal had top priority in Africa. For the British, the Gambia was the least important area. Furthermore, the British did not want the responsibility and the expense of governing and defending an African population. In 1832, after a conflict with Niumi (Barra), they had taken over the Ceded Mile, a stretch one mile deep

---

[h] Sources for this period are limited. Reports sent to Paris often said little about affairs in neighboring African states. This does not mean that no traders ever aided a preferred candidate with money, but if this took place, it probably did not take place on a large scale. The Gorée traders did not have large sums available for purchasing the friendship of local rulers.

[i] The British had signed a commercial treaty with Sine in 1856.

along the shore opposite Bathurst, but they made no real effort to govern this area. Otherwise, British policy was restricted to the use of diplomacy and the granting of subsidies to African rulers to ensure the safety of British traders. In 1855, the British even had to call for French military assistance when Bathurst unwittingly got itself involved in a religious conflict in Kombo, the neighboring Mandinka state.[35] At the same time, Britain and France moved toward resolution of long-standing conflicts. In 1857, the two countries signed a treaty stipulating that Portendik, a British factory that tapped the gum trade on the Mauritanian coast, be exchanged for Albreda, the French factory on the Gambia River. However, this treaty gave French merchants the right to trade in the Gambia, and permitted French commercial houses to extend their domination of the peanut trade.

In May 1859, Faidherbe decided to deal a quick blow in Sine-Saloum before the rains. As he explained to Paris:

> Our goal is to traverse these countries with our forces, to declare null treaties and conventions passed in recent years for the regulation of customs to be paid to chiefs of the country in exchange for security promised by the latter—treaties and conventions repeatedly violated by them—and to establish our future relations on new and more dignified terms, which we will see are strictly observed. I would hope to achieve these results without hostility, solely by proving to these people that we are capable of penetrating their lands and willing to do so.[36]

Faidherbe arrived in Gorée with 200 *tirailleurs* and 160 marines.[j] He added the Gorée garrison to his forces, and announced to the people of Gorée that he was inviting them to participate. This meant a hundred "volunteers." At Dakar, only recently occupied by France, Faidherbe gathered the Lebu inhabitants. He reports:

> I told them that they were French, and that for this reason they had to take arms to join us and had to participate in the

---

[j] The *tirailleurs,* or sharpshooters, made up most of the Senegalese military force. Most West Africans who served in French forces during the two wars served in the Senegalese Tirailleurs.

expedition that we were going to make against their neighbors to obtain reparation for wrongs those people had done us. This demand astonished them a little, but they did not dare to refuse.[37]

The Lebu "volunteers" were added to the ranks, and then all proceeded to Rufisque, where Faidherbe arrested one of the Damel's representatives, whom he declared guilty of "all kinds of violence," and a member of the tyeddo who had participated in an attempt to kill a French trader. Here, too, Faidherbe gathered the population:

> I declared that duties collected until this day were too high. I suppressed all taxes on the importation of our merchandise and the embarkment of products. I left only a small export duty on the products of Cayor, and I cut that approximately in half in order to reduce it to the same level as the export tax collected in the St. Louis area. . . . This tax will be collected by any agent of the Damel acceptable to us.[38]

Faidherbe also announced that a blockhouse would be built in Rufisque and that henceforth French subjects would build in masonry. France was asserting her sovereignty over the Petite Côte with a sudden and forceful gesture. From Rufisque he proceeded to Joal. As the French camp was being set up, a patrol ran into Bumi Sanoumon Faye and a band of tyeddo, who were apparently ignorant of the French presence. Sanoumon escaped, but two men were captured. One of these men was entrusted with a message for the Bur to the effect that Faidherbe would be in Fatick in three days. Faidherbe stated that he would make peace or war with the Bur according to whether or not the Bur granted the reparations and concessions that Faidherbe had demanded of him.[k]

During the march, the French force was constantly watched by horsemen from Sine. On the morning of March 18, the French

[k] Report to Minister of Algeria and the Colonies, 14 June 1859, FOM, Sénégal IV 50 a. Faidherbe justified his assertion of French sovereignty along the Petite Côte by several treaties, supposedly signed by the African rulers in 1679, which gave France sovereignty over a strip of coast six leagues deep. See Abdoulaye Ly, La Compagnie du Sénégal (Paris, 1958), pp. 144–47.

reached Fatick and took positions. At 9 A.M. the army of Sine suddenly emerged from the forest. For twenty minutes the two armies engaged in combat, and then the Sine cavalry retreated, only to try two more charges. Unable to dent the French ranks, the Bur's forces retreated, and Faidherbe burned the village of Fatick. Faidherbe claimed that the French had either killed or wounded 150 Sine men, but that the French force had only five wounded. The warriors of Sine loaded their weapons with too many balls, he said, so that they were lethal only at very close range.

From Fatick, the French army moved overland to Kaolack without waiting for the Bur's response to Faidherbe's demands. In Saloum, the situation was very different. Bur Saloum Coumba N'Dama had died only a month earlier. Samba Laobé Fall, the next in line among the Diogop Bigué, was hard-pressed to defend his throne, and could not afford to do battle with the French. He quickly accepted the terms.

When Faidherbe arrived back at Gorée, there was a message from the Bur Sine. Coumba N'Doffène accused the French Governor of acting in Sine without notifying him of the issues, but his acceptance of the French ultimatum was unconditional: "Send me a paper. Grant us peace. We have learned and we accept, O all powerful Sultan, O King of Kings! We beg pardon from God and from you."[39] The treaties with Sine and Saloum, almost identical in wording, guaranteed the freedom of French commerce, allowed the French a monopoly of trade, and gave to French traders the rights to build in masonry and to buy land. The only tax was to be a 3 per cent export duty, and French subjects were to be tried only before French courts.[40]

When Faidherbe was criticized by Paris for undertaking a military campaign without notifying his superiors, he wrote back that he had only intended "a peaceful tour in order to show our forces." The expedition, he explained, did not necessitate the reoccupation of old posts, but rather permitted small units to reoccupy an area that had belonged to France since 1679.[41] Faidherbe was playing with words in an effort to deny that he was making basic policy in Senegal. The invasion had clearly

been planned to force a conflict that could be resolved on Faidherbe's terms. It resulted in the occupation of an area never
ruled by the French, and the suppression of duties usually paid
in exchange for the right to trade.

The posts at Joal and Rufisque were built before the rains began, the posts at Kaolack and Portudal not long after. With the
construction of these posts, French sovereignty was effectively
exercised along the coast, though by the middle of 1860 the Bur
Sine was challenging French rights over several villages just inland from Joal. In July 1860, Gorée received a letter from the
Bur, who threatened to kill every white man in Sine if he was not
permitted to exercise his traditional rights:

> We wish neither gold, nor silver, nor diamonds; we wish only
> the inhabitants of Diavalo and Fadioudj; we wish to do with
> them as we have always done. . . . Those people are my slaves.
> I will take their property, their children, and their millet.[42]

To force French acquiescence, the Bur stopped all movement
of Serer flocks to Joal and began to harass the traders at Fatick.[43]

In Saloum, things became equally bad. The treaty was followed faithfully for about a year, and then the Bur suspended
trade and announced that commercial relations would be resumed after the French military post had been razed.[44] This time
it was Pinet-Laprade who acted. At 1 A.M. on February 28, 1861,
French troops debarked near Kaolack. They divided into two
forces, one attacking Kaolack, the other Kahone. Over 450 prisoners were taken, including the Linguère and several of the Bur's
other relatives, and the two villages were sacked and burned.
While waiting for Saloum to accept his terms, Pinet-Laprade
and part of his column began moving on Diakhao. Before they
arrived, they were met by Coumba N'Doffène's marabout, who
announced that Sine had accepted the terms.

The new treaties involved the reaffirmation of the 1859 treaties and the imposition of indemnities, 500 cattle for Saloum, 200
for Sine. Sine gave to the French the right to build a military
post at Fatick, and Saloum relinquished all land within 600
meters of the post at Kaolack. The Fatick tower was never built,
but the post at Kaolack remained a lone symbol of the French

presence in Saloum for 26 years. The two military campaigns and the resulting treaties did not establish French sovereignty, in spite of their nominal reference to a protectorate, nor did they break the determination of the Serer states to maintain their independence. The Serer rulers clearly understood the implications of the French victory. Circumstances later on would leave Saloum little freedom of action in dealing with the French, but Sine continued seeking to conciliate, to limit, and where possible, to use the French.

Even before the end of 1861, Coumba N'Doffène was trying to negotiate implementation of the treaties as he interpreted them. Some cattle had been stolen, and when the French protested, he wrote Faidherbe, indicating his willingness to make good the stolen cattle:

> The goal of this letter is to let you know that I have understood your words. These affairs of cattle are nothing; they are easy to resolve. The question of N'Diouk and Fadioudj is more important for us. . . . Peace between us is on the condition that N'Diouk and Fadioudj continue to pay me their tribute as in the past. We have not taken the property of any whites. . . . Nobody will be pillaged except the people of Joal, who are not my subjects. I am angry with these people because they have taken N'Diouk and Fadioudj from me. Only peace exists between me and the whites, but peace according to the usages of this land. There are many men between us who lie, and it is necessary not to listen to them.[45]

Coumba N'Doffène was seeking to make the security of trade depend on his right to collect taxes in the disputed villages. Coumba N'Doffène's effort to control these villages ended only when a more dangerous enemy forced him to seek French assistance.

Neither Faidherbe nor Pinet-Laprade wanted to get further involved in Sine and Saloum. Both sought security for French commerce, but French resources did not permit the occupation of more than the Petite Côte, largely because other areas seemed more important. Cayor was of particular strategic importance because it lay largely between the two important cities of St. Louis and Dakar, and because peanut cultivation there was developing more rapidly than in Saloum. In 1859, Damel Biraima of Cayor agreed to let the French build a telegraph line from St. Louis to Dakar. In 1860, when they were ready to proceed, the new Damel, Macodou, refused to approve the project. The result was war. In 1861 the French expelled Macodou and imposed a puppet Damel. The same year they occupied Diander, the southernmost part of Cayor, thereby moving toward achievement of Pinet-Laprade's desire to dismember Cayor.

In 1862, Lat Dior Diop, a new and more vigorous claimant to the throne of Cayor, appeared on the scene, and in the next two years waged a determined campaign against the French. The French were having trouble also with the Nones, who in 1863 wiped out the newly established post at Pout in a surprise attack. The French responded with a punitive expedition and the establishment of a stronger post at Thiès. (The posts at Pout and Thiès were designed to protect the increasingly important trade route between Baol and Rufisque, which was blossoming in the 1860's as the major peanut-exporting port of Senegal.) In December 1863, Lat Dior and his men inflicted a severe defeat on the French, but a month later, in a bitter battle that left over five hundred dead on the battlefield, Lat Dior was defeated and driven from Cayor. The victory gave the French effective control of Cayor for a time, but the battles were not over. The field of conflict had only shifted further south, and Lat Dior was to trouble the French for another twenty years.[46]

After the military campaign of 1859, Joal and the Catholic missionary effort become unimportant for the purposes of this study. The campaign detached Joal from Sine and placed it under direct French administration. As for the missionaries, their failure was costly to the Catholic effort in Senegal. The Serer were the best prospects for proselytizing in Senegal. Now, when a more successful effort is under way, the Moslems are more numerous in Sine. We should not, however, be too harsh in judging the early missionaries. They were seeking to enter a world radically different from their own. In view of the hostility they faced, it is not surprising that they failed to see clearly the opportunities that existed. Nor is it surprising that they had only modest success, when limited to the Petite Côte. In a society that places great value on offspring, the missionaries stood out as men without children. Moreover, they demanded monogamy and sought an African priesthood, even though the number of African males willing to accept celibacy and thus cut themselves off from the possibility of offspring was limited. In this respect, the Catholics were at a much greater disadvantage than the Protestants.

Faidherbe's conquests gave France a sizable mainland domain for the first time. In Diander, along the Petite Côte, and in other mainland areas, French officials were able to experiment with methods of governing alien peoples. During the early 1860's, these regions were divided into cantons, each under an African *chef du canton,* who supervised the collection of the personal taxes that the French instituted.[1] Little effort was made to invest in these areas or to change the ways of their peoples. The French yoke was light during the generation that followed, and was probably welcomed by some of the peoples involved, especially those living on the periphery of established states, who were subject to frequent raids.

Small as this domain was, Faidherbe's conquests made Senegal the largest European colony in West Africa. The European presence in West Africa did not yet amount to much—a few coastal islands, a series of forts and trading stations, a small peninsula. (Lagos was first occupied by the British in 1861.) However, the importance of Faidherbe's conquests was not in the extent of area occupied, but in the reversal of time-honored policies. First, where France previously had claimed to rule only two islands, it now ruled several mainland territories. Second, where it had paid for the privilege of trading, it now asserted the right to control trade and, to a lesser degree, politics.

The scramble for Africa has often been treated as a phenomenon which suddenly manifested itself about 1880, but the expansive impulse was fully developed in Faidherbe's Senegal. It

[1] After the French conquest of Saloum in 1887, Senegal was divided into *cercles,* each governed by a *Commandant du Cercle.* Each cercle was in turn broken up into cantons. In addition, there were often intermediate circumscriptions called either provinces or subdivisions.

was restrained only by the reluctance of governments in Paris to appropriate funds for African adventures and by the high cost in lives of occupying an interior area.[m] The Kaolack garrison was often changed every six months, and it was generally manned by Senegalese troops during the rainy season.

Though the area occupied was limited, French power was unrivaled there, and modern science was rapidly increasing the disparities between the French and the Africans. Superior weapons technology gave the French complete supremacy on any field of battle they chose, and at any point they could supply. Once committed to the mainland, France could no longer limit her forward movement—any more than Britain could stop with half of India. David Landes has written thus about such unstable ballances of power:

> In the long run, the weaker party will never accept his inferiority, first because of the material disadvantages it entails, but even more because of the humiliation it imposes. In return, the stronger party must ceaselessly concern itself with the security of its position.[47]

Landes goes on to suggest that even when the metropolitan power tries to exercise restraint, her citizens seek to negate its policy by exploiting the disparity of power. But even apart from such exploitation, the mere fact of the French presence meant that France had to involve herself in internal power conflicts and in struggles between African states. Faidherbe's successful occupation of Oualo and Diander forced him, a bit later, to become involved with a new and more potent enemy, a militant and expansive Islam.

[m] The death rate of Europeans in West Africa declined rapidly after the middle of the nineteenth century, largely because of the increased prophylactic use of quinine to prevent malaria. Nevertheless, epidemics of other diseases, especially yellow fever, remained costly and were a major factor inhibiting European expansion. See Philip D. Curtin, *The Image of Africa* (Madison, Wis., 1964), chaps. 7 and 14.

MA BA AND RELIGIOUS WAR
1861–1867

Background of the Revolution

ISLAM WAS FIRST BROUGHT to West Africa by traders on the trans-Sahara routes, and it early established a base in the southern termini of those routes. In the eleventh century, the ruler of Takrur, a trading state that straddled the Senegal River, was converted. In the same century, the puritanical Almoravid movement made its appearance among the Berber tribes of southern Mauritania.[1] Though the Almoravids directed their most important efforts to the north, they left a strongly Moslem imprint on the area, and Mauritanian marabouts introduced Islam to many areas south of the Senegal River. The Mali Empire, which was established in the thirteenth century and which controlled the Gambia River, also played a major role in Islamization, especially among the Mandinkas.

When the Portuguese arrived in the fifteenth century, there were marabouts attached to most of the Senegambian courts. These marabouts prayed for the chiefs and handled correspondence. As a reward for their services, they received land and were permitted to found villages. By the seventeenth century their villages had become substantial islands of Islam. The Moslem community supported Koranic schools, kept the fast of Ramadan, and followed the Moslem dietary laws. Although Islam first took hold in the chiefly entourages, it increasingly found its greatest success among the jambur (free peasants). The tyeddo became the group most refractory to Islam. The bulk of the population mixed traditional pagan beliefs with Islam, and purchased gris-gris from the marabouts.[a]

[a] See my article "The Moslem Revolution in Nineteenth-Century Senegambia" in *Boston University Papers on Africa: History*, eds., Daniel McCall, Jeffrey But-

Thus an African Islam evolved very early in Senegambia. It was characterized by, among other things, the importance of religious fraternities known as *tariqas*. The tariqas developed out of Sufism—Islamic mysticism—which first appeared in the Arab world in the second century after the hegira as a reaction to the coldness of orthodox rationalistic theology. Much of Islamic intellectual history consists of a dialogue between Sufism and orthodox theology, but while orthodoxy has maintained its hold over the better-educated classes in the Middle East, Sufism has shaped both popular religious beliefs and the adaptation of Islam to non-Arab cultures and beliefs. Sufi mystics have been influenced by sources as diverse as the early Christian monastics, the Hindu Upanishads, and Berber animists.

Among the Sufis, loose and voluntary associations of pious men evolved; they often formed around a teacher known for his piety or his ability to work miracles. The disciples sought initiation into the master's *tariqa*, or "way." The disciple who had been completely initiated often went forth to found a new community and spread the master's teachings. In this way, networks of religious communities developed, often extending from one end of the Islamic world to the other. In some areas, alms permitted the Sufis to form monastic organizations, which freed the masters and their disciples from the necessity of earning a living, and left them free to devote full time to pious exercises and meditation. The tariqas were especially important to Berber North Africa, where Islam was characterized by saint worship, and where the tombs of holy men are often the sites of regular pilgrimages.

From North Africa, the tariqas spread south, though monastic organization has been very rare and saint worship is found only among a few peoples, like the Wolof, who have been influenced

---

ler, and Norman Bennett, Vol. IV in a series (New York, in prep.). Some Europeans were quite struck by the Moslems' absolute refusal to touch alcoholic drink. In the early 1800's, Francis Moore described the Mandinka of the Gambia thus: "Those who can write Arabick are very strict at their devotion 3 or 4 times a Day, and are very sober and abstemious in their way of living, chusing rather to die than drink strong liquors, and rather fast than eat anything which is not killed by one of their own Way of Thinking. They have great veneration paid them by all the Mundingoes, insomuch that if any of them are ill, they apply to a Mahometan for cure." (Moore, *Travels into the Inland Part of Africa*, p. 28.)

by the Moors. Most West African Moslems have been affiliated with one of the major tariqas through their ties with a local marabout. The believer is a *talibé*[b] of his marabout, just as the marabout is the talibé of his teacher. The "chain" of initiation that ties the individual marabout to one of the more famous religious teachers is an important source of prestige. Membership in a tariqa requires accepting the guidance of the marabout, using a distinctive set of prayer beads, and participating in special religious exercises.[2]

The first major tariqa to establish roots in West Africa was the *Qadiriyya,* an othodox order little inclined to fanaticism. It was largely Qadiriyya marabouts who led the first wave of revolts in West Africa in the late eighteenth and early nineteenth centuries. The marabouts based their revolution on a coherent set of ideas that insisted not only on the rejection of any states that did not enforce Moslem law, but also on the forcible conversion of pagans.[3] The first revolts took place among the Poular-speaking peoples, but the ideology on which these revolts were based soon spread to other ethnic groups. New states were formed under marabout leadership in Fouta Djallon in 1725 and Fouta Toro in 1776, in northern Nigeria in 1804, and in Macina in 1810. One of the major results of the revolution, in addition to the formation of the new states, was the creation of a new Moslem aristocracy.

In the early nineteenth century, a new tariqa, the *Tijaniyya,* was introduced into West Africa, and it gave new life to the revolutionary impulse that seemed to have faded after the revolutionary regimes had established themselves.[4] Founded in the late eighteenth century by a North African cleric, the Tijaniyya is more democratic in its conception of Islam, is simpler, and imposes fewer obligations on the believer, though at the same time it is more puritanical, as in its prohibition of tobacco. Not all branches of the Tijaniyya were involved in the resistance to

[b] The word *talibé* comes from the Arabic *talib.* It can be translated either student or disciple, and refers to the relationship between a student and his teacher, a man and his marabout, and the Moslem and the Prophet. In his letters, Ma Bâ repeatedly refers to himself as a *talibé,* which is to say that he was only doing God's Will as made manifest by the Prophet.

French expansion in Senegal, but France's most vigorous opponents were almost all *Tijani,* and many early French administrators feared the passion that Tijani marabouts were able to arouse
in their followers.

The most important of the Tijani leaders was Al Hajj Umar
Tall.[c] Umar was born in Fouta Toro in 1797, the son of a marabout. He was a member of the *torodbe,* the Toucouleur society's
clerical class, which had overthrown the *denianke* rulers of the
Fouta in 1776 and created a theocratic state. (The denianke were
members of a dynasty that had ruled the Fouta since the sixteenth century.) In the 1820's, Umar made the pilgrimage to
Mecca, a feat undertaken infrequently at that time from the
western Sudan, and while he was in Arabia, he was initiated into
the Tijaniyya and appointed Khalif for the western Sudan. After
returning, Umar lived at or visited the major Moslem courts of
West Africa—Kanem, Sokoto, Macina, and Fouta Djallon. Within a short time, the Tijaniyya replaced the Qadiriyya as the
dominant tariqa in both Fouta Djallon and Fouta Toro. Umar
established a religious center at Dinguiraye, in the foothills of
Fouta Djallon, and it was here that he began his religious crusade
in 1852. He intended to create an Islamic empire that would restore the unity that the western Sudan had had in the time of the
Mali Empire. Though the nucleus of his army was recruited in
Fouta Toro, he was opposed by the rulers of the Fouta, and his
failure to take Medina from the French in 1857 doomed his effort to conquer the region where he was born.[5]

While Umar was conquering much of the western Sudan, a
parallel effort was being undertaken in Senegambia by a man
who had met Umar only once. This was Amath Bâ, better known
as Ma Bâ Diakhou. Ma Bâ was born into a denianke family from
Fouta Toro.[d] His father migrated to Rip, or Badibu, where he
taught the Koran. Ma Bâ received his Koranic education at a

---

[c] The Tijaniyya was first introduced to West Africa by Mohammed Al-Hajes,
a Moor, but Umar played the key role in its extension. See Jamil Abun-Nasr, *The
Tijaniyya* (London, 1965), chap. 5.

[d] Ma Bâ's grandfather, Paté Douloh, converted to the orthodox Islam of the
torodbe shortly after the Fouta Toro revolt of 1776. Ma Bâ's father, N'Dougou
Penda Bâ, spent his life teaching the Koran in a largely Wolof area of Rip. Ma Bâ,

school in Cayor, and then taught the Koran himself in Djoloff. After several decades of study and teaching in the Wolof states, he returned to Rip at the request of a younger brother to take over his father's position. About 1850, in the village of Kabakoto, Ma Bâ had his only interview with Umar. According to Tamsir Bâ, Umar chose Ma Bâ as the Tijani representative in the area, and the two prayed together for three days and three nights.[6] There is little indication of later contact between the two Tijani reformers, but their goals were similar, and Ma Bâ chose the name of Umar's capital, Nioro, for his own capital. During the decade that followed this interview, Ma Bâ devoted himself not to revolution but to teaching the Koran.

The Tijani phase of the Islamic revolution was developing at the same time that French imperialism was becoming a powerful force. Umar's war of conquest began three years before Faidherbe established French claims over Oualo. The connection between the two expansive forces was, however, limited. Undoubtedly, profits from the peanut trade made it possible for frugal Moslem peasants to buy guns and ammunition, which could transform the peasants into warriors. Undoubtedly too, some African leaders saw in Islam a unifying force and a base for resistance to French imperialism. On the other hand, the religious revolution took form long before the new, expansionist imperialism did, and therefore it did not take shape in response to the problems caused either by the end of the slave trade or by the growth of legitimate commerce. The revolution was essentially a product of certain internal tensions within important West

---

the oldest son, was sent to M'Bayène in Cayor for his Koranic studies, and when N'Dougou died, a younger son took over the father's responsibilities so that the oldest son could continue his studies. After completing his education, Ma Bâ moved to Djoloff, where his mother had been born, and began teaching. He was joined there by his brother, Mamour N'Dari, who had been educated in Mauritania. Ma Bâ married Maty N'Diaye, niece of the Burba Djoloff, and forged ties in both Cayor and Djoloff that were to be useful in later years. Maty was the mother of Saër Maty Bâ, who later became Ma Bâ's chosen heir. It is striking that Ma Bâ's family had not been in Rip as long as other marabout families; Ma Bâ's personal ascendancy was established in a very short period of time. See Tamsir Ousmane Bâ, "Essai historique sur le Rip (Sénégal)," BIFAN, XIX (1957), 564–91; Lieutenant Chaudron, "Etude sur le cercle du Nioro du Rip," manuscript, ARS, 1 G 283.

African societies and of the efforts of powerful groups within those societies to resolve those tensions.

To understand the revolution, we must examine the societies affected by it. Of the four agricultural peoples who concern us, the Serer were the only ones with no Moslem community. The Toucouleur were deeply committed to Islam, as Carrère and Holle explained in 1855:

> The Koran is the only law in the political and civil order there; all social life is regulated according to the principles, more or less well understood, of their sacred book.
>
> Only the Moslem religion is tolerated in the Fouta. Every individual who lives in the territory of the Fouta must publicly make the salaam and meticulously observe the external practices of Moslem idolatry; if he refuses these marks of adhesion, he runs the risk of confiscation of property and exile.[7]

The Toucouleur aristocracy, which took power in the revolution of 1776, briefly sought to spread its conception of Islam to neighboring states, but after meeting little success, lost much of its crusading spirit. Fouta Toro remained a source of marabouts who started Koranic schools in other areas, and spread the ideology of the Moslem revolution.

Among the Mandinka and the Wolof, there was tension between Moslem minorities and traditional elites, who were either pagans or very lax Moslems. In 1818, Mollien described the Wolof Moslems of Diambour, a province of Cayor, thus:

> Mahometanism will soon become the universal religion of the country of Cayor. The court indeed remains attached to paganism, probably as more indulgent to the passions. Circumcision is practiced among the Joloffs universally; this, with the public schools kept by the marabouts, and frequented by all children, and the persons of the Mahometan priests being sacred even among the pagans, must powerfully operate to extend Islamism among these people. The Mahometan Negroes are devout votaries to the external forms of their religion. They will rise frequently in the night to chant chapters of the Koran, and one part of the day is allotted to repeating prayers on a long chaplet suspended from their girdle.

The Mahometan priests possess an authority almost unlimited. They alone interpret the will of heaven, and this they can well turn to account. The Negroes have a blind confidence in certain papers, which they call gris-gris, on which are written Arabic prayers. . . .

To procure admissions into the class of marabouts, an irreproachable character and some knowledge of the Arabic language are requisite. The candidate must not only retain several chapters of the Koran in his memory, but must acquire the knowledge of certain Arabic books, which treat of the history of the world and of arithmetic.[8]

There were frequent conflicts between the Moslems and the tyeddo. The Moslems tended to be the most hardworking and frugal villagers, and therefore the wealthiest. This made them a target for tyeddo pillage. It also created a frustrating situation for the Moslems, who felt themselves culturally superior to their pagan overlords and had in the Koran a justification for revolution. Senegambian history is dotted with Moslem revolts. In the 1670's, a marabout overthrew the Damel Cayor and kept him out of power for a brief period. Over a century later, the Lebu peoples of Cape Verde, under marabout leadership, asserted their independence of Cayor. There were marabout-led revolts in Ouli in 1842, in Kombo in 1855, and in Cayor in 1859. In 1862, Governor D'Arcy of the Gambia described the mixture of respect and hostility apparent in the two communities there as follows:

The Mandingoes are Mahomedans but divided . . . into two sections, Marabouts and Soninkes.[e] The former tell their beads, are careful in their public devotions, abstain from drink, are industrious but crafty, ambitious and sensual, besides being given to slavedealing. The latter, on the other hand, are law-

---

[e] The term "marabout" (in Wolof, "serigne") was generally used throughout Senegambia for any supporter of the marabout-led faction. Those who remained loyal to the traditional elites were called "soninke" in the Gambia, "tyeddo" in Senegal. The term "soninke" comes from "so-ni," the Mandinka word for sacrifice or libation. It means "one who gives libations," that is, a Moslem in name alone. These soninke are not to be confused with the people of the same name who live in the upper Senegal river valley. (They were also called the Sarakollé.) See J. S. Trimingham, *Islam in West Africa* (Oxford, 1959). p. 246; and Harry Gailey, *A History of the Gambia* (London, 1964), chap. 3.

less and dissipated, plundering when they can from the European trade or from the industrious Marabout—[are] warlike drones in fact. Yet, from this wild, unthinking people the Kings have hitherto been elected. . . .

The two adverse parties can scarcely be called castes as in India; a Mandingoe at birth is circumcized, and brought up by the village Fodey, or Schoolmaster, as a Marabout, but on arriving at Manhood he decides whether he will renounce the faith and its strict observance by becoming a Soninke, abandoned to vice in every kind.[9]

The spread of Islamic culture in Wolof society was speeded up among those who migrated into the Serer and Mandinka states. For centuries, the Wolof had been moving south, largely from Djoloff into better-watered lands in Saloum and the Mandinka states. Here they seem to have become largely Moslem, if they were not so already, and they affiliated with marabout factions. It was in a Wolof area of Rip that Ma Bâ began his revolution. While his forces included both Wolof and Mandinka, the largest group was Wolof.

The Moslem communities were structured so that they could easily be organized into a revolutionary movement. Many of the Moslems lived in villages separate from the pagan majority; and the marabouts exercised both religious and political authority in these villages. A well-known marabout would have a network of talibé, whose loyalty he could usually count on. These entirely Moslem communities existed in all of the Senegambian states except Sine, and since they were more or less constantly threatened by tyeddo attacks, they were hostile to the ruling elite.

The Religious Revolution

Ma Bâ's revolt began with an attack on Passy Khour, a village in Badibu—the Mandinka term was more commonly used in this area—but sources differ on what set off this attack. Abdou Boury Bâ says that the decision to revolt had been made several years before the attack, and that Ma Bâ, after being chosen leader, had begun to collect arms and ammunition. However, most versions discount the idea of a carefully planned conspiracy, and place emphasis instead on a series of triggering events that Ma Bâ could not have foreseen. According to Tamsir Bâ's account, the son of the Mansa Badibu was initially responsible for the revolt. Math Diaker, the Mansa's son, seized the wife of a Moslem and demanded that Ma Bâ send a cow for the marriage celebration. Ma Bâ responded to the indignity with an insult, sending a bowl of porridge and beans. His emissary, a half brother, Amath Khodia Bâ, was held as a hostage. That night, Moslem forces attacked Passy Khour, killing Math Diaker and beginning their devastation of Badibu.[10]

However, the most likely account suggests that the event triggering the action was a British decision to punish Badibu for harassing some Bathurst traders. The attack was planned to coordinate with Pinet-Laprade's 1861 invasion of Saloum, and a token French force joined the British.[11] During the operations, Ma Bâ came aboard the Governor's boat and agreed to accompany the expedition if his village were spared. The Mansa Badibu was easily defeated, and Ma Bâ helped to arrange the peace terms. Then, according to Governor D'Arcy, the Mansa sent his son to kill Ma Bâ. Math Diaker had had too much to drink the night before he was to commit the deed, and had bragged about his intentions. Instead of killing Ma Bâ, he himself was killed, and the revolt began.[12]

An examination of all the differing accounts suggests that the Mansa, Diéreba Marone, feared the increasing power and independence of marabout-led forces, and decided to move against them, either by trying to kill the outstanding leader or by forcing a symbolic gesture of submission on that leader. This strategy succeeded only in launching the marabouts on a rampage that made them aware, apparently for the first time, of their very real power. Once they knew what they could do, they could not be stopped.[f] Their forces swept through Badibu, burning villages that did not willingly accept the new order. The Mansa was

---

[f] Belated attempts by existing regimes to repress marabout power were important stimuli to many of the Moslem revolts, for example, those led by Uthman dan Fodio in northern Nigeria and Cheikhou Amadou in Macina. See J. S. Trimingham, *A History of Islam in West Africa* (London, 1962), pp. 177, 198.

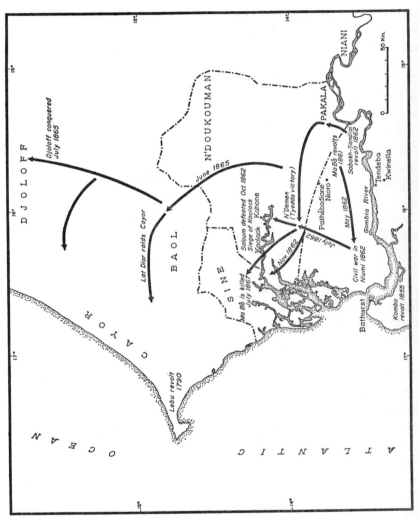

Ma Bâ's Wars and Related Conflicts

killed, and after a series of battles the old warrior aristocracy was driven across the Gambia River into exile. Over six hundred refugees fled to the British post at Tendeba. Others found their way to Bathurst or took refuge in Saloum. The British viewed Islam as a progressive force favorable to commerce, and they looked with approval on the Moslem victories, in spite of the refugee hordes.[13] The predominantly Moslem population of the French and English trading settlements also was sympathetic to the Tijani reformer.[14]

Ma Bâ's success caused others to look to him for aid. Shortly after the civil war began in Badibu, the Mansa Niumi died. A local marabout leader took advantage of the interregnum and revolted. Not finding success, he called on Ma Bâ for aid. Ma Bâ answered the call, and in May 1862 the new Mansa of Niumi, Buntu Gamey, took refuge with the British. When the British sought to mediate, Ma Bâ told them, as he later told French representatives, that he would spare the lives only of those who converted. In June, at about the time when Bathurst heard rumors that Saloum had invaded Badibu, Ma Bâ retreated, and Buntu Gamey and his chiefs returned to their badly ravaged villages.[15] In February 1863, the independence of Niumi as a pagan state was guaranteed in a treaty Ma Bâ signed with the British.[16] In general, though Ma Bâ collected tribute from large parts of Niumi through Amer Fall, a marabout leader there, he avoided challenging British control of the area. Ma Bâ bought most of his arms and ammunition in Bathurst, and could not afford to alienate the British.

Ma Bâ's battles were something new in Senegambia. The area had long known revolts and plunderings. It had not known revolution and total war. Ma Bâ destroyed and pillaged, burned villages, sold slaves, and killed pagans, not for greed, but for the power and glory of God. When a British emissary told him that famine would result from his ravaging, he answered simply, "God is our Father, and he has brought this war. We are in his hands."[17] He was successful because his charisma was strong and because a large Moslem population believed that the existing sociopolitical order was an affront to God. Ma Bâ's use of his religious prestige has been described by D'Arcy as follows:

On approaching a town he intends to destroy, he dismounts from his horse, orders his praying carpet to be spread, and calls for writing materials. A staff of blind marabouts now surround him, repeating in a low chant that God is great, and that there is only one God and Mahomet is his prophet. Mahaba then most earnestly writes *grees* [gris-gris], or charms, which he hastily distributes to his warriors, who, as they now imagine themselves doubly armed, rush to victory or heaven.[18]

Prisoners were given the choice of death or shaving their heads. Many chose death rather than token submission.[19] Though often politically astute, Ma Bâ was more interested in leading a militant crusade to establish a Moslem community ruled by Koranic law than he was in constructing a political structure that would survive him. To the chiefs that were the target of his crusading zeal, he addressed letters that protested in appropriately Moslem style his own humble status and the divine mission he had assumed. To the Burba Djoloff, he wrote in 1864, "You are greater than I and than all of the kings of the East. . . . Come simply to me as a Moslem, and God will serve as a witness between us."[20]

Saloum at this time was a richer and more challenging prize than Niumi. The Bur Saloum was Samba Laobé Fall, a young man of about nineteen, who was, like many of his predecessors, a heavy drinker. Crowned in 1859, he defended his throne against Coumba Dianké and the Kévé Bigué. Then, when he was saddled with the heavy reparations exacted by the French after Pinet-Laprade's night attack, Samba Laobé had to defend Saloum against an invasion by his father, Macodou, the former Damel Cayor. Macodou had earlier turned down the throne of Saloum for that of Cayor,[21] but in 1861, he opposed French plans to build a telegraph line across Cayor and was driven into exile by French arms. Supported by the Beleup N'Doukouman, he twice tried to attack Kahone, and twice his son's forces drove his army back to N'Doukouman.[g]

---

[g] Commandant of Kaolack to Commandant of Gorée, 4 Apr. 1862, ARS, 13 G 319; also versions given by Al Hajj N'Diack Samb, of Kaolack, and Abdou Boury Bâ, of Birkelane, in interviews. Beleup N'Doukouman was the title of one of the most powerful eastern Saloum chiefs.

At this time, another Moslem revolt erupted in Sabakh and Sandial, two small states tributary to the Mansa Badibu. The revolt was independent of Ma Bâ, and was led by three marabouts —Cheikhou Ousman Diop, Sambou Oumané Touré, and Mandiaye Khoredia.[h] After their initial victory, the marabout-led forces swept into Kaymor, a Saloum province that had a large Moslem population, and defeated the Bumi Kaymor. The tyeddo forces of Kaymor fell back on Kahone, and Samba Laobé gathered his army to help them. In a battle near N'Demen, a third Moslem area, Samba Laobé's tyeddo prevailed, and two of the marabout leaders, Sambou Oumané Touré and Mandiaye Khoredia, were killed.

The result of the tyeddo victory was another call to Ma Bâ. The remnants of the defeated force joined Ma Bâ's growing army, and Sambou Oumané's sons, Sed Kani and N'Deri Kani Touré, henceforth played an important role in Rip politics. It was probably the defeat at N'Demen that induced Ma Bâ to pull his forces out of Niumi in June 1862. Shortly thereafter, Macodou and his followers shaved their heads, and Ma Bâ agreed to put the former Damel on the throne of Saloum. The dissidents in Coumba Dianké's faction (the Kévé Bigué) also joined the marabouts. In July 1862, the tyeddo of Sambo Laobé attacked marabout positions south of the Saloum River, and were repulsed. Their retreat was cut off by Macodou, and the Saloum army suffered heavy losses. This battle more than any other seems to have broken the Saloum tyeddo's will to fight.[22] On the other hand, the battle did little good for Macodou. That night he got drunk in a victory celebration, and Ma Bâ, a good Molsem throughout, gathered his army and pulled out. Macodou was unable to hold Kahone himself, and Samba Laobé regained his capital without any difficulty.

[h] Though there are references to "Ousman" in the French archives, it is very difficult to put together an accurate description of this faction, which was later to cause Ma Bâ a great deal of difficulty. The only extensive information on Ousman is in A. Le Chatelier, *L'Islam dans l'Afrique Occidentale* (Paris, 1899), pp. 204–9. Unfortunately, this account was written years after the events, and it attributes to Ousman Diop some actions clearly Ma Bâ's. Diop was a Wolof born in Balagnar, a village near the Gambia, and educated in Cayor and Fouta Toro. Accord-

French policy was primarily concerned with Macodou. The Saloum River was still an area of only secondary interest. France wanted to control commerce without making extensive political commitments, but Macodou, as a former Damel, was a potential threat in the Cayor-Baol area that was central to French political and commercial interests. Governor Jauréguibéry wrote Paris after Samba Laobé's defeat, "Macodou, our former enemy, supported by a fanatic marabout who is worrying the English factories in the Gambia, has just posted a strong victory over the king of Saloum, and it is to be feared that he will try to penetrate Baol."[23] The hostility of the French toward Macodou was countered only by their conviction that Islam represented progress and would be favorable to commerce. Pinet-Laprade wrote in September 1862:

> I think that a revolution accomplished in the name of Moslem civilization against the blind and brutal despotism of the tyeddo would be favorable to the Wolof populations submitted to this despotism and, as a result, to the development of commerce.[24]

He went on to say that the French could not deal with Macodou, and should make it clear to the Moslems that they would remain neutral only if he were expelled from Moslem ranks.

While not actively taking sides, the French hindered Samba Laobé. The French raid in 1861 resulted in large losses, which, coupled with the reparations demanded, left Saloum little to spend on guns and horses. Furthermore, Samba Laobé could no longer step up his demands on the merchants without their making immediate, and often excessive, demands for reimbursement. The French Commandant collected export duties in Kaolack, and until January 1863, did not have orders to immediately give these needed revenues to the Bur.[25] In the months before the rains in 1862, Samba Laobé and the tyeddo were ravaging the

---

ing to Le Chatelier, Diop was personally initiated into the Tijaniyya by Umar and was appointed its representative in the area. This claim was also made by Ma Bâ. Further research on family and village traditions might cast more light on these forces.

countryside for food. At the same time, the Commandant reported that hunger was striking the peasantry.[4]

Famine was several times reported in Rip too, but in general
Ma Bâ's position was stronger. The stifling of the coastal slave
trade limited the market, but slaves could easily be sold to a number of neighboring societies. Although the French considered
Ma Bâ's killing and enslavement of pagans evidence of his lack
of religious principles, neither practice was explicitly forbidden
by his faith, and enslavement had long been one of the hazards
of war. The continuation of the war demanded a constant flow
of arms, horses, and ammunition, which could be bought with
the income from the sale of slaves and cattle.[26] Samba Laobé had
little to sell, and he spent some of his resources on liquor. A British emissary reported that there were three to four thousand
cattle in Ma Bâ's camp in February 1863, mostly taken in raids
on Saloum.[27] The task of supplying an army was complicated on
both sides by regular natural catastrophes. For example, locusts
struck large areas in 1862, 1864, and 1865.

In September 1862, Macodou's tyeddo shaved their heads
again, and resumed their alliance with Ma Bâ.[28] On October 6,
as refugees fleeing from Ma Bâ's forces poured into Kaolack,
Samba Laobé's forces took up a defensive position at Tikat, carefully chosen to allow flight to Kaolack. Badly outnumbered, with
fifteen hundred men to Ma Bâ's four thousand, Samba Laobé's
forces did not resist for long. The marabouts followed the fleeing
tyeddo to Kaolack, and then attacked the French post there. All
day long, the twelve-man garrison held off marabout attacks.
When Ma Bâ withdrew his forces that night, there were over 250
bodies on the field.[29] The French commanded only the area within cannon shot of the post, but that much was securely theirs. The
battle over, Ma Bâ pulled his army back to Nioro, and Macodou
returned to eastern Saloum, where he died in June 1863. Samba
Laobé died the following February and was succeeded by his
brother, Fakha Fall.

[4] 11 Mar. and 9 Sept. 1862, ARS, 13 G 319. Economic difficulties did not, of
course, stop trade, which involved mostly the trading of cattle for guns. Trade
with Saloum reached 200,000 francs in 1862. 31 May 1863, ARS, 13 G 319.

In November 1862, marabout forces destroyed the small state of Coular and moved north into Djilor.[30] According to oral accounts, the tyeddo of Djilor fought fiercely, but after a series of battles they were driven north across the Saloum River, and Mama Gaolo Niang, a marabout of griot origin, was chosen chief of Djilor. This solidly Serer and pagan area was one of those most extensively devastated by marabout attacks.[31] The Mandinka villages of Niombato swore allegiance to Ma Bâ and took part in operations against the tyeddo. Several of the Serer-speaking Niominka villages on the Saloum delta islands followed suit.[32] It is probable that conversions in this area were influenced by a shared hostility to the tyeddo—Saloum had long tried to control the Saloum delta islands. The alliance of Ma Bâ with the coastal peoples reversed traditional relationships—the attacked were now the attackers—and led to the lasting conversion of the area. In Djilor and central Saloum, many Serer peasants fled, taking refuge in Sine, in Kaolack, or along the French-protected Petite Côte. Monsignor Kobès, who was trying to introduce large-scale cotton plantations, had more refugees willing to work his fields than he could use.[33] Some Serer villages resisted the marabout forces. In May 1863, one of Ma Bâ's bands was repulsed by five villages north of Kaolack. The victory was short-lived, for a larger band returned and destroyed the villages. Reports drifted into Kaolack that more than a thousand peasants had been killed.[34]

By the time the rains came in 1863, the marabouts controlled everything between the Gambia and Saloum rivers except part of Niumi, and their lands extended north in eastern Saloum to the Djoloff frontier. Moslem forces in eastern Saloum were joined by the Serigne Pakala,[j] and successfully drove the other traditional chiefs out of the area. In the same year, 1863, marabout bands began operating further north, raiding in Sine and in the Wolof states, but they also faced one more challenge from the former Mandinka rulers of Badibu. Mandinka warriors, supported by men from Ouli, up the river, and Kiang, on the other bank, crossed the Gambia and fortified Tounkou. They were attacked

---

[j] The Serigne Pakala was a Moslem chief, but for over a century he was subject to the Bur Saloum.

and driven back south of the river, but when Ma Bâ tried to follow up his victory, he suffered one of his few defeats, reportedly leaving five hundred of his men dead on the south bank.[k] The marabout army seems to have successfully recovered from such costly battles. In February 1863, a British visitor to Ma Bâ's camp estimated his force at about eleven thousand men,[l] and a year later the Commandant at Kaolack believed Ma Bâ's troops to number seventeen to twenty thousand.[35]

Ma Bâ and the French

Even after the attack on Kaolack, the French were reluctant to take action against Ma Bâ. Jauréguibéry, who replaced Faidherbe as Governor from December 1861 to July 1863, was not interested in further expansion. Both Faidherbe and Pinet-Laprade preferred the Moslems to the tyeddo, and were disturbed only by the presence of Macodou in the marabout camp. In explaining the events of 1863 to Paris, Pinet-Laprade wrote:

> The marabouts—faithful observers of the Koran, who are tired of the violence inflicted on them by bands of drunkards like the tyeddo of Cayor, Baol, Sine, and Saloum, who live only by thievery—resolved about a year ago to convert or destroy this brutalized and useless race.[36]

As the marabout bands began to move farther north, the French administration began to see in Ma Bâ a barrier to the expansion of commerce, and its favorable attitude changed. Faidherbe wrote in 1864, "The destruction of the tyeddo kings is a good thing in itself; but by the methods he uses, Ma Bâ becomes a plague still worse than the tyeddo kings."[37]

Faidherbe's change of heart was influenced by an alliance Ma Bâ had formed with Lat Dior. Like Macodou, Lat Dior opposed the French telegraph line. He defeated a French column in De-

[k] Gray, A History of the Gambia, pp. 423–24; Bâ, BIFAN, XIX, 578. Gray thinks that this battle broke Ma Bâ's power. This is not true, but then, Gray's book is based only on the Gambia archives.

[l] C. Beresford Primet to Governor of Gambia, 9 Mar. 1863, ARS, 1 F 6. According to the oral tradition, Ma Bâ had only 313 men when he first did battle with the Mansa Badibu in 1861.

cember 1863, but the French drove him from Cayor the following month, and he fled to Sine. Coumba N'Doffène, who was beginning to feel the sting of Ma Bâ's raids, feared to antagonize French power, so he wrote Gorée asking that the French permit Lat Dior to remain in Sine.[38] The permission was not given, and the former Damel was forced to seek shelter elsewhere. Ma Bâ's response to the demand that he expel Lat Dior was very different. He said, "Lat Dior has converted, and he lives with me, but we have no commerce together. If he stays with me in order to make his salaam and read the Koran, we will be friends, because I love only the truth."[39]

The conversion of Lat Dior, Macodou, and the Niominka villages involved the Moslem revolution in traditional leadership conflicts. Both Macodou and Lat Dior converted for political reasons: they needed support against the French and against traditional rivals in Cayor whom the French were supporting. (The difference between the two lay in the degrees of their commitments to Islam: Macodou was interested in the religion only insofar as adherence to it gained him Ma Bâ's support; Lat Dior remained a practicing Moslem for the rest of his life and used Islam to reinforce his power.) The long-standing lineage conflicts that emerged in all Senegambian states when a ruler died created opportunities for interference in the selection of Burs. Islamic leaders, and later the French, seized these opportunities, perhaps without clearly realizing what they were doing. From 1860 on, out-of-power factions sought aid either from the French or from the marabouts, if not from both.

Although Ma Bâ continued to be allied with Lat Dior, he began negotiations with the French in May 1864.[40] Shortly after defeating the tyeddo again, Ma Bâ wrote Faidherbe, outlining his objectives thus:

I, Ma Bâ, do not see what concerns you in the affairs of Djoloff, Cayor, Baol, Sine, and the rest of Saloum. Tell me what concerns you. Are they Moslems or Christians? Do you love the infidels and detest the believers? . . . As for me, I find in the laws of the Prophet that we should declare war on the infidels who are near you. . . . We have confidence in God because he who is immortal has told us to count on him. Because it is God, and not his servants, who will bring us great well-being.[41]

When Faidherbe met with his council of administration, he was ready for action, if only because he believed that "The Negroes will doubt our power against Ma Bâ, and that will increase his forces and his authority in a manner dangerous for the future."[42] The consensus of the council was that Sine and Saloum should be conceded to Ma Bâ if he recognized earlier treaties, but that the commercially important states of Cayor and Baol should be defended. Faidherbe explained his terms to Ma Bâ in this way:

> You have written me that you are working only for a commendable goal—that of ending permanently the domination of the tyeddo, who under the influence of alcoholic drink commit all sorts of crimes, and who are a very real calamity for the country they dominate. We are trying to do the same thing; we have overturned the two most detestable tyeddo, Macodou and Lat Dior, in order to put in their place a man who will govern under our protection and suppress plunder. . . . You are not one of those false marabouts who, under the pretext of holy war, make war simply to plunder the country and seize women and children in order to sell them. . . . Saloum was a country daily destroyed by its own chiefs. Today you are the master. I hope that you are going to make peace, justice, work, and commerce flourish there. Begin by organizing Saloum before undertaking the conquest of other countries with which we have close ties of friendship, and which no person may touch. As for Baol and Cayor, touching them is like attacking St. Louis itself. . . . Respect everywhere our nationals, our posts, and our territory.[43]

Ma Bâ would not break his ties with Lat Dior, but he saw the possibility of coming to terms with the French as he already had with the British. His correspondence with Faidherbe lasted through the rainy season and eventually produced a treaty. Though both sides sought to avoid a conflict, this correspondence made it evident that a lasting compromise was impossible. Both Faidherbe and Ma Bâ were motivated by messianic ideals—Ma

Bâ believed in his divine mission, Faidherbe believed that he represented peace, order, commerce, and civilization. Faidherbe insisted on the power to protect commerce, and Ma Bâ demanded the freedom to pursue religious and political objectives that were incompatible with peaceful commercial development. Neither man was able to comprehend the other's ideals. To Faidherbe, Ma Bâ seemed politically ambitious, since he could be appealed to only by a guarantee of those conquests he had already made. To Ma Bâ, the French were traders; he was quite willing to guarantee their trading privileges, saying "I am only a talibé and you are a merchant," and, "Do not put yourself on the side of infidels, but only on the side of your property when damage is done you. . . . There can only exist between us good commercial relations."[44]

The French had given up on the tyeddo of Saloum. They persuaded Fakha Fall, the Bur, to leave the post at Kaolack so that they could make an agreement with the marabouts. In July 1864, Ma Bâ was informed that the tyeddo had gone. He, in turn, permitted the fields near Kaolack to be worked in peace, and let his people trade gold and hides at Kaolack for the grain that his forces apparently needed during the "hungry season."

Neither Faidherbe nor Ma Bâ counted on the negotiations. Marabout bands raided in Baol and Sine, and Lat Dior was several times reported in Djoloff.[m] At the same time, Faidherbe was negotiating with Governor D'Arcy of the Gambia for permission to use the Gambia River for a two-pronged attack on Rip. D'Arcy, who had been sending Faidherbe information about Ma Bâ, wanted to destroy the marabout's power. In July 1864, he wrote of his anger against

anarchy, confusion, spoliation, and all the horrors of a savage war, which has now lasted nearly three years, filling our settlement with the poor and the destitute, destroying our trade, giving to the more ignorant pastoral tribes who surround us, such as the Foulahs and the Jaffers, at least an appearance that

[m] Lat Dior, who often commanded Ma Bâ's forces in the north, usually used M'Backé, a village in eastern Baol founded by the marabout family of that name, as his base.

the white man approves by his silence and inaction . . . the horrors committed on them in the name of religion.[45]

Her Majesty's Government, however, was unhappy about losses in the Ashanti War of 1863, and would not even permit the French to move supplies up the Gambia.[46]

Even before London killed the Gambia invasion plan, the correspondence with Ma Bâ took a favorable turn, perhaps because locusts had damaged crops, perhaps because Ma Bâ needed time to prepare new projects. In October 1864, a treaty was signed by Ma Bâ, France, Cayor, Sine, Baol, and Djoloff. It recognized Ma Bâ as the Almamy of Badibu and Saloum, confirmed the rights of French commerce in Saloum, and guaranteed existing frontiers. All rulers promised to permit free trade and not to discriminate against either pagan or Moslem. It was not a treaty either side expected to keep for long. During the negotiations, Pinet-Laprade had written Faidherbe that France would have to act "as soon as he [Ma Bâ] has accomplished the useful part of his mission, that is to say the destruction of the tyeddo of Sine and Saloum."[47] And Faidherbe wrote Pinet-Laprade shortly after the treaty was signed:

> I am as certain as you that we cannot count on the good faith of Ma Bâ any more than on that of the majority of other chiefs with whom we have to deal in this country, but at the same time I cannot undertake a war without urgent reasons, and solely to escape an uncertain future. It is necessary not to forget that if Ma Bâ is a man of bad faith, the tyeddo chiefs whom we let him replace were as much thieves as he, and were just as detestable and far more brutalized.[48]

For Ma Bâ, the treaty was a way of gaining time to build up a grand alliance capable of checking the French. He came surprisingly close to success, and might have made it had he waited two years; for after 1867 the crisis in Europe completely immobilized French forces in Senegal. More important, he failed because he did not devote enough attention to political questions, and did not completely control his marabout allies.

Early in 1865 there were scattered reports of bands moving

through Baol and Djoloff, but large-scale operations did not begin until the rains started in June. Ma Bâ chose his time well, for the climate condemned the French to four months of inaction. Pinet-Laprade, the new Governor, was not willing to send out a column made up entirely of Senegalese tirailleurs, but neither could he commit his white troops to a month-long campaign during the rains. Instead, he set up a line of posts on the Cayor-Djoloff frontier. Arms were sent to Baol and Sine, and letters followed promising action at the end of the rains. In addition, boats were sent to patrol the river and keep Fouta Toro quiet.[49] On July 22 Pinet-Laprade reported that Ma Bâ was in complete control of Djoloff,[50] where the Burba's forces had been defeated several times by the marabout army.

At least one of the French posts found itself in an area of "dubious loyalty." The Commandant at Niomré in Moslem Diambour wrote Pinet-Laprade that the local people kept protesting their friendship but never carried out his requests. He reported of one meeting: "I tried to make them understand that we all had only one chief, and that it was you. They answered me that for them the chief of N'Diambour was the Serigne Louga, and that they would not budge without his order."[51]

From his new base, Ma Bâ sought an alliance with the Moors of Trarza and with the people of Fouta Toro. In August, the French learned that Trarza had promised to send twenty horsemen as soon as the Emir collected the duties due on gum. After a bitter three-year war with the French in the 1850's, the Trarza Moors were cautious about committing a large force to an anti-French coalition.[52] What is more, they seem to have changed their minds about sending any at all before the time came. The same month, the French also got hold of a circular that Ma Bâ's talibés were distributing in Fouta Toro:

> You, the people of the Fouta, as well as the Lam Toro, you are my equals and my brothers before Mahomet. I am sending this message to tell you that I am a man of little value, but one who calls you to God and his prophet. . . . People of the Fouta, all those among you who have something to sell, sell it to me; that will serve the religion of our God, who has promised to protect all those who defend his religion. Whoever among you

has something that can be useful to the defense of our religion, let him bring it to me.[53]

Ma Bâ probably received some aid and some recruits from the Fouta, but Umar had also recruited his forces there, and it is unlikely that there were many more potential recruits. Moreover, before his alliance could take form, Ma Bâ had to return to Saloum to deal with a revolt by Cheikhou Ousman Diop.[n] Lat Dior remained in Djoloff, but Diop's revolt doomed Ma Bâ's bid for an empire in the north.

Pinet-Laprade depended on the flooded river to keep the Moors from attacking before mid-January. At the end of the rains, he strengthened his garrison at Dagana in order to keep the Fouta quiet, and moved the bulk of his forces—about two thousand cavalry and four thousand infantry—overland to Kaolack, in a show of force designed to immobilize Ma Bâ's potential allies. On November 24 he destroyed the *tata*, masonry fortifications one meter thick, which Ma Bâ had built at Maka, near Kahone. There was no resistance. Four days later, as the army moved south toward Nioro, it was attacked at Pathébadiane. Pinet-Laprade's account describes heavy fighting, in which there were over a hundred casualties, including himself. That night French forces went on to burn Nioro, and the next day the African auxiliaries—tyeddo from allied states—were turned loose on the countryside. Over thirty villages were burned, the report stated.[54]

All the versions of the oral tradition that I collected treat Pathébadiane as a victory for the marabouts. Lat Dior, who had fought the French before, was the marabout strategist. To nullify greater French firepower and longer-range rifles, he planned

---

[n] Commandant of Merinaghen to Governor of Senegal, 8 Aug. 1865, ARS, 1 D 27. The oral tradition attributes this revolt to Matar Kalla. See also Bâ, *BIFAN*, XIX, 581–83. The opposition of this faction limited Nioro's operations until 1868. After Diop's death in 1866, opposition was led by Matar Kalla and Mamour Samba Diobaye. One Kaolack Commandant referred to them as "the national party," which would suggest a predominantly Mandinka faction, but Diop was Wolof. Commandant of Kaolack to Governor of Senegal, 15 Oct. 1867, ARS, unclassified. It is not clear whether the French had accurate information on conflicts within the Moslem camp, and my oral informants cast little light on the dissidents. According to Le Chatelier, *L'Islam dans l'Afrique Occidentale*, Matar Kalla was not allied to Diop at this time, but sought to arbitrate the conflict.

an ambush in the forest. However, tradition has it that a warrior who had never seen white men became very curious and raised his head, thereby alerting the French. The fighting was joined too soon, but the Moslems eventually prevailed. The French were able to pull out and burn several villages, but did not achieve their objectives.[55] I was inclined to accept the French account until I looked at the British archives in the Gambia. There were three references to the battle. The first was to a French victory "in a terrible battle."[56] The second was to French prisoners: "French officers taken by Ma Bâ last December were tied to a tree and his Warriors fired at them as they rode by at a gallop. . . . The expedition was taken at an unfavorable season of the year and did not produce the results expected from it."[57] The third described the marabout forces celebrating: "Proud of their alleged triumph over the French last December, they actually at Tubarcolong dressed up their warriors in caps taken from the baggage of the French army."[o]

Pinet-Laprade's report was not simply a lie. His letters to post Commandants the following year showed surprise that Ma Bâ continued strong. However, Pinet-Laprade did not try another invasion, even though Ma Bâ's power had not been destroyed. The battle made it clear that in spite of their technological superiority, the French did not have the military power to assert themselves very far inland. France could not afford to supply a large fighting force in the field indefinitely, and when the French withdrew, burned villages could be rebuilt and enemy forces could reestablish themselves. For Ma Bâ, success in holding Rip was not as important as failure to hold the Wolof north. Moslem villages allied to the marabout cause were forced to migrate to Rip rather than expose themselves to retaliation. During 1865, Ma Bâ's position in the north had grown weaker.

The Bull of Diakhou Dies

Early in 1866, Pinet-Laprade urged the Commandant at Gorée to encourage resettlement of the area around Kaolack and to seek the restoration of order and commerce there. He also wrote the Bur Sine:

[o] July 3, 1866, AG. The French also lost at least one large gun.

Our long friendship has made me think of you to restore this ancient Serer kingdom. I authorize you to enter this country with your army, to expel from it the several thieves who are to be found there, and to found villages at your convenience. You will be wise to give Fakha Fall a command.[58]

But Fakha Fall refused to obey the Bur Sine,[59] and in later years Pinet-Laprade's successors were to deny his grant to the Bur, partly because the policy was a failure. Two months after it was made, the Governor wrote another letter to the Bur Sine:

Saloum can only become rich through agriculture; in order to attract farmers, it is necessary for you to leave them their harvests. Thus, the people of Saloum who have farmed at Gandiaye or elsewhere should bring in their harvests; I do not want them to be troubled. Now that the country is growing and becoming quieter, it is necessary to make [the farmers] cultivate peanuts. That is what I wanted done when I confided Saloum to you.[60]

It is probable that the Bur was unwilling to move his people into a threatened area, and thus tried to establish his authority in the only way he knew, by sending his tyeddo in to collect taxes.

In 1866 Ma Bâ was not the threat he had been a year earlier, but his bands moved at will through much of Senegal. The French had an intelligence network that included every chief who protested friendship, but the network provided only confusing and erratic information on Ma Bâ's movements. Pinet-Laprade ordered post commanders to send out spies and to shoot Ma Bâ's agents, but at least one commander complained that he did not have an interpreter and did not even know what was going on in the village next to the post.[61] When Lat Dior moved through southern Cayor, a supposedly pro-French chief explained that there was no resistance because Lat Dior's men had relatives in the area.[62] In the Gambia, marabout forces under Amer Fall went into action again in Niumi. When the marabouts invaded the Ceded Mile, the British burned several of their villages in retaliation, and extracted from Ma Bâ a promise not to molest the area further.[63] The reason for Ma Bâ's quick acceptance of British demands may have been the large arms purchases he was making in the Gambia.[64]

After Pathébadiane, Pinet-Laprade was reluctant to commit his forces. Instead of trying to destroy Ma Bâ or come to terms with him, Pinet-Laprade strengthened his fortifications, tying down men in posts that controlled very limited areas, and carried out a raid, which did not dent Ma Bâ's power. In April 1867, Flize, the Commandant at Gorée, led a 270-man force into the Saloum delta, and burned a number of pro-marabout villages.[p] Flize then left 160 men at Kaolack, hoping to block a reported invasion of Sine. Captain Le Creurer, who commanded the group, had orders to make periodic military excursions, but not to spend the night outside of the camp and not to commit his troops unless absolutely sure of victory. On April 20, upon receiving reports about an enemy band in the area, he left the post with his whole force. Ten kilometers from Kaolack, the outfit walked into a marabout ambush. About forty of Le Creurer's men succeeded in fighting their way back.[q]

Pinet-Laprade was determined to defend Sine, but even before Paris received word of the disaster at Kaolack, the Minister turned down his request for more troops and ordered him to avoid new involvements, saying:

> I do not disregard the inconveniences that can result from this aggression from the point of view of our influence on these populations, and of the interests involved in several of our factories. But we have more grave subjects of preoccupation: Europe at this time is going through a serious political crisis. In the presence of possibilities that could develop in spite of the spirit of moderation and conciliation that animates the government of the Emperor, it is absolutely necessary that you carefully avoid new complications. Until new orders, as soon

---

[p] *Moniteur du Sénégal*, Vol. XII (23 Apr. 1867); Commandant of Gorée to Governor of Senegal, 12 Apr. 1867, ARS, 1 D 30. The area attacked was not important to Ma Bâ.

[q] Commandant of Kaolack to Commandant of Gorée, 20 Apr. 1867, ARS, 13 G 320. According to an article in the *Moniteur du Sénégal*, Vol. XII (30 Apr. 1867), total casualties amounted to 60 killed and 30 wounded. Le Creurer, who was responsible for the defeat, was killed in action, so Flize, who was not responsible, became the scapegoat and was removed from his post.

as the expedition now in progress has been completed, you will remain on the defensive.[65]

Several days later, Pinet-Laprade was told that he would not even receive replacements for white troops who got sick or died. When Ma Bâ invaded Sine, Pinet-Laprade was in Paris vainly trying to get those instructions rescinded.

Pinet-Laprade wanted to defend Sine with French forces because he believed that Ma Bâ was otherwise a certain victor. His conviction was based on a misinterpretation of Sine's policies regarding Ma Bâ. During the six years before Ma Bâ invaded Sine, the Bur Sine seemed reluctant to fight him. Pinet-Laprade mistook his reluctance for cowardice, and assumed that Sine would not offer strong resistance to an attack. It now seems more likely that Sine's policy toward Ma Bâ was motivated by a combination of discretion and the belief that France was the greater enemy. For more than two years after the 1861 treaty, Sine concentrated on whittling away its concessions to the French. The Bur appointed chiefs for the disputed villages, collected taxes in them, and exercised his judicial authority over the people living there. During the same period, traders at Fatick were made to pay taxes higher than those set up in the treaty. Jauréguibéry criticized the traders for paying, but he refused their demands for a post at Fatick.[r] The Bur also tried to restrict peanut cultivation in the hope that if there were no peanuts, the French would go away.[s] Pinet-Laprade's response to this was direct:

> If you wish us to protect you against interior as well as exterior enemies, you will have to follow my advice and do everything you can to increase the well-being of your subjects

---

[r] He explained his refusal by insisting that this would constitute "a precedent dangerous to the general interests of the colony and to the firmness of our relations with the natives." Governor of Senegal to Commandant of Gorée, 24 Jan. and 11 Mar. 1862, ARS, 3 B 81.

[s] Commandant of Kaolack to Commandant of Gorée, 18 Aug. 1862, ARS, 13 G 319; Commandant of Gorée to Governor of Senegal, 22 Aug. 1862, ARS, 1 D 22. This effort to limit cultivation in the hope that France would then go away was not at all unusual, though it is impossible to estimate how much such policies succeeded in limiting cultivation.

and the wealth of your country. You will attain [these goals] by careful cultivation of the products that are objects of commerce.[66]

By early 1864, the tone of the Bur's letters had changed. The Bur assured Faidherbe: "You dominate all of the black princes, and it is from you alone that I expect the increase of my power. . . . I will look with pleasure upon the creation of a French establishment in my country."[67] From 1864 on, the Bur continually protested his readiness to fight, bragged about victories in small engagements, and pleaded for horses, guns, and ammunition. Late in the year he wrote: "Tell me what I should do, what is the line of conduct that I should take toward Ma Bâ, and just what you intend to do. My great desire is to go to Saloum."[68] Apparently the French, and particularly Pinet-Laprade, remained unimpressed by the Bur's protestations.

For six years, Ma Bâ avoided a direct confrontation with pagan Sine. The oral tradition explains that he had heard a prediction that he would die in Sine. It is more likely that he postponed a confrontation with Sine because he wanted to concentrate first on areas where he could fight alongside a local Moslem population. Then, in 1867, his strategy changed. Several days after his victory at Kaolack, a band of his followers entered Sine, but after an indecisive battle, it withdrew. Two months later, the marabouts burned Diakhao in a surprise attack. Tradition has it that Coumba N'Doffène was away at a funeral. After the marabout victory, the story goes, Coumba N'Doffène sent a messenger who told Ma Bâ that such an attack was undignified, and that if he were a man, he would come back and meet the army of Sine in open battle.[t] In the middle of July, he came.

According to the oral tradition, the Bur called together his counselors when the word came that the Rip army was in Sine. They met for a long time, and the Bur himself was indecisive

---

[t] Bâ, *BIFAN*, XIX, 584–85; oral versions from Abdou Boury Bâ, Bur Sine Mahecor Diouf, and Latgarand N'Diaye, *chef d'arrondissement* at Sokone. Funerals are the occasion of much eating and drinking, and thus, a funeral would have caught Sine with its defenses down.

until one of the chiefs planted a spear in the ground and announced that he saw victory. The clairvoyant warrior was given
command of the army, and the drums began to beat to call together the men of Sine.[69] Written sources provide a description
of the battle itself. That night there was a heavy rain. Much of
Ma Bâ's powder got wet, and his forces stopped to dry it out.
When Sine scouts reported this, a band of tyeddo attacked the
marabouts. The tyeddo were repulsed, and they quickly rejoined
the main force of the Sine army. Ma Bâ's forces pursued them,
and the battle at Somb began. The marabouts prevailed in the
early hours of the fighting, but the tyeddo held firm, and as the
day grew hotter, men arrived from all parts of Sine to join the
fray. Early in the afternoon, Lat Dior fled, probably recognizing
that the cause was lost. About the same time, Ma Bâ laid out his
prayer mat and began praying in a loud voice. His body was
found on the prayer mat when the battle was over. The Bur Sine
did not at first believe that Ma Bâ was dead. When the body was
identified, he had the head cut off and sent to Joal as proof of
his victory.[70]

The griots of Sine still chant these verses in praise of Coumba
N'Doffène:

> At the marigot of Fandane, hé!
> The drums beat loud
> Masamba is sealed
> Diakhou begins to cry
> The talibé leave us in peace.
>
> Hé! My mother! There's no time for anger
>
> But to laugh:
> It is God's will that M'Bay, brother of Nadié,
> Has killed the Marabout.
>
> Hé Yasine! Hé Mbombé!
> Coumba N'Doffène has killed Ma Bâ
> Your husband!

His head is in Europe! His hand at Sedhiou!
His feet at Rufisque!
The bull of Diakhou Dob
Will nevermore offend the Bur."

In later letters, Coumba N'Doffène reminded the French that when they were called, they did not come. According to the Bur's account, over five hundred marabout bodies were left on the field of battle. Although the Bur was wounded and seven of his chiefs were killed, it was a proud day for Sine.

The battle at Somb was also a victory for the French. It removed from the scene a leader who had almost reunited the old Djoloff empire in the name of militant Islam, and it did so, ironically, at a time when St. Louis had very explicit orders not to get involved in mainland military conquests. Neither Ma Bâ's successors nor any other Senegambian leaders came close to unifying Senegambia so that it might resist French imperialism. Ma Bâ failed to establish a powerful Moslem empire, but he succeeded in shattering a number of states and in nearly destroying a traditional political order that had stood for five centuries. Several more states collapsed before the Moslem onslaught in the 1870's. After this, the traditional states could offer little resistance to French military and political expansion and, in fact, often looked to the French for help.

The political structure that Ma Bâ left behind in Rip, the state he created, was less stable than the one he had destroyed, but a new Moslem elite had seized power, and had clearly rejected the traditional state and the sanctions that made its authority secure. In the religious wars, the area that today makes up the cercle of Nioro received the strongly Moslem and puritanical imprint it still retains. Ma Bâ the teacher and religious leader was in the long run more important than Ma Bâ the general and statesman. With Ma Bâ, the Moslem revolution spread beyond the Toucouleur and Fulbe peoples who had earlier provided its base. After his death, several of his lieutenants moved over to

---

" Henri Gravrand, *Horizons Africains*, No. 68, p. 15. A marigot is a small stream. Diakhou Dob was the name of Ma Bâ's mother.

the south bank of the Gambia and into the upper river area to extend Moslem control. Two others, Lat Dior of Cayor and Alboury N'Diaye of Djoloff, returned to power in their home states, and played an important role in the Islamization of those areas.[71] Even after the French conquest, Islam continued to gain adherents, largely as a result of efforts made by a number of marabout families connected with Rip to seek converts by peaceful methods.[v]

[v] Of particular importance were the M'Backé family of Porokhane and the Niasses of Niacene, who will be discussed in the last chapter. On the M'Backé family, see Vincent Monteil, "Une Confrérie musulmane: Les Mourides du Sénégal," *Archives de Sociologie des Religions*, No. 14, 1962, pp. 77–101.

AFTER MA BA, 1867–1885

THE GENERATION after Ma Bâ's death was a generation of re-prieves for the traditional political systems of Senegambia. The Moslems and the French imperialists, the two expansive forces operating within Senegambia, eased their pressure on each other, as well as on the older political systems. Long-range goals were not changed, but the imperialists found themselves shackled by very explicit orders from above, and the marabout leaders were increasingly distracted from their crusade by in-ternal difficulties. It was an uncertain generation during which both the Moslem and the traditional states sought security in a series of shifting alliances. Shifting coalitions were formed for the purpose of limiting either marabout power or French power, but in the long run these were of little avail.

The crisis in Europe led Paris to restrict the activities of her colonial proconsuls, and her defeat in the Franco-Prussian War forced her to devote her resources to reconstruction at home. In the wake of the traumatic loss of Alsace and Lorraine, many Frenchmen regarded anything that diverted France from re-gaining the two lost provinces as treason. When French colonial officers in Africa pleaded for men and weapons, their requests were denied, and they were again ordered not to enter new en-gagements. During the 1860's, anticolonial currents were run-ning high in Britain also. The antislavery crusade was over, and the British were becoming skeptical about the advantages of colonies. Strong forces not only opposed any extension of empire, but advocated a policy of retrenchment on the West African coast. All regular troops were withdrawn from Bathurst, and the Administrator was told that he could count on aid from the

Royal Navy only if Bathurst itself were threatened.[a] The Administrators saw the economic development of the Gambia limited by the marabout-soninke wars, but they could do little more than try to mediate.

The restraints imposed on the French administration forced Governor François Xavier Valière (1869–76) to return several areas France had taken over to African rule. More important, he came to terms with Lat Dior, who had returned to Cayor after Ma Bâ's defeat. Cayor could not be occupied, and Lat Dior could not be defeated without a greater military commitment than Valière was free to make. In the entourage of the restored Damel were a number of marabouts formerly associated with Ma Bâ.[b] After becoming a practicing Moslem, Lat Dior tried to push a profound social and religious revolution in Cayor. He sought the conversion of the remaining pagans, the imposition of Moslem law, and the creation of a more egalitarian and more authoritarian sociopolitical order. In Vincent Monteil's words, he attempted to become an "oriental monarch."[1] To do so, he had to trim the privileges of his tyeddo and counterbalance tyeddo power with that of the Moslem peasantry.

In 1875, Lat Dior joined the French to defeat Amadou Cheikhou, a Toucouleur marabout who controlled much of Djoloff and Fouta Toro, and who threatened Cayor. The Franco-Cayor victory led to the election of Alboury N'Diaye as Burba Djoloff. Alboury, who was Lat Dior's nephew and Ma Bâ's brother-in-law, was a devout Moslem and a sturdy war leader, who wrote the French friendly letters and carefully avoided conflict. For many years the French considered him an ally, but in the 1880's

[a] In 1865, the colonial administration in West Africa was reorganized. All colonies were placed under a Governor-in-Chief in Freetown. The highest official in Bathurst was an Administrator. On British and French attitudes and policies toward West Africa, see J. D. Hargreaves, *Prelude to the Partition of West Africa* (London, 1963), chaps. 2 and 3.

[b] Lat Dior's first *qadi* (judge) was Momar Anta Sali M'Backé of Porokhane, who had taught the Koran to Ma Bâ's son. The son of Momar Anta Sali was Amadou Bamba M'Backé, who founded the powerful Mouride tariqa. In later years, Lat Dior's qadi was Khali Ma Diakhaté, who is known in Cayor tradition both for the poems he wrote in alternating verses of Arabic and Wolof and for his just decisions as qadi. Both judges were stern exponents of the reformed Moslem creed.

he became the leader of a Tijani coalition that tried to resist the encroachments of French power.

In the period before 1879, French officers in Senegal were dissatisfied with policies dictated by Paris, and revealed their restlessness by occasionally taking limited initiatives; but no new military posts were built, no new areas were occupied, and all military actions were defensive. While both Paris and London were keeping a tight leash on their proconsuls, the African states had time to work out many of their problems. Time was especially important to Rip—which, like many other states created in the West African Moslem revolution, was forced to make the transition from government based on charismatic authority to a more stable form of bureaucratic organization.

The Marabout State

Ma Bâ's state had depended on his charisma and his ability to harness to the service of his crusade both the religious zeal of the Moslems and their resentment of the traditional elites. While his military campaigns were going well, he was able to bring together a series of leaders, each of whom had a large following and controlled a given area and its revenues. The wars gave each of these men a chance to increase his wealth and power. It seems likely that Ma Bâ's political objectives were never as clearly thought through as his religious goals. He sought a society in which the laws of Islam would be enforced and accepted, and he saw himself as the means to this end, but he seems to have devoted little attention to political structure or to the nature of the state that would survive him. The movement was constantly concerned with the next military campaign and not with what should be done in areas already won.

As a result, the political structure of Rip had a directness and simplicity quite different from the complex mechanisms of the traditional states. In both, two types of political ties were important—the tie between the chief and his retainers and the tie between the chief and the territory he ruled; but in the traditional state, loyalty to the kingship was superimposed on this. Tied to the kingship was a title system. Each status group participated in the state as a corporate group and was represented at court by a chief.

The marabout state did not incorporate the status groups, though it did not deny their existence. In fact, the marabout state hardly acknowledged its status as a state at all. It recognized the simple patrimonial ties between the chief and his retainers and between the chief and his villages, as well as the more universal tie between all Moslems; but the leaders did not conceive of these ties as being elements of a state with its own claims to loyalty. A charismatic leader like Ma Bâ could unite the Moslem community, but Ma Bâ died before he could begin to establish stable bureaucratic institutions. In the state he left behind, each of his lieutenants controlled a body of retainers and a province.[c] Each collected the taxes authorized by the Koran, distributed the booty he received, and appointed his own qadi. Important disputes were taken to the qadi of Nioro. (Nioro was still recognized as the marabouts' capital.) Although a successor to Ma Bâ was chosen, there seems to have been no central administration, and no provisions were made for controlling the component units and collecting revenues from them.

After Ma Bâ's death, a council of major chiefs chose his brother, Mamour N'Dari, as his successor. Ma Bâ's son, Saër Maty, was probably too young to have been considered, though later disputes revolved around the question of whether Mamour N'Dari was chosen in his own right or as regent for Saër Maty. Mamour Samba Diobaye and Matar Kalla, who had been allies of Cheikhou Ousman Diop, refused to recognize the succession, but they were defeated in battle in 1868 by Mamour N'Dari and his supporters. Ma Bâ had used the title "Almamy" (derived from Imam), but Mamour N'Dari was called the "Eliman."

[c] Ma Bâ's lieutenants each had different claims to power. Mandiack Cissé, the Serigne Pakala, was a traditional chief whose family had held the title under the Bur Saloum. Others, like Biram Cissé of Kaymor and Sed Kani Touré of Sabakh, came from important marabout families, each of which had long commanded a group of Moslem villages. Amath, Ali, and Omar Khodia Bâ, who ruled Laghem, the area between Nioro and Kaolack, were members of Ma Bâ's family. Military ability seems to have made possible the rise of Goumbo Gueye, who ruled Sandial, and of Mama Gaolo Niang, a Mandinka of griot origin, who received the thankless job of trying to rule pagan Djilor.

Ma Bâ had been motivated by a deep faith in himself, and by a belief in his mission that led him to overreach himself. In contrast, the cautious and wily Mamour N'Dari had a sense of his own limitations.[d] Yet this sense of his own limitations made his task more difficult, for the *jihad* was the very cement of the state. Mamour N'Dari was surrounded by men who had acquired a taste for war and who wanted to continue their crusade, either out of religious zeal or out of a desire for booty. His success depended on channeling the energies of these war hawks into areas where they would not threaten his authority. It also depended on continued victories. In January 1868, before Mamour N'Dari's conflict with Mamour Samba Diobaye had been resolved, Bathurst sources reported that marabout bands were making raids in Niani, apparently at the invitation of local marabout leaders. Shortly thereafter, both Niani and Ouli (see map, page 6) were torn apart by the same soninke-marabout conflict that had destroyed the other Mandinka states.[e] By 1873, forces loyal to Mamour N'Dari exercised an uneasy sovereignty over both Niani and Ouli, and Mamour N'Dari could claim authority over an area extending from the Atlantic Ocean to the Tambacounda region.

Marabout forces were also busy on other fronts. In 1869, they sought to avenge Ma Bâ by invading Sine, but the invasion failed. There was also constant raiding by all sides, which disturbed trade and provoked the Administrator of the Gambia to complain in 1869:

> It appears that as long as the Mahomedans and Pagans inhabit the same country, so long will it be devastated by war, as it is the creed of the former to exterminate the latter. The Pagans, being given to drink, are at a disadvantage, and they

---

[d] Mamour N'Dari had studied the Koran in Mauritania, and had helped Ma Bâ operate a school in Djoloff. After the fighting began, Mamour N'Dari made frequent trips to Bathurst to purchase the arms and ammunition Ma Bâ's army needed. Like his brother, he seems to have been a strict Moslem, austere in dress, simple in manner, puritanical in his personal habits. Much of my information about Mamour N'Dari comes from his knowledgeable grandson, Abdou Boury Bâ, *chef d'arrondissement* at Birkelane.

[e] Administrator of Gambia to Governor-in-Chief, 23, 27, and 31 Jan. 1868, AG. The marabout factions fighting in Niani and Ouli were led by two of the Eliman's potential rivals—his brother, Abdou Bâ, and Biram Cissé.

are gradually but surely disappearing before the aggressions of the Mahomedans and their own discretion. But to the Pagans we have to look for our own trade, as they pay far greater attention to the soil than their opponents, who as soon as each has been able to purchase a horse and a gun, considers himself a warrior, lives by plunder and works his fields by the slaves he captures in his expeditions, and thinks it beneath his dignity to perform any work whatsoever, which is left to women and slaves.[1]

With no British troops in the Gambia, marabout forces were active near Bathurst, and even collected taxes within the Ceded Mile. Conflicts with the British almost erupted in 1871 and again in 1872, the first over the assertion of marabout control in Niumi, and the second over a projected marabout invasion of Kombo. The arrival of a British gunboat persuaded the marabouts to give up their plans of crossing the Gambia, and Mamour N'Dari wrote a conciliatory letter to the Administrator (given here in its translation by a semiliterate interpreter):

What lives on this side of the river he has nothing to do with. His way is by N'Youmey, Salum, Bambook, Woolley, Bundoo, Fooler & Torrow [all states north of the Gambia]. He has no canoe to cross to Combo to enter Goonjoor— that Country is the British Governor's his friends [sic], and it is not good for two friends to disagree between themselves.[9]

In early 1873, when the British again feared a marabout invasion, the Administrator asked the aid of a French gunboat, and one sailed into the Bathurst harbor and stayed until the crisis ended.

[1] Administrator of Gambia to Governor-in-Chief, 26 July 1869, AG. The most interesting point here is that where the British had looked to the marabout communities for their trade before 1860, they now found the pagans the most diligent farmers. The Moslem peasants had become warriors.

[9] Mamour N'Dari Bâ to Administrator of Gambia, 5 July 1872, AG. Several years later a force did cross the river. It was led by Fodé Kabba, who had been the Kombo marabout leader in an 1855 conflict, and had later joined Ma Bâ. This time, Kabba succeeded in building a Kombo-based marabout state in Bathurst's backyard. At about the same time, Moussa Molo, a Fulah from Fouta Djallon, moved into the Gambia area further up river. For many years, Kabba and Molo contested control of the south bank. Both participated also in conflicts north of the river. See Administrator of Gambia to Governor-in-Chief, 5 Dec. 1877, AG. On Moussa Molo, see Le Chatelier, *L'Islam dans l'Afrique Occidentale*, p. 172.

To Colonel Canard, the Commandant at Gorée, this proved the necessity of an armed force to protect commerce:

> I strongly hope that the new affairs that are taking place in the Gambia finally prove to the English, and also to some Frenchmen, that it is ridiculous to try to trade along the rivers of the west coast of Africa without any military protection.[h]

The British, however, preferred diplomacy to military force. They had two cards to play. First, they could threaten to limit or cease trading with the marabouts. Second, they could control the river with a gunboat when they wanted to do so. Though there were problems, the British generally found the chiefs in the river areas willing to meet their demands. In late 1873, the British signed a treaty with Mamour N'Dari, in which they recognized him as the ruler of the north bank from Swarracunda Creek to Ouli—that is, all regions except Niumi—and gave him an annual stipend of 110 pounds. In return, Mamour N'Dari promised to protect British subjects and their property on lands under his control, and to charge only the usual customs.[2] There were some violations of this treaty, but generally Mamour N'Dari paid for whatever had been taken from the traders in question. When an outbreak of fighting among the Africans was imminent, one of the chiefs usually dispatched a letter to Bathurst, and the British put up posters warning of the danger.

Mamour N'Dari frequently addressed letters to the French asking that traders be kept out of war zones, and like Ma Bâ before him, he repeatedly promised to protect French property and trading privileges:

> Praises to God, creator of the seas and of the earth, which he has divided among the whites and the blacks, who has decided that the rivers would be commanded by whites and that the deserts would become the property of the Moslems.[3]

---

[h] Commandant of Gorée to Governor of Senegal, 25 Jan. 1873, ARS, 1 F 7. Many French officers reacted to the British with both hostility and suspiciousness. Others, like Canard, thought that Africans had to be taught to fear and respect all Europeans, and thus looked on a show of force by any European power as a good thing.

Mamour N'Dari was proposing the same arrangement he had
with the British: waterways to the whites, land to the blacks.
The French, however, no longer felt threatened by the marabouts of Nioro, and showed little interest in coming to terms
with them.

Nevertheless Mamour N'Dari's accomplishments were substantial. He established his personal supremacy, channeled the
crusading fervor of the war hawks into conflicts that did not
threaten him, and worked out a profitable relationship with the
British. Trade was increasing, and it offered him certain rewards
if he could continue to control the situation. He did not, however, create bureaucratic institutions that might have made his
state more effective. His problem was the same one faced by all
of the Moslem revolutionaries—institutions that could transcend
the power of a series of patrimonial chiefs. In northern Nigeria,
Uthman dan Fodio's heirs were successful partly because they
built on Hausa bureaucratic models. Fouta Toro and Fouta Djallon developed elective monarchies, in which the Moslem clerics
became land-owning aristocrats committed to the perpetuation
of a state that confirmed their privileges. Rip never evolved such
a consensus on political institutions.

Having established their power, the chiefs of Rip wished to
enjoy it. Assertive, self-confident men, they were not willing to
accept Mamour N'Dari as more than *primus inter pares,* and
since each commanded a band of retainers, Mamour N'Dari
lacked the force to effectively restrict their freedom of action.
In 1877, one of the most independent, Biram Cissé of Kaymor,
built his own tata. When Mamour N'Dari ordered him to tear
it down, the fight began.[4] Cissé had the support of several of Ma
Bâ's lieutenants, including Sed Kani Touré and N'Deri Kani
Touré of Sabakh. The Cissé and Touré families had settled in
the area before the arrival of the Bâ family, and had a sure base
of power.[4]

[4] Biram Cissé, born at Keur Samba Yacine, was the son of Andalla Boury Cissé,
an important local marabout. The Cissés of Keur Samba Yacine, like the Cissés
from Pakala, were of Mande origin, but they lived in an area with a large Wolof
population and probably spoke Wolof in the nineteenth century. Biram Cissé had

From the first, the British and several Moslem leaders tried to mediate the conflict, but it proved impossible to reestablish good faith between the rivals. "The greatest obstacle to peace being established," Gambia Administrator V. S. Gouldsbury wrote, "proceeds from the fear on either side that the other side would deal treacherously."[5] The fighting in its early phases was not as impassioned and cruel as it had been in the religious wars, but it did fragment the marabout state. The chiefs furthest from Nioro became virtually independent, and the Nioro regime left Niani and Ouli to their own wars. Both factions sought allies. Mamour N'Dari allied himself to Fodé Kabba, and Biram Cissé to Moussa Molo and Bur Saloum Guédel M'Bodj. With this, the religious crusade took a strange turn.[j]

Saloum

The death of Ma Bâ and the long succession struggle of his heirs permitted the traditional elite of Saloum to reassert its control over the ravaged Serer areas north of the Saloum River. The wars had driven tyeddo as well as peasants from this area, and resettlement was a slow process. In 1868, peasants who had fled Saloum began drifting back to their homes, and those who had converted to Catholicism reverted to their pagan faith. The French encouraged Fakha Fall to resettle villages, but they could give the peasants few incentives to speed up this process, and Fakha had difficulty even luring back his tyeddo. In 1871, there were still many empty villages and unused fields in Saloum.[6]

Fakha was an uninspiring leader who spent much of his time

---

studied the Koran with Ma Bâ, and had been with him from the start. A hardy warrior, he had received the rich province of Kaymor; and upon the death of Ma Bâ he was one of the arbiters of the succession. The descriptions we have of Cissé differ radically. At least one British Administrator found him a just and reasonable man, which is to say that he did not trouble commerce. The French, on the other hand, consistently treated him as a war hawk and a troublemaker. In any case, we know that throughout Cissé's long career there was rarely a year when he was not involved in one or another of the Gambian wars.

  j It is not clear how close the Guédel-Cissé alliance was, but Cissé and Guédel coordinated operations on several occasions. Cissé's alliance with Moussa Molo was closer, and involved substantial loans of men. At one time, nine hundred of Molo's men were in Cissé's forces. Moussa Molo was involved in a struggle with Fodé Kabba for control of the south bank of the Gambia. Sgt. Pearce to Administrator of Gambia, Report on Mission to Nioro, May 1879, PRO, CO 87/113; Governor-in-Chief to Minister, 14 May 1885, PRO, CO 87/124.

in the security of the French post. This displeased both his French allies and a small band of nobles and tyeddo determined to continue the fight for Saloum. In June 1871, Fakha shot and killed one of his lesser chiefs, and Fakha's opponents moved against him. A crowd of over a thousand people chased him from his residence, and he fled to the delta.[7] This was the only time in the nineteenth century when an ineffectual leader was removed as Serer political theory says he should be removed—when he is no longer successful. Fakha later joined the Nioro marabouts, but his defection did not make him a threat to Saloum's leaders. His successor, Niahoul Coumba Daga M'Bodj had no difficulty maintaining himself in power.

Niahoul was the oldest of three brothers who occupied the throne of Saloum in succession and briefly restored its power in the Serer areas of central Saloum. The sons of guelowar princess Coumba Daga N'Dao, they all came to power young, fought hard, and died before reaching their prime. Niahoul was the leader of a contingent of Saloum tyeddo, who helped defeat Ma Bâ at Somb in 1867. The sons of Coumba Daga reacted to the militance of the Moslem religious crusade with a militance of their own, and the army they led was willing to fight just as hard as the Moslems to defend its traditional ways of living and believing.

Within a month after taking power, Niahoul and his tyeddo, accompanied by a force of Sine-Sine,[k] attacked a marabout force at Tiofat, near Kaolack.[8] Though the battle was inconclusive, Niahoul was able soon afterward to build a wooden stockade at Tiofat, which was to serve as the tyeddo base for many years.[9] Niahoul also rebuilt villages and demanded higher customs payments from traders operating in Saloum.

The renewed fighting consisted mostly of raiding and counter-raiding, usually initiated by the tyeddo until 1873, when a large marabout force moved north for a confrontation. The French expected the tyeddo to flee as soon as heavy fighting began,[l] but

[k] "Sine-Sine," a Serer plural form, means "more than one person from Sine."
[l] Commandant of Gorée to Governor of Senegal, 12 Apr. 1873, ARS, 4 B 48. The French were very contemptuous of the tyeddo, and never quite believed that a tyeddo renaissance was taking place.

they did not do so. The marabouts apparently won the first few
battles, but Niahoul was determined to resist. On one occasion,
when many tyeddo took refuge at Kaolack, he asked that the
Commandant place in irons all tyeddo who refused to join him
in the stockade at Tiofat.[10] The tide was soon reversed. Late in
1874, after several defeats, Mamour N'Dari pulled out of his tata.
But the victory was short-lived, for Niahoul died on December
4, 1874.

Under Sadiouka (1874–79) and the third brother, Guédel
(1879–94), the fight continued, though it was henceforth conducted within a very small area—Laghem, the region just south
of Kaolack. In 1882, Guédel M'Bodj was able to win control of
Dagaminian (south of Kaolack), and made the fort there his
base, but he never won control of the rest of Laghem or of any of
the Wolof areas of eastern Saloum, which were by then solidly
Moslem. Of the major chiefs, only the Bur Djilor returned to his
lands, and he made his capital at M'Bam, a trading and fishing
village near Foundiougne. It is not clear from French reports
how much fighting was done in this area, but in 1891, Djilor contained only eight villages and about twelve hundred people.

Guédel, a short, slender man with a stutter, was not impres-
sive in conferences, but he acquitted himself well on the battlefield. He was very sober in his personal habits, a trait rare among
the Serer nobles. He gave up drink (drinking may have killed
his two brothers), and induced some of his warriors to do like-
wise. He was frequently intransigent where he saw his interests
involved, but he was flexible in dealing with internal conflict.
Guédel won many of the Kévé Bigué back from their marabout
alliance, and over the opposition of many of his chiefs, he chose
as his Bumi one of the Kévé Bigué, Semou Djimit Diouf. Semou
Djimit had a reputation as an effective military leader. Because
of his marabout ties, Semou Djimit was often in charge of the
tyeddo contingents that fought alongside Biram Cissé.

Sine

For the Sine-Sine, the years after Ma Bâ's death were years of
triumph. Coumba N'Doffène boasted in letter after letter that he

had beaten Ma Bâ, and when the marabouts returned in April 1869, they were again defeated.[11] After being repulsed by Sine's army, the marabouts retreated, and were attacked by the Saloum army led by Fakha Fall. Coumba N'Doffène tried to use his position of strength to pursue two policies. First, he tried again to cut the substance out of earlier concessions to the French and reassert his claims to the villages near Joal. A sakh-sakh was established in Fadial, and despite French promises of protection, the village paid taxes to both the Bur and the French, and carefully stayed out of the fight.[12] The Bur Sine wrote to both Gorée and St. Louis:

> The inhabitants, as you well know, are my subjects, as are the people of Joal. At a time when you are raising me above all of the Negro kings, I plead with you to return these villages to me. I will name the chiefs myself.[13]

At the same time, Coumba N'Doffène was trying to parlay his victory over the marabouts into an extension of his power. He addressed many letters to the French, reminding them of his victory and asking their aid for an attack on Rip. If they would not send troops, he said, then he needed guns and horses. Each letter spoke of his determination to avenge earlier attacks by the marabouts; but the aid did not come, and Coumba N'Doffène judiciously chose not to act on his own.[14] Pinet-Laprade flatly denied the validity of the Bur's claims to Fadial and Joal, insisting that the matter had already been decided by the treaties. At the same time, he urged the Bur to move into Saloum:

> As for Saloum, I have authorized you to found villages there, and I will keep my promise as long as you respect the treaties. ... It is up to you to attract them [the Saloum peasants who had fled elsewhere], if you can, by the benefits of your government.[15]

As we have seen, the Bur's response to these suggestions was not what Pinet-Laprade wanted. Both partners sought to exploit the alliance, and neither trusted the other.

Coumba N'Doffène was willing to maintain good relations

with Gorée as long as Sine's independence—in particular, control over commercial activity within its borders—was respected by the French. In 1869, the Bur briefly suspended trade for reasons that were not clearly explained.[16] In spite of this, the French continued to encourage the Bur to attack Rip. In 1870, Governor Valière wrote:

> I am in no way opposed to your entering Rip; I told you this at the time I chased Lat Dior from Cayor, and I repeat it to you today: everything that you can do against Rip will be good, and I will be pleased if you take booty and captives there. For me, the moment has not yet come to act in this country.[17]

The letter was accompanied by gifts of cloth, powder, and ammunition.

The power of the diminutive Serer state was dependent on its stability, a stability based partly on the leadership of a strong Bur. In August 1871, in conscious violation of the 1859 treaty, Coumba N'Doffène arrived at Joal with a large entourage. The small garrison was powerless to act when the Bur and his tyeddo demanded "gifts" from many of the traders. One of them, Beccaria, a man with a reputation as a troublemaker, shot the Bur and wounded him fatally.[m] The resulting events showed some of the weaknesses of the Serer political system.

Coumba N'Doffène's Bumi, Sanoumon Faye, was in exile at this time. He was a renowned warrior, but was also the scourge of peasants, traders, and missionaries. The choice of the Grand Jaraf was not Sanoumon, but a younger man, Semou Mack Diouf.[18] Sanoumon gathered his forces in Baol, and three weeks later he chased his rival from Sine. Semou Mack fled to Saloum, gathered his forces, and returned, but was soundly beaten.[19] He then appealed to the French for aid, but Sanoumon had already moved to establish his credit with the new arbiters of power. Even before he received the Governor's letter demanding com-

[m] Commandant of Gorée to Governor of Senegal, 24 Aug. 1871, ARS, 4 B 48. The French treated Coumba N'Doffène's visit as another example of tyeddo thievery, but it is more likely that it was another attempt by the Bur to show the French that he could be a valuable friend or a potent enemy. Coumba N'Doffène's demand was simple: clear recognition of the Bur's supremacy within Sine.

plete restitution of everything stolen in Joal during the visit of
Coumba N'Doffène and his entourage, Sanoumon began paying
the damages including debts to the trader who had killed Coumba N'Doffène.[20] Largely because of this action, the French were
sympathetic to Sanoumon through the conflicts that followed.

Sanoumon has held a strange fascination for the oral tradition. He is the sadist par excellence: there are dozens of stories
of his arbitrary and sadistic tortures and murders. Some of these
tales are supported by contemporary accounts—in particular, by
letters from missionaries and post commanders.[21]

In 1876, the Grand Farba wrote to the French, announcing
that he had gone over to Semou Mack. His letter itemized Sanoumon's depraved and sadistic actions, and then went on to
say:

> The leading men and notables of Sine, seeing the many in-
> famous and wicked actions of Bur Sanoumon Faye, [say], "Let
> the curse of God fall on him!" Seeing the deplorable situation
> in which the territory of Sine finds itself, a situation caused by
> him, and not knowing what remedy should be employed to
> save us from the unhappiness that menaces the country, the
> notables complained sorrowfully to me, Farba M'Bar, asking
> me what means might be employed to cure the unhappiness
> that threatens the country and to remove completely this evil
> king. Then I said to them, "The best way is for us to join to-
> gether to go look for Semou Mack in Baol, and place him on
> the throne." They then answered me: "Since you are the Grand
> Farba of Sine, you go first with your army to camp outside the
> country; then we will join you to go find Semou Mack as soon
> as it is agreed."[22]

The letter also assured the French that the rebels were in favor
of trade, and would protect the interests and property of French
traders. The Grand Farba was playing a role here that traditionally belonged to the Grand Jaraf. In theory, the Grand Farba,
as a slave, was the Bur's man, whereas the Grand Jaraf, as chief
of the jambur was independent. In practice, the slaves of the
crown (tyeddo) were powerful, and the Grand Farba, who represented them, could act independently.

Farba M'Bar's letter evoked no response. Traders had seldom been harassed since the new Bur had taken over, and Sanoumon had been careful to keep up a steady correspondence with the French authorities.[23] The Commandant at Joal had great difficulty finding couriers to run messages to Diakhao because the couriers feared Sanoumon and his men;[24] but the military authorities, who felt they had nothing to gain from involvement in the conflict, took a very practical attitude and did nothing to support the opposition. In spite of the failure of the French to help them, the Farba and other defectors attacked Sanoumon. The attack was not successful, but Sanoumon's opposition remained potent.

Sanoumon's letters increasingly reflected worries about his own safety because of the defections from his camp. In April 1877, he wrote Canard, who was now Commandant at Dakar, asking the protection of the French government for himself and his family. Canard, long frustrated in his desire for a more active policy, jumped at the opportunity and suggested a new treaty.[25] Sanoumon quickly accepted the draft treaty Canard sent him, saying:

> In order to enjoy the most perfect tranquillity and ease during my life, I accept and I agree to all of the conditions that you have proposed in your letter, because I only demand today to be under the protection of the French government during my life, so that after my death, my family will not be chased from Sine. . . . The king of Sine submits himself and his country to the sovereignty of France, and will remain under its domination during all of his life and after his death.[26]

The treaty had been agreed on in principle, and the only question was where it would be signed. Sanoumon refused to go to Gorée because Burs were forbidden by custom to see the ocean, and he would not go to Joal because his predecessor had been killed there. When the French suggested Fadial, Sanoumon insisted that Canard's emissary come to Faouey in Sine.

Lt. Colonel Reybaud, the emissary, arrived at Faouey with the final treaty on a wet September day. Sanoumon came that evening, accompanied by the usual band of griots and warriors.

Their talks were short, and Sanoumon quickly accepted the treaty without asking for changes. It provided that France would recognize Sanoumon as the Bur, and it promised him French protection as long as he undertook no military actions without consulting the Governor. The 1859 and 1861 treaties were reaffirmed, and Sanoumon explicitly accepted the right of traders at Fatick and Silif to build in stone. No armed warriors were to enter these villages, no taxes above 3 per cent were to be levied, and no gifts were to be demanded from traders.[27] The Bur drank steadily during the talks, but Reybaud's judgment of him was favorable. Reybaud described him as tall and erect, intelligent and courageous, though unfortunately little aware of his own limitations.

Shortly after the treaty was signed, Sanoumon sent the Commandant at Dakar 25 cows as a gift, but the gesture was no herald of compliance with the terms of the treaty. By the end of the year, the traders were complaining of harassment by Sanoumon's tyeddo. Three months later, the Commandant wrote: "The trade along the Sine River is always very difficult. The Bur Sine writes me beautiful letters, but it seems that he is not respecting the terms of the treaty."[28] Canard repeated his warnings that traders would be protected only within cannon range of French posts, but he also considered either closing the factories at Fatick and Silif or supporting Semou Mack.[29] Before taking a more radical course, Canard wrote Sanoumon, reminding him, "A treaty is a sacred thing, and you must respect it or you will bring war into your country."[30] Sanoumon paid the reparations demanded.[31]

If the treaty was of little use to the French, it was even less beneficial for Sanoumon. In February 1878, he killed an emissary of Sadiouka M'Bodj, the Bur Saloum.[32] Sadiouka immediately allied himself with Semou Mack and the Sine rebels. In the ensuing battle, Sanoumon was defeated and killed.[33] Semou Mack clearly recognized the changing shape of power in Senegal. One of his first actions was to assure the Commandant at Dakar of his love for the French and his desire to protect commerce. At the insistence of the French, he signed the Reybaud treaty.[34]

Unfortunately, the French archives are incomplete for the decade before the conquest, and they give us little information about Semou Mack and his successors. We know that Semou Mack protected the traders—the only important claim against him came from a trader with a reputation for making fraudulent claims—and we know that he took his own life with a revolver in November 1881.[35]

The death of Semou Mack began a period of civil war during which five men became Bur within five years. Regular succession conflicts had not hitherto threatened the existence of the state, but this time there were two unusual circumstances. First, the two leading factions were evenly matched. Second, the conflict was exacerbated by the constant interference of outsiders. During this period, increasing French activity—in particular, the conquest of Cayor (1882–86)—produced an alliance of Tijani chiefs against the extension of French authority. Though reluctant to force a showdown with the French, the Tijani league was interested in supporting potential allies throughout Senegambia. The situation in Sine was ripe for its interference.

There is a tradition in Sine that, when Semou Mack Diouf, Amadi Baro Diouf, and M'Backé Mack[n] N'Diaye were boys, Coumba N'Doffène asked them to take an oath never to fight each other for the throne. However, when Semou Mack died, Amadi Baro was chosen as Bur, and M'Backé Mack became Bumi. Urged on by his entourage, M'Backé Mack broke with Amadi Baro.[36] In the seesaw conflicts that followed, Amadi Baro allied himself with the marabouts of Nioro. Bur Saloum Guédel M'Bodj could not tolerate a hostile state to his north, so he backed M'Backé. Amadi Baro prevailed in the first battles, and in May 1882 he wrote the French Governor that he was in power and wished to continue the good relations that princes of his family always had with the French.[37] By May 1884, when Lt. Governor Jean Bayol visited Sine, M'Backé was back in power.

Though the pro-marabout factions continually assured Gorée of their love and friendship, the anti-marabout forces in Sine in-

[n] Mack means "the elder."

creasingly looked to the French for aid. This aid was generally
not forthcoming, but the possibility of French activity strongly
influenced the diplomacy of both factions. When M'Backé Mack
N'Diaye, shortly after his victory over Amadi Baro early in 1884,
met with Lt. Governor Bayol, he made generous promises in the
hope of getting French aid. He willingly granted permission for
traders at Fatick and Silif to build in stone, and for the Governor
to have two posts built at whatever places best suited French interests.[o] Several months later, when M'Backé felt more secure,
he reverted to Sine's traditional policy of denying foreigners the
right to build in stone.[38] His change of policy was a mistake, for
by July 1885 he too had fallen.

Bayol had seriously considered M'Backé's request for aid, and
had M'Backé not reneged on his original grant, France might
have provided the aid he needed. As it was, though the French
very much feared the militance of M'Backé's Tijani opposition,
they kept out of the conflict. M'Backé was deposed by Dialigui
Sira Diouf, Amadi Baro's nephew, with the aid of contingents
from Djoloff, Cayor, and Baol.[p] Dialigui was not able to hold on
without outside aid. In February 1886, he was killed in battle,
and M'Backé returned to power.[39] The leadership of the pro-
marabout faction was taken over by Niokhorbaye Diouf, whose
mother was married to Alboury N'Diaye, the Burba Djoloff, who
had loaned Niokhorbaye 150 horses.[40] In August, M'Backé was
finally killed, and Niokhorbaye became Bur. Leadership of the
pro-Saloum (anti-marabout) faction then passed to M'Backé
Deb ("the younger") N'Diaye.[q] The forces of M'Backé Deb de-

[o] Lt. Governor of Rivières du Sud to Governor of Senegal, 7 May 1884, Papers
of Victor Ballot, No. 171, ARS and AN. The right of the traders to build in stone
had been conceded by Sanoumon, but efforts to do so seem to have been regularly blocked.

[p] Lt. Governor of Rivières du Sud to Governor of Senegal, 8 July 1885, ARS,
4 B 74. The pro-marabout rulers of Sine seem to have remained pagan—though,
interestingly, Amadi Baro bears a variant of the name of a great Moslem state
builder, Cheikhou Amadou of Macina.

[q] Governor of Senegal to Minister, 13 Aug. 1886, ARS, 2 B 64. It is not clear
whether M'Backé Deb was the nephew or son of M'Backé Mack. Though it was
remotely possible for a son to succeed his father, it was very unusual and did not
happen on any other occasion in the nineteenth century.

feated the pro-marabout troops, and M'Backé Deb became the
fifth Bur in five years. But Niokhorbaye's power was not destroyed, and as a French column began moving south, Sine's
civil war seemed far from over.

Through all of these struggles, French activity consisted primarily of efforts to keep outside elements out of Sine.[41] Since
France had more influence with Guédel and could restrain him
more easily than it could the marabouts, French policy unwittingly favored the pro-marabout faction. In general, French diplomacy failed to take advantage of its strong position, and the
failure of the French to aid their "allies" caused a great deal of
bitterness in both Sine and Saloum.[r] Though French dispatches
spoke of different chiefs as being friendly to France or to the
cause of "civilization," the French often failed to see that a ruler's
policies reflected not his sympathy or lack of sympathy with
France, but his own real interests. Thus, they did not always
distinguish between chiefs who wrote friendly letters to keep
France out and those who wrote friendly letters to pull France
into local conflicts.

The Serer leaders clearly saw the threat posed by French military power. This is implicit in their actions and statements. However, they gave low priority to warding off the French—partly
because they saw the French as traders and felt it was in their
own interest to concede favorable trading conditions, but also
because they were absorbed in other issues. In Saloum, which
was free of succession conflicts after the expulsion of Fakha Fall
in 1871, the leaders had to concentrate on war with the Moslems.
Sine was not threatened by Moslem forces, but in Sine internal
conflicts took priority over defense against the French. The problem was that loyalty to family and faction was stronger than
loyalty to the state. The kingship—and therefore, the existence
—of the state was confirmed by power struggles; yet in seeking
power, most contestants made concessions to traditional enemies

---

[r] The sergeant in command at Kaolack generally had orders not to help Saloum.
When Niahoul asked permission to place his mother, his children, and the old
women at the post during a battle, the Commandant was told to refuse. Commandant of Gorée to Commandant of Kaolack, 17 Feb. 1874, ARS, 4 B 51.

that they might later have regretted. Given a clear victory and a secure title, any of the candidates would have vigorously pursued the interests of the state, as Coumba N'Doffène had done, but the intervention of outside forces in the succession conflicts made a clear resolution of the succession impossible.

Only Islam could transcend the many particularistic interests that kept Senegal fragmented, and even Islam could operate only through conquest and with a charismatic leader. Umar's failure in the 1850's and Ma Bâ's unsuccessful campaign in 1865 doomed Senegambia to division. After 1865, various Moslem chiefs tried to create broad alliances, but these alliance systems ran afoul of the traditional rivalries and the particular interests of the different chiefs, and they did not effectively bar French expansion.[8]

[8] J. C. Anene sees a similar relationship between structural weaknesses in the Niger Delta states and the extension of British power there. See his *Southern Nigeria in Transition, 1885–1906* (Cambridge, Eng., 1966).

THE FRENCH IN SINE-SALOUM

1865–1887

THE FAILURE OF THE MARABOUT FORCES to finish off what Ma Bâ had started, and the resulting series of stalemates within the Senegalese political systems, led many leaders to look to either the French or the British for aid. The possibility that such aid might be forthcoming, and the fact that only the Europeans had guns and ammunition to sell to them made it difficult for any groups to pursue an overtly anti-European policy. Thus, no rulers, marabout or anti-marabout, were in a position to restrict or control a commercial penetration that many feared. This penetration undoubtedly seemed the lesser of many evils in a strife-torn situation, but it drew both peasants and chiefs into the world market and made them dependent for income on prices set in distant European commercial centers.

Forts and Trading Posts

The French military presence during this period was represented by a series of small forts, each with a garrison of about twelve men commanded by a sergeant. The forts were usually staffed by African soldiers during the rainy season and by a mixed garrison during the dry season. Even when garrisons were changed every three months, the rate of death from malaria was high among the French soldiers. Of the three posts on the Petite Côte, the most important was at Rufisque, where Mauritanian camel drivers delivered the peanut crop from southern Cayor and Baol. The little city, which became a commune in 1880, was exporting 22,000 to 25,000 tons of peanuts a year by 1885. French officers regularly cited its growth to justify the aggressive policies of the Faidherbe era, although Pinet-Laprade was unhappy because the traders were not using Dakar, which he had planned as the major French base in West Africa.[1]

Further south, there were posts at Portudal and Joal, neither of which was an important trading center at this time. Portudal, for centuries Baol's major seaport, was suddenly deserted in the 1870's when sleeping sickness reached epidemic proportions.[2] The Portudal traders moved to Nianing, which was handling two thousand tons of peanuts a year by 1879. When they asked that the post be officially moved to Nianing, the French administration refused the request, and told them to trade where the post was.[3] This does not seem to have seriously limited the trade at Nianing. Further down the coast, Joal remained active, but the trade in most of its hinterland went to factories located on the interior water routes of Sine. In 1885, the forts at Joal and Portudal were closed.

In spite of warnings that their protection could not be guaranteed, Fatick and Silif grew in importance. By 1871, Fatick was handling more trade than Joal.[a] In Saloum, the village of Foundiougne showed similar commercial growth. Situated on a body of land that was cut off from Djilor by several creeks, Foundiougne faced the Sine River; it was thus in an excellent position for the transshipment of peanuts moved from Fatick and Silif by small boats. Substantial fighting had taken place in this area during 1863 and 1864, resulting in some depopulation, but marabout raiders seem to have left it alone after Ma Bâ's death.

There was also a fort at Thiès, just inland from Cape Verde. Thiès was the place where camel caravans coming from Baol banded together before crossing the unsafe country of the Nones. France exercised nominal sovereignty over the area between Thiès and Cape Verde and over the strip along the Petite Côte. Within these areas, the villages were grouped into cantons, which were supervised by chiefs, usually appointed from im-

[a] Commandant of Gorée to Governor of Senegal, 30 Dec. 1871, ARS, 4 B 48. Silif subsequently declined and is now practically uninhabited.

portant families.[b] Sovereignty—for the French as for the Bur Sine—involved the collection of a head tax and an effort to keep order.

The situation in Kaolack was different. Only the adjacent village was under French sovereignty and paid the tax of 1.5 francs per person. The *escale*, or port, extended for about five hundred meters along the river and was protected by solid earthwork fortifications.[4] The post at Kaolack had difficulty developing its commercial potential because wars raged constantly in its hinterland, but the area's agricultural possibilities were greater than those of the area from which Rufisque drew trade. In spite of the fighting, the traders at Kaolack did a steady business in cattle, alcohol, military supplies, and peanuts.

The Kaolack post played only a negative role in the area's development, mostly because its Commandants were sergeants who were often barely literate and usually lacked the judgment needed for any political undertakings. The authorities at Gorée and St. Louis were well aware of the limitations of their agents. They continually instructed the Commandants never to leave the post or engage in correspondence with African chiefs. All letters received from chiefs were to be forwarded to Gorée or, after 1876, to Dakar. Commandants were criticized for arbitrary actions, and were told never to try to mediate commercial disputes except by agreement of both sides.[c] At least twice, over-eager Commandants with orders to deny the tyeddo access to the post, fired on their supposed allies. Many of the French officers at Gorée and Dakar wanted to bring the area under stricter and more intelligent control. Canard, in particular, wanted an officer at Kaolack and regular gunboat visits to the Saloum River —a show of force to impress tyeddo and marabouts alike.[5] Paris,

[b] The Nones and the Serer N'Diéghem, who made up much of the population in this area, had never known the authority of a complex state system, and often ignored efforts to impose an external organization. The Nones, in particular, refused to pay taxes, and continued to raid caravans and shoot strangers who approached their villages.

[c] Commandant of Gorée to Commandant of Kaolack, 21 Aug. 1872, ARS, 4 B 51. In 1876 Dakar became the headquarters of the second arrondissement, which included Gorée and its coastal dependencies.

however, was not willing to provide more funds, and St. Louis chose to spend existing funds to struggle for position with the English in the Rivières du Sud.

The usefulness of the Kaolack post for intelligence purposes was limited by the complete absence of independent sources of information. It is doubtful whether any of the Commandants spoke either Wolof or Serer. Therefore, they were completely dependent on the traders for information. One Commandant complained that he could not trust the village chief, who was also his interpreter, because the chief traded with both Sine and Nioro.[6] Most of the traders at Kaolack were Moslem, and the Bur Saloum also distrusted them. On one occasion, Niahoul sent a mission to N'Gasobil to ask that a letter be written to Gorée. The missionaries gladly complied.[d]

Citizens and Traders

The French presence consisted not only of the posts, but also of those who availed themselves of the posts' protection. These included the French traders who went to Africa in quest of fortune, and the missionaries. It also included a sizable African community, most of whom were from the Four Communes (St. Louis, Gorée, Dakar, and Rufisque) and were, therefore citizens of France.[7] These *citoyens* were the beneficiaries of the only consistent policy of assimilation ever carried out by the French in Negro Africa; they were protected by French law and had representative institutions. They received this favored position not because the colonial administration wanted to reward faithful intermediaries, but because the logic of French republican ideology demanded that these rights be given to peoples ruled by the French. In the 1870's, few Frenchmen expected that France was going to erect a massive empire in which an island of citizenship might prove embarrassing.

French colonial theory has been assimilationist since the French Revolution. Colonies were considered extensions of

[d] "Annales Religieuses de St. Joseph de N'Gasobil," manuscript, ARS. With the Petite Côte under French control, the Church returned to N'Gasobil in 1863.

France, and the peoples of French colonies were granted the rights of citizens. This policy caused few complications as long as the colonies were few, and as long as French law was appropriate to their administration. Thus, the Third Republic encountered no serious problems when it extended to the Communes of Senegal first the right to elect municipal councils (1872), then the right to elect a *Conseil Général* and a deputy to represent Senegal in Paris (1879). The Conseil Général had control over certain revenues, a control that brought it into constant conflict with the colonial administration. From 1879, when French policy became more expansionist, constant efforts were made to limit the authority of the Conseil Général and prevent the extension of similar rights and privileges. But the administration was not in a position to limit the exercise of civil rights by the citoyens. In fact, citoyens were able to preserve their privileges even when they lived outside the Four Communes. And if ever a citoyen felt that his rights were being violated, he could bring his grievances to the attention of Paris through his elected deputy there.

The citoyens played an important role in the extension of French commerce. Many were entrepreneurs trading on their own. Others worked for French commercial houses as salaried agents or as subtraders selling goods provided on credit. Tied to this trading community were small settlements of African traders and peasants that clustered around the various posts and ports. Many of them traded imported goods, like liquor and cloth, as well as more traditional items, like palm wine and dried fish. A mulatto social and financial elite developed within the Four Communes, partly as a result of business ties and intermarriage between Africans and Bordeaux commercial families. Both the mulatto elite and the Communes' largely Moslem Negro community helped advance the political and economic growth of France's African empire.

The small trader's position in African commerce improved greatly in the 1850's, when steam navigation to West Africa began. The steamships radically reduced the cost of shipping peanuts to Europe, and made it easier for the small entrepreneur to compete with large companies.[8] Hitherto, the trader either needed his own ships, or he found it necessary to group together with other small operators to hire a ship. The steamship lines made any quantity of space available to the small trader. Only toward the end of the century did economies of scale enable the larger houses to reestablish their advantage and force the smaller houses back into a dependent relationship.

In this period, however, a number of large new houses came into existence. For example, Chéri Peyrissac arrived in St. Louis in 1862 with little money. He took a job as a clerk, and soon got into the buying and selling of gum. Later on, the organization he started branched out into peanuts, salt, electricity, transportation, rubber, bananas, and cloth, among other things. (This type of diversity has characterized most commercial houses in the twentieth century.)[9]

The reduction of shipping costs and European industry's rising demand for vegetable oils created a favorable situation for traders in Senegal. Because of the heavy demand, prices for peanuts remained high until after 1880.[e] This gave traders an incentive to extend their operations and gave peasants a reason to devote increasing amounts of land to peanuts. Then, after the opening of the Suez Canal in 1869, peanuts from India began to appear on the Marseilles market in steadily increasing amounts, along with several other competing vegetable oils—cottonseed oil from the United States and sesame from Egypt. The price of peanuts in Senegal declined slowly from its peak of 27.50 francs per hundred kilos, and then, in 1883, took a plunge down to 15. Coming at a time when warfare, both between the African states and between Africans and the French, was increasing, the price drop led to a serious economic crisis. Within a four-year period,

[e] The following were the average prices paid at Rufisque in the mid-nineteenth century (Jean Adam, *L'Arachide* [Paris, 1908], pp. 124–27):

Year	Francs per hundred kilos
1843–45	16
1846	20
1857	26
1860–67	25 to 27.50
1868–77	20.80

exports from Senegal dropped to a quarter of what they had been. In the Gambia, the falloff was even more radical.[1]

This economic crisis increased the pressure for French action. In particular, the Senegalese commercial community demanded a railroad across Cayor, which would connect St. Louis with Dakar and reduce the cost of transporting peanuts from the area that was then the largest producer. The French gave the railroad high priority in their strategic considerations, and though they had to go to war with Lat Dior before they could begin building it, they completed it in 1885.[9] The commercial community also pressed for action to guarantee the security of traders in other areas.

A peculiarity of the trade is that peanuts were exported in the shell and pressed in France, though only the oil (which accounted for little more than a third of the weight) was really desired. This was largely because olive oil interests in southern France were successful in pressuring the government to maintain a high duty on oil imports. As a result, there was no local pressing industry, and Senegal had to import cottonseed oil for cooking. Several efforts were made to press oil in Senegal for local markets, but they were rarely successful until World War I. Performing simple transformation processes in France rather than in the colonies was one of the most striking characteristics of the colonial economy.[10]

Organization of Commerce

The posts protected the traders and served as important supply bases, but the traders were often told that they would be

---

[1] In Senegal, peanut exports dropped from 83,000 tons in 1882 to 21,729 tons in 1886; in the Gambia they dropped from 18,000 tons in 1884 to 2,900 tons in 1887. (Figures from Senegal are in metric tons; those for the Gambia are in long tons, or 1.016 metric tons.) The British tended to blame the step-up of the marabout-soninke wars and the civil war in Rip for this, but the drop was too great and occurred throughout too large an area to be explained so easily. The price had been high just before the drop. In 1880 and 1882, peanuts were bringing 25 francs per 100 kilos at Rufisque, and in 1882, 22.50 francs per 100 kilos on the Petite Côte. Governor of Senegal to Minister, 22 Feb. 1882, FOM, Sénégal, I 66 b.

[9] The railroad achieved what the traders wanted. The Cayor-Baol region, which was already the most important peanut-producing area, saw its exports jump from 12 million kilos in 1885 to 98 million kilos in 1900. This was about two-thirds of the total export from Senegal. (Adam, pp. 121–23.)

protected only within range of French cannon. But they were willing to take their risks, and generally went wherever they could make a profit. Thus, each of the four major houses operating near the Saloum River had factories at four places within the area: Kaolack, Foundiougne, Fatick, and Silif.[h] The agents at these points were all either Frenchmen or citoyens. There were also eighteen other sites in the area where trading was done by representatives of these houses and by smaller operators. All of these were Senegalese operating with goods advanced on credit. Most of the trading was done on or near a body of water, and the largest part of the crop was transported by boat. At several of these trading sites, including two in Laghem, the risk of being raided during the time of marabout-tyeddo conflicts was great, but in general, the warring factions seem not to have attacked the traders.

When the houses began granting goods on credit to the small traders, and the traders in turn granted them to peasants, another kind of risk came into the trade. Nevertheless, any trader who wanted to compete had to operate this way. In fact, credit became part of the annual cycle of peasant life in areas near the factories, especially during the "hungry season"—the months before the first harvest, when the peasant was working hard, but often lacked food. The peasant would give the trader some piece of cloth or jewelry as collateral, and in return would receive either food or seed nuts, which he would then have to repay at the end of the season with exorbitant interest. For the small African traders operating in remote areas, the rules were often more flexible. The trader whose goods were stolen or who gave them on credit to unreliable peasants often found it advantageous simply to disappear.[11]

In French factories, trade was largely by weight. This led

[h] The four big houses were Maurel and Prom, Maurel Frères, Buhan and Teisseire, and Compagnie du Sénégal et de la Côte Occidentale d'Afrique (a Marseille-based company, which became Compagnie Française de l'Afrique Occidentale). Lt. Governor to Governor, 14 Oct. 1886, FOM, Sénégal, I 87 c. The trade in Senegal tended to be dominated by Bordeaux commercial houses, though most of the peanut crop was sent to Marseille. In spite of the rivalry between the French ports, the different French commercial houses in Senegal cooperated in setting prices. See Eugene Lagrillière-Beauclerc, *Mission au Sénégal et au Soudan* (Paris, 1897), pp. 102–3.

to two kinds of fraud, both of which seem to have been wide-spread: the rigging of scales by the merchants and the addition of foreign matter to sacks of peanuts by the peasants.[i] In the English factories and in a few of the French centers, the trade was by the bushel. In the Gambia, when the world price of peanuts went down, traders often simply tried to increase the size of the bushel, leaving the price the same. This usually led to a seller's strike (called *tong* or *laff*).

In spite of the reluctance of French administration to see that commerce was protected beyond "the range of French cannon," it did get involved with commerce in another way. In 1872 Canard authorized the Commandant at Kaolack to guarantee advances by the commercial houses to certain chiefs in whom he had confidence, i.e., to co-sign for loans made to the chiefs. The interest rate was not to exceed 5 per cent on money loans or 100 per cent on loans in kind, which were the majority. All loans were to be repaid from the first harvest, and the Commandant was instructed to use all legal means at his disposal to see that they were. Canard also authorized a direct loan of millet seed worth five hundred francs to Niahoul, the Bur Saloum.[j]

However, the traders wanted more than loans. They wanted protection, especially at Foundiougne. By 1880, Foundiougne had replaced Kaolack as the most important trade center on the Saloum River. The increase in trade brought demands for an increase in protection. Though Saloum needed French friend-ship, the traders were a source of valuable revenue, and were frequently asked to pay more than the 3 per cent export duty that was stipulated by the 1859 and 1861 treaties. Boilève, the

---

[i] In 1866 the amount of permissible foreign matter was fixed by law at 2 per cent. The law did not succeed in ending the practice. (Joseph Fouquet, *La Traite des Arachides dans le Pays de Kaolack*, vol. 8 of *Etudes Sénégalaises*, St. Louis, Senegal, 1958, pp. 45–46.)

[j] Commandant of Gorée to Commandant of Kaolack, 25 May 1872, ARS, 4 B 51. Like so many other policies, the granting of loans for seed can be traced back to Faidherbe, who sponsored loans of seed to famine-stricken peasants in Cayor in 1863 and 1864. Faidherbe wanted both to increase cultivation and to make the Cayor peasants more dependent on France. But Cayor was under French administration at that time, and French control of Saloum in 1872 was, at best, very tenuous.

interim Commandant at Dakar, was like Canard in wanting regular gunboat visits, as much to warn the tyeddo to leave the traders alone as to protect the traders from the marabouts.[k] The traders themselves felt that stone buildings, at the least, were necessary for self-protection, but the Burs consistently refused to permit construction in stone. So, in 1879, Boilève visited the river to talk the matter over with Guédel M'Bodj. Guédel had little reason to feel grateful toward the French, for, as his Grand Jaraf pointed out in a bitter speech at the meeting, Saloum had received no aid from the French for the past twelve years, in spite of treaties and promises.[12] Nevertheless, Guédel was hard-pressed and did not want to offend the French, so he withdrew his prohibition, on the condition that no fort would be built at Foundiougne.

But the right to build in stone was not enough for the traders. The policy of the commercial community was to trade wherever it could, and seek the protection of the state whenever it could get it. In late 1881, the traders of Foundiougne presented their grievances to the Conseil Général as follows:

These two countries [Sine and Saloum] have acquired a wealth that, instead of making them peaceful, has rendered them very arrogant toward the traders who frequent these parts; the claims of the chiefs are becoming exorbitant; at will they decide on customs and gifts contrary to treaties that they have concluded with the French government. But not content with this constant plunder, they have continually harassed the merchants, whose very existence is in danger. . . .

Every moment, we are afraid of learning that our property has been plundered and our personnel mistreated. Faced with the menacing attitude of these kings, we expect at a time not far distant to be forced to abandon all [outlying] trading sites, and to group ourselves around Kaolack so that we may be protected by the French flag; but [even] that post appears insufficient to safeguard the interests of commerce, because

---

[k] Commandant of Dakar to Governor of Senegal, 9 Jan., 21 Jan., and 19 June 1879, ARS, 4 B 64. The tyeddo probably harassed traders more than the marabouts did.

the proximity of the king of Saloum will always cause a legitimate distrust.[13]

The Conseil Général approved the construction of a military post at Foundiougne, and it probably would have been constructed if the Conseil had been willing to provide the funds. The administration was unwilling to move the Kaolack post there because of the absence of fresh water.[14] As it was, Foundiougne received a customs post several years later, and became the center of the cercle of Sine-Saloum in 1887.

Toward Intervention

The camel caravans that went from village to village do not seem to have entered Sine until the late 1870's. Nevertheless, the flow of peanuts was steadily increasing, and with it, the French commitment in the area increased. Soon every little squabble was taken to the French military authorities. Gifts and pillage were once considered part of the costs of doing business, but as French power increased, the traders began to seek compensation for all losses. Even though both French and British authorities knew that the traders often lied about damages, they generally supported the traders' claims with letters to the chiefs involved; the French traders usually received compensation from the tyeddo, and the British traders from the marabouts.

Many of the military men in Senegal disliked the traders as a group, but they willingly listened to their complaints.[1] For these empire-minded proconsuls, restraint was a difficult virtue. Rare was the Governor or Commandant who did not ask his superiors for more soldiers, more gunboats, and more freedom of action. François Valière, who was Governor from 1869 to 1876, was of

---

[1] Thus, Governor Brière de l'Isle wrote of the French traders: "One cannot count on the wisdom of our nationals who live in these unpleasant climates only so that they can live well, and return to France with a fortune accumulated in the shortest possible time. It is essential that the administration, vigilant guardian of the general interest, oppose passion and greed with calm and equity, and not let itself be troubled by these false tears when we should be marching forward according to the true principles of civilization, which dictate our duties in the colony." (Governor of Senegal to Minister, 21 Apr. 1878, FOM, Sénégal, I 61 c.)

necessity the most pacific, since France was recovering from defeat in Europe during his administration. In 1874 he wrote:

> In this country, more than anywhere else, in order to assure peace, it is necessary to be always ready to make war and to be able to make rather frequent military demonstrations whenever the natives feel themselves ready to become effective.[m]

Valière was asking only that his outfits be kept up to full strength and that he be given four or five gunboats. His successor, Colonel Brière de l'Isle, wrote two years later in defense of a more active policy:

> In Senegal, there are two ways to arrive at war—that is, either to openly seek a quarrel with whomever you wish to fight or to completely efface yourself until you are obliged to end that reserve too long imposed on by the tensions of being a conqueror and by the dangerous proximity of a state that is too powerful and proud, a seat of religious hatred directed at Christians.[15]

Brière de l'Isle, who had much greater freedom of action and was much more aggressive than Valière, might be considered the first of the "new imperialists" in Senegal. Strongly influenced by Faidherbe's ideas, he wanted to resume the push into the Sudan and assert French control over the mouths of various coastal rivers. Though frequently restrained by Paris, he signed treaties and strengthened the French military presence along the coast from Cape Verde to Sierra Leone. He also proposed that three railroad lines be constructed, one from St. Louis to Dakar, a second from Dakar to Medina or Kayes on the upper Senegal River, and a third tying the Senegal River to the Niger. In 1880, Jauréguibéry, Minister of the Navy and a former Gov-

---

[m] Governor of Senegal to Minister, 13 May 1874, ARS, "Situation politique." The effective strength of the Senegal garrison in 1874 was listed at 1,798, but it was seldom up to full strength. More than half were *spahis* (African cavalrymen) or tirailleurs recruited in Senegal. Most of the rest were *disciplinaires,* men sent to Senegal in punishment for misdeeds in France. FOM, Sénégal, IX 7 bis.

ernor of Senegal, presented Brière de l'Isle's plan in Paris, and received authorization for building the three railroads.[n] This, more than any other decision, committed France to the quest for empire. Hitherto, commercial activities had been carried on with limited capital investment, and traders had used existing means of transport; but a railroad required a large commitment of resources, and could be built only if its security could be assured by French troops. African leaders were well aware of the military implications of a railroad. Conquest usually preceded construction, and further military action was necessary afterwards to make sure that the investment would be secure and remunerative.

The British in the Gambia do not seem to have been aware of the danger to British interests that changes in French policy represented. The British had no desire for territorial responsibilities. They were interested in keeping control of the Gambia River for their trade, but they did not want to embroil themselves in African conflicts. At one point, Bathurst was ready to turn the Ceded Mile over to Mamour N'Dari, but London vetoed the proposal because of talks with France on exchanging the Gambia for French possessions elsewhere.[16]

The Gambia exchange was proposed almost simultaneously by both Faidherbe and D'Arcy. The reasons were many. Bathurst was the lone British settlement on a stretch of coast dominated by the French. Three-fourths of the peanuts exported from the Gambia went to France, and much of the buying on the river was done by French commercial houses. Many British colonial officials, both in London and in Sierra Leone, felt that Britain's

[n] John D. Hargreaves, *Prelude to the Partition of West Africa*, pp. 253-71. Historians have spent much time trying to decide what event began the scramble. Unfortunately, there is no neat answer, for there was a series of events, each of which committed one or more European powers to further action. For the French in West Africa, the decision to penetrate the Niger River area was a key one, but it was the logical outgrowth of Faidherbe's annexations, and followed certain strategic lines he had laid out. In fact, most French activity in West Africa during the scramble for colonies was merely the implementation of ideas proposed earlier by Faidherbe and Bouët-Willaumez. The question is not why a new forward movement began, but rather why metropolitan governments relaxed their restraints on the adventurous policies of the colonial officials.

profits from the trade did not justify the defense efforts that the Gambia demanded. At the same time, the French knew that if they controlled the Gambia, they could more easily strike out at their African enemies, in particular, the marabouts at Nioro.

France started in 1866 by offering its three posts on the Ivory Coast in exchange for the Gambia, and then threw in Gabon. The French were also willing to concede certain areas of the Rivières du Sud, where Gorée and Freetown trade spheres overlapped. For ten years the French and the British exchanged proposals and counterproposals; at times the proposals were limited in scope, and at other times they were tied to broader settlements of issues in different parts of the world. In spite of the many reasons for making the trade, the negotiations failed, partly because of the machinations of a small but adept Gambia lobby in London, and partly because the Colonial Office insisted on asking for too much in return for the Gambia. The proposal was dropped after 1876, though French representatives in St. Louis and Kaolack continued to address passionate pleas to Paris on the subject until after World War I.[17] The failure of the negotiations exacerbated the suspicion with which most French and British representatives in West Africa regarded each other; and this suspicion created a pressure on each to act first, and influenced the speed with which these once reticent colonial powers grabbed economically unproductive territories during the generation that followed.

There is no single point at which France or Great Britain switched to an aggressive forward policy. Rather, with the growing fear that rivals might successfully exploit advantages in areas only partially explored, Paris was increasingly willing to permit colonial officials to do the things they had always wanted to do. The more authority the men on the spot received, the more they wanted. At the same time, the ministries, which came and went continually in Paris, varied radically in their willingness to authorize new initiatives.

The new imperialism expressed itself not only in new conquests, but also in reorganization of the existing colonial domain. In 1882, the short-lived ministry of Léon Gambetta reorganized the management of the colonies, and sent out René Servatius, the first civilian Governor.[o] The military retained control of the Sudan and of certain areas where French control was only lightly seated, but most of the empire was speedily placed under the authority of a corps of civilian administrators. In 1889 the Ecole Coloniale was founded in Paris to train professional administrators.

The transfer to civilian control was a sign that Paris was becoming more concerned with colonial matters, and a series of organizational changes within Africa followed this transfer. The telegraph made it unnecessary to have two commands, so in 1882 the second arrondissement, in Dakar, was placed directly under St. Louis. At the same time, increasing French use of the coastal rivers led to the appointment of a Lieutenant Governor of Rivières du Sud, in command of the area from Saloum to Sierra Leone.

Because Dr. Jean Bayol, the new Lieutenant Governor, was on tour most of the year, matters concerning Saloum tended to fall between desks. The communications problem that resulted was only partially solved when Kaolack was placed under St. Louis in 1884.[p]

The Catholic Mission

The missionaries benefited very little from the extension of French power. However, the treaties of 1859 and 1861 did give the mission a protected base on the Petite Côte, within which they were able to build a small Christian community. They did this, in general, without the aid of the administration, which was generally careful not to antagonize the Moslems. When Father Lamoise asked the administration to forbid construction of a

[o] Gambetta also took the *Direction des Colonies* from the Ministry of the Navy and placed it under the Ministry of Commerce. The transfer was temporary, and in 1894 a separate colonial ministry was founded.

[p] Undersecretary of State to Governor of Senegal, 31 Mar. 1884, FOM, Sénégal, I 71 a. Some communications difficulties remained, with the result that the Governor's reports to Paris up until the conquest in 1887 contain very little information about Saloum. The historian's problem is further complicated by the absence in both Paris and Dakar of certain important documents, which seem to have simply been lost.

mosque in Joal, his request was turned down, and the administration further angered him by appointing Moslems as chiefs in
Joal. The Church's most striking success was the large-scale conversion of Fadioute, an island fishing village opposite Joal, which
had often sought to remain independent of Sine.[18]

In Sine, the area that had the greatest potential for the
Church, the missionaries had become anathema to the Serer
chiefs during the 1850's. In 1881, when Father Léopold Diouf,
an African priest, persuaded the Bur to permit a mission in
Palmarin, not far from Joal, the opposition of the Bur's chiefs
forced the abandonment of the project.[19] A mission was founded
there several years later, but the real penetration of Sine did not
begin until the twentieth century, by which time the Moslems
had established a larger beachhead.

Saloum offered better possibilities. When Ma Bâ was ravaging
Saloum, many of the Saloum-Saloum took refuge at the Petite
Côte missions, and some were converted, only to drop from the
fold when Ma Bâ's death (in 1867) permitted them to return to
their ancestral villages. Nevertheless, when Father Diouf visited
Sadiouka M'Bodj at Tiofat, he was received warmly. The Bur
attended mass and catechism class, and invited Diouf to stay in
his own compound. Diouf received a horse as a gift, and was
escorted back to the Petite Côte by Sadiouka's men. He carried
a letter thanking the missionaries for all they had done for his
people, and asking them to intercede on Sadiouka's behalf with
the current administration.[20] In spite of this encouragement, no
regular mission was established in Saloum until 1910, long after
the pacification of the area.

Thus, when crises arose, the missionaries were not in a position to mediate or to influence French policy. France's dominant military position regulated relations with the Senegambian
states, and contact was maintained by direct correspondence
between Senegambian rulers and colonial officers. The missionaries had little to say about what the administration did.

VII

THE CONQUEST OF SALOUM

The Tijani League

SENEGAL WAS FRANCE'S MAJOR BASE in West Africa, the one area
where her claims were largely staked out long before the "scramble" began. As a result, there were few struggles for territory
in that area between the French and the British. In Senegal,
the new imperialism first manifested itself in Brière de l'Isle's
railroad projects. Construction of the railroads had at first been
vigorously resisted by Lat Dior. But in 1879, while involved
in a conflict with the major tyeddo chiefs, Lat Dior signed a
treaty authorizing the French to build a railroad across Cayor.
Two years later, when he was more sure of himself and of the
mood of his followers, he expelled the surveyors and renounced
the treaty. For five years, Lat Dior alternately resisted and
evaded French power while construction of the railroad proceeded under an armed guard and the French sought docile
collaborators.[1] When a French-backed puppet ruler in Cayor
proved incompetent, the French allied themselves with Lat
Dior's popular nephew, Samba Laobé Fall, but Samba Laobé
found himself caught between French military power and his
own people, who pulled up survey stakes, attacked locomotives,
and deliberately violated trespass rules. Finally, in 1886, in separate battles several weeks apart, both Lat Dior and Samba
Laobé were killed.[a] The French broke Cayor up into six cantons,

[a] Julian Witherell, "The Response of the Peoples of Cayor to French Penetration," unpub. diss. (University of Wisconsin, 1964), chaps. 4 and 5; Vincent
Monteil, "Lat Dyor ...," *Archives de Sociologie des Religions*, No. 16 (1963),
77–104. Lat Dior has become a Senegalese national hero. He plays a large role in
the oral tradition, and Senegal's major military base bears his name.

but in order to avoid having to free the slaves, they called it a protectorate.[b]

Lat Dior's closest ally during these last bitter years was the man he had installed as Burba Djoloff, Alboury N'Diaye. Alboury was fortunate in that Djoloff's sandy wastes attracted few covetous glances. He was unchallenged there, he had a disciplined band of warriors at his command, and he seems to have been one of the few rulers in Senegal with a surplus of horses. By judiciously loaning men and horses to other Senegambian leaders, Alboury contributed to the development of what one French Governor called "a sort of Tijani league bitterly resisting our civilizing influence."[2] But he was unwilling to commit his forces to a battle he could not win, and he watched the French defeat his two closest allies, Lat Dior and Saër Maty Bâ. He even accepted a treaty that made his state a French protectorate; but finally, in 1890, the inevitable conflict came. As a French column moved on his capital, Yang-Yang, Alboury fled to the east, where he eventually joined Ahmadou, the son of Al Hajj Umar Tall, in a final bitter gesture of defiance.

The ties that bound the different members of the Tijani league varied in strength. Each of the leaders was torn between his local interests and his commitment to Islam. Lat Dior fought alongside the French against the Toucouleur marabout Amadou Cheikhou in 1875; and Abdoul Boubakar, the Toucouleur leader in Fouta Toro, who was one of the most committed of the Tijani leaders, cooperated with the French in their 1887 campaign against the Sarakollé marabout, Mamadou Lamine. But though the marabouts fought each other at times, French fears of a "Tijani league" were clearly not exaggerated. Alboury loaned men and horses to Saër Maty and to pro-marabout forces in Sine. Saër Maty and Fodé Kabba both loaned each other forces. Alboury allied himself to Abdoul Boubakar, and when he was chased from Djoloff, he took refuge in Fouta Toro with the

---

[b] The law of 1848 that abolished slavery was considered valid only in areas of direct administration. To avoid social disruption and the hostility of ruling elites, areas where slavery was entrenched were placed under protectorate.

Toucouleur leader. Alboury also became an ally of the Teigne Baol, and he corresponded with Mamadou Lamine, the man whom Abdoul Boubakar had fought in cooperation with the French.

Arbitration

If the Tijani alliance was to be effective, it had to present the French with a united front. To do this, it was necessary to restore unity in Rip. Lat Dior, Alboury, and Abdoul Boubakar all tried to mediate the conflict that had broken out among Ma Bâ's lieutenants between 1878 and 1887. None of the three Tijani leaders committed forces to the conflict in the early years because they wanted to reconcile Mamour N'Dari and Biram Cissé, not to crush Cissé, who was a valuable military leader. In this attempt to mediate, the Tijani were trying what the British and French had tried, though their goals were radically different. The British wanted peace on the banks of the Gambia, the French in Saloum, so that the economic development of these valuable areas might proceed without interruption.

But Biram Cissé could not retract his original act of rebellion against Mamour N'Dari. Once the conflict began, there were only two possible outcomes. Either one side had to accept the domination of the other, or each had to accept the other's independence. Neither Mamour N'Dari nor Saër Maty could accept Cissé's right to build his own fortifications, but if Cissé tore down his fortifications, he would have been inviting his enemies to destroy his power. A reconciliation was made all the more unlikely by Biram Cissé's initial successes. V. S. Gouldsbury, the Gambian Administrator, described the situation in 1879 this way:

> Beram Ceesay has taken, and is in possession of, nearly all the towns and villages in Baddiboo adjacent to the [Gambia] river, and his rule is well spoken of by the traders at several trading wharfs. He is a man of enlightened ideas, and of considerable ability as a general and a statesman. Were he to succeed in the present struggle for supremacy—and success appears possible—I think it would be the most desirable termination to the present state of affairs that could occur.[3]

When Cissé met Gouldsbury in 1879, he demanded a share of the stipend given to Mamour N'Dari for protecting commerce.[4] Sir Samuel Rowe, Governor-in-Chief of the British West African settlements, refused to approve such a grant until the war was resolved, but he suggested that a "gift" be offered to Cissé and that Mamour N'Dari be informed of the gift.[5]

Gouldsbury was convinced that the major barrier to compromise was Saër Maty, the leader of the war hawks at Nioro. He explained to Rowe that Mamour N'Dari was disposed to compromise, but that he was a "weak, quiet old man . . . entirely in the hands of Said Matty [Saër Maty] and his adherents."[6] Gouldsbury considered Saër Maty "a man of a most treacherous, mean, savage, and withal cowardly disposition."[c] In 1879, Saër Maty killed two of Cissé's hostages.[d] Later that year, one of Saër Maty's aides allegedly took the property of some Bathurst traders when he sacked a Gambian village. Gouldsbury made little effort to verify the traders' claims, and insisted that Mamour N'Dari compensate them and pay a fine.[7] The fine was set at five hundred pounds, and Mamour N'Dari was ordered to either surrender the culprit or pay another eighty pounds.[8] Fearing that he might lose his stipend, Mamour N'Dari complied; and in doing so he probably weakened his own power, which depended in part on his wealth and his ability to reward his entourage.

The peace terms that Mamour N'Dari offered Cissé were unreasonable. He demanded that Cissé level all of his fortresses, totally disarm, and re-dig wells he had filled in.[9] Cissé was willing only if the British would guarantee his life and property and the lives and property of his followers. The British did not want

[c] Administrator of Gambia to Governor-in-Chief, 18 Nov. 1879, PRO, CO 87/115, No. 34. Although Gouldsbury was very biased, the oral tradition has preserved a picture of Saër Maty that is not very different from his—a picture of a man of action who was impulsive, cruel, and uncompromising. The tradition contains more stories of Saër Maty and gives a more vivid impression of him than it does of his uncle, Mamour N'Dari. The oral account makes it clear that Saër Maty attracted a following both because he was Ma Bâ's son and because he had undeniable leadership ability.

[d] *Ibid.* According to Gouldsbury, Cissé countered this by returning unharmed to Mamour N'Dari the two hostages he held.

to do this. In 1880, Cissé asked for a British protectorate, but this too was refused.[10] Cissé did, however, force a truce in 1883; but it was a truce that did little more than temporarily affirm the status quo.

Severely limited by his superiors in Freetown and London, Gouldsbury could only plead for a reconciliation, write letters, and offer his services as an arbitrator. Late in 1879, he complained to Rowe:

> The interests involved in the struggle between the contending parties being varied, and important, and weighty, it is perhaps no cause of wonder that I have failed to succeed where I had nothing to promise, no threat of punishment to pronounce, no assurances of protection against treachery and bad faith to offer, and no equivalent to tender for concession or sacrifice on either side. . . .
>
> Where a kingdom, and a wealthy and powerful one, is fought for, and where not alone the wishes and ambition of one man to retain and the other to grasp power and dominion are involved, but where, as an important factor in the conflict, the wishes and aspirations of numerous and powerful adherents on either side are intimately concerned, exhortation has, as might be expected, proved powerless, and the prospect of an inconclusive peace has failed to present to the opponents such attractive features as could compensate them for all they might lose, or for all they might gain.[11]

Up to 1884, the French did not involve themselves in the conflicts of Saloum except to advise the warring parties to fight less and farm more. Then, in 1884, Lt. Governor Jean Bayol visited both Sine and Saloum. His visit reflected the more lively interest France was taking in the African states because of her increasing involvement in the economy of the region.[e] The fight-

---

[e] Approximately three thousand tons of peanuts and three hundred tons of millet were shipped out of the Saloum River in 1875. In 1884, according to Bayol, this sum had risen to nine thousand tons of peanuts and five hundred tons of millet. Almost half of this came from Fatick, which would suggest that Sine's succession conflicts limited economic development much less than the religious war in Saloum did. Nevertheless, the French were attracted to Saloum's extensive fertile and well-watered lands. Lt. Governor of Rivières du Sud to Governor of Senegal, 7 May 1884, Papers of Victor Ballot, No. 171, ARS and AN.

ing in Saloum was much less savage than it had been during the height of Ma Bâ's crusades, but the French stake was much greater. Bayol had lengthy talks with the traders at Kaolack, with Guédel, and with Ali Khodia Bâ, the marabout chief of Laghem. Ali Khodia was a nephew of Ma Bâ and Mamour N'Dari, and was apparently also related to Guédel. A tall, pock-marked man of about forty-five, severe and dignified in appearance, he had an entourage of fifty infantrymen and two hundred horsemen, and had been closely tied to Mamour N'Dari. Bayol left his conference with Ali Khodia convinced that he had an ally in his peacemaking efforts. He also won from Guédel the right to construct new posts and to negotiate with the marabouts in Saloum's name.

Bayol arranged a meeting with Mamour N'Dari. When Mamour N'Dari did not show up and instead sent a letter suggesting another meeting place, Bayol, convinced that his prestige was at stake, returned to Kaolack, and threatened to pay another visit with a force of tyeddo and tirailleurs. The second time, the meeting went off on schedule. It opened coldly when Saër Maty announced that the war would end only when Guédel had become a Moslem. Bayol got up to leave, but Mamour N'Dari quickly silenced his nephew. After lengthy discussions, the Nioro leaders presented their terms. These were: (1) destruction of the tata at Dagaminian, which had been Guédel's base, (2) Guédel's renunciation of the south bank of the Saloum, and (3) the return of all prisoners. Guédel's response to these terms was that he could not leave lands his ancestors had ruled. The best Bayol could do was to get both sides to agree to an uneasy truce. He did not expect it to last.[12]

On his return from Saloum, Bayol suggested that a fort at Fatick and a customs post at Foundiougne be built, and that the French occupy the south bank of the Saloum. A British officer had visited Sine in 1881 to find out if the area was really under French control. Bayol wanted to assert French claims before the British decided to move in. Bayol also wanted to replace the sergeant in Kaolack with a Commandant du Cercle capable of assuming political and administrative responsibilities.[13]

The different African factions remained on the alert, and may have done some raiding, but full-scale war did not break out until March 27, 1885, when Ali Khodia Bâ was murdered by Saër Maty Bâ. Saër Maty charged that Ali Khodia's relations with the French had been tantamount to treason. The murder brought Biram Cissé back from the south bank of the Gambia, where he had been helping Moussa Molo against Fodé Kabba, and it brought Mamour N'Dari, who had now lost everything but the village of Nioro, into a coalition with Cissé and Guédel.[14] This last stage of the war was the bitterest and most destructive after Ma Bâ passed from the scene.

The first months of the war went badly for Saër Maty. Enemy warriors swept through southern Rip, sacking and burning most of his villages.[15] By July, he had been defeated in nine battles.[16] But Saër Maty's fortunes were suddenly reversed when he was given outside aid—mainly by his uncle, Alboury N'Diaye. In August, Saër Maty attacked and burned Kau-Ur, Biram Cissé's most important trading wharf. He immediately dashed off a letter to Bathurst, bragging of his victory and promising compensation to any traders who had lost goods: "Know this, that I have burned Cawer. Should any of your people's property [have been] spoilt there, I shall settle [with] them before it comes to your hearing."[17]

By the end of the rains, another truce had been arranged. The French and the British were trying to mediate, as were many Moslem leaders. Abdoul Boubakar, who visited Rip in February 1886, divided his forces between the two Moslem rivals with instructions that his men were to fight only for the side that was attacked. When Saër Maty attacked, half of Abdoul's warriors were fighting alongside Cissé.[18]

Bathurst blamed the war for the large drop in peanut exports.[f] The usually profitable Gambia colony was dependent on the export tax on peanuts, and it suddenly found itself operating in the red. In spite of the fighting, however, the traders seem to

---

[f] *Annual Report*, 1887, AG. From 18,404 tons in 1884, exports declined to 2,986 tons in 1887. See also my chapter 6, p. 120n.

have been relatively safe. Bathurst was notified about the war
zones, and posters went up warning the traders to stay away.
Some years before, when the fighting had just begun, Gouldsbury had noted that the marabouts took great care to keep the
wars from disturbing commerce. He reported in 1877:

> None of the chiefs on either side of the river are opposed to
> trade; on the contrary they are desirous that it should flourish
> in their kingdoms; [however] it is difficult, if not impossible,
> for any chief to ensure the safety of traders' property therein,
> or to protect their goods from marauders, so long as such a
> district is the scene of warfare. The various warnings which
> have been given from time to time by the chiefs as to the
> removal of traders' goods to places of safety have been held
> out for purposes of preventing complications and trouble with
> our governments, and have been, I consider, very promptly
> given.[19]

Ten years later Genouille, the French Governor, grudgingly observed the same respect for trade in territories north of the Gambia. Though he was bitterly hostile to Saër Maty, Genouille
wrote: "I confess that up to the present Saër Maty, either because of his prudence or because of his interests, has not molested our traders very much. But he can scarcely hide his
aversion for whites."[20]

There were incidents, however. During Biram Cissé's sweep
through Rip in May and June 1885, several factories at N'Diayen
were sacked. A few traders were enslaved, and the rest lost their
goods.[21] The hapless Mamour N'Dari, who was still nominally
the Eliman Nioro and was thus held responsible for any damage
done in his area, was faced with yet another demand for reparations. He promised to make good the losses, but was unable to
do so.[22] In January 1886, the following notice was posted:

> It is hereby notified for general information that Chief
> Mahmoud N'Dery Bah, in treaty with this government to
> protect British interests in the Kingdom of Baddiboo, has
> announced his inability for the present, on account of war in
> his country, to take the responsibility of affording protection

to Traders, and the Mercantile public in particular are requested to be guided accordingly.[g]

The British were to regret this action. Both Biram Cissé and
Saër Maty petitioned for Mamour N'Dari's stipend. Administrator Alfred Maloney favored Saër Maty, mostly because he
believed the young chief's statement that Mamour N'Dari had
held power only as regent.[23] While Maloney was sending the
marabout chiefs sanctimonious lectures on international law, the
various levels at the Colonial Office were exchanging memoran-
da on how to keep control of the Gambia without governing it
as a territory.

Late in 1886, a French Administrator, Lucien Rabourdin, was
dispatched to Sine-Saloum, and he claimed to have reestablished
a peace that would permit the trading season to pass quietly.
Rabourdin reported that there were British emissaries in Saër
Maty's camp.[24] These British emissaries were able to win more
substantial concessions from the marabouts than were the
French. Saër Maty refused a British protectorate, but both he
and Cissé finally signed treaties with Bathurst in February 1887.
Both chiefs agreed to protect British subjects, to guarantee the
safety of Mamour N'Dari, and to enter into a treaty of peace
and friendship with each other. Each was to receive one hundred
pounds a year. The treaties confirmed Cissé's control of an area
much larger than that controlled by his rival.[25]

The Campaign of 1887

On about the first of April, Saër Maty sacked Kahone. Guédel
immediately sent a plea to Dakar for help. His letter came at the
right moment. The trading season was almost over, but the
peasants were not yet ready to plant. The weather was hot, but
still dry. Even more favorable for French intervention than the
climate were the political factors. First, Genouille, the French
Governor, wanted to get into Rip before the British did. He did

[g] PRO., CO 87/127, No. 7. Saër Maty had been collecting the customs in the
Gambia trading wharfs of Badibu since 1883. Administrator of Gambia to Governor-in-Chief, 3 June 1885, PRO, CO 87/124.

not know what kind of treaty arrangements the British had with their Gambian neighbors, but he believed, correctly, that they would have no legal basis for protesting a fait accompli. Second, the French were worried about the "Tijani league." Alboury N'Diaye was aiding Saër Maty and corresponding with Mamadou Lamine, the Sarakollé marabout who had dealt the French a surprising defeat at Bakel on the upper Senegal River. In early 1887, General Joseph Gallieni led a column against Mamadou Lamine, who seemed to be moving toward Rip. The French wanted to prevent their two enemies from joining, and wanted to take Saër Maty out of action before Alboury got involved personally in the fighting. During the 1887 campaign all posts in northern Senegal carefully watched Alboury's activities in Djoloff.[26]

Genouille gave Colonel Coronnat, who was commanding the column, instructions to investigate carefully the ties between the English and the chiefs. "But," Genouille continued, "the goal to be attained immediately is to give to commerce, which has demanded it for a long time, a security that is absolute and will be fruitful."[27] The 1887 campaign displayed meticulous planning and a knowledge of the countryside; both had been lacking in the 1865 campaign. Before any troop movement was made, a camp with fresh water was chosen for the night. Starting on April 5, Coronnat moved his troops to Kaolack. Plans were made for his Saloum tyeddo allies to go on ahead of the column, digging wells and setting up camp. On April 16, Coronnat wrote Saër Maty that, as a result of his raids, the Governor had decided "to put Rip under a French protectorate, and to give the power in Rip to a prince who was devoted to the French and who had proved his devotion by acts and not only by words."[28] The letter told Saër Maty that Guédel had been designated to rule Saloum, and that he could avoid war with Guédel and the French by surrendering.

On April 20, Coronnat moved his column of almost five hundred men, more than half of them Africans. Supported by the tyeddo of Saloum, they attacked the tata at Goumbof, east of Kahone. Saër Maty had massed most of his forces there. As the

French took positions and prepared their artillery, Saër Maty carefully stationed his horsemen outside the tata, so they could flee if necessary. The marabouts fired on the French as they approached the fort, but they failed to do much damage because the French rifles had greater range. Next the marabouts tried brush fires, but this tactic failed when the wind shifted. Finally Coronnat's attack column stormed the tata and easily breached its stone walls. Before the fighting was over, the marabouts had lost over 250 men. Only three of Coronnat's soldiers were dead and fifteen wounded. Within twenty-four hours of the victory at Goumbof, six tatas in northern Rip with walls averaging more than sixteen feet high had been taken and were being torn down. The tyeddo handled these mopping-up operations, and, where possible, used the occasion to settle old accounts, amass booty, and take slaves.

Saër Maty pulled his forces back, and Coronnat retreated toward Kaolack, moving toward Nioro by a route along which there would be fresh water. The column moved slowly, careful not to outdistance supplies of food and water. On May 3, Saër Maty's capital, Keur Ma Bâ (Ma Bâ's village) was yielded without a fight. His tata there had walls about twelve feet high, flanked by eight thirty-foot towers. Saër Maty was carefully keeping two days march from Coronnat. After taking Keur Ma Bâ, Coronnat set up a flying column of 105 men and one artillery piece under Captain Villiers. Leaving tents and bedding behind, the column took off in pursuit of the marabout chief. It covered more than seventy miles in twenty-eight hours, and caught up with Saër Maty at Bantanding, not far from Bathurst. Saër Maty fled with thirty men and made it safely to the Ceded Mile, which Villiers did not enter. Instead, he sent a letter to the Administrator asking that Saër Maty be turned over to him. The British, indignant about the whole operation, flatly refused, and Saër Maty was ferried across the river. He lived in a village near Bathurst until his death in 1897.

For Guédel's tyeddo, the operation was very successful. They took many cattle and about five hundred women and children, and they shot more than one hundred male prisoners.[29]

Neither Biram Cissé nor Mamour N'Dari was mentioned in reports of the campaign. On April 17, Cissé had written the Administrator in Bathurst that the French were at Kaolack preparing to attack Saër Maty (the faulty grammar is the interpreter's, not Cissé's):

> For I believed that if the French commence to war with Saide Mattie, no longer will they distorbe me. And I am in the hand of her Majesty the Queen. Watering to [sic] the advice of His Excellency. For the French will not fail to war with us. And I am in my house disturbing no man.[80]

The Administrator wrote back to Cissé that he had "taken steps to ascertain the real intentions of the French people" and would let him know "in good time" what these intentions were. He went on to say that the French people were friendly with the English people and would not be likely to invade Badibu. The letter was written the day Goumbof fell.[h]

The French campaign was also a surprise to Paris. Earlier in the year, when the cercle of Sine-Saloum was set up, Paris withheld authorization of the new circumscription. The Governor was told that funds were limited, but that he could either apply for funds for the new cercle or proceed by rearranging existing cercles.[31] When the letter arrived, Coronnat's troops were already on the way. Paris seldom repudiated victories, and had little further to say on the subject.

On May 11, the tricolor was run up above Nioro's highest tower while Biram Cissé, Mamour N'Dari, Omar Khodia Bâ, and Guédel M'Bodj looked on. When questioned by the French, Cissé denied having any treaty ties with the British. On the following day, the three marabout chiefs met with a French officer

[h] Administrator of Gambia to Biram Cissé, sent in dispatch of 25 Apr. 1887, PRO, CO 87/130, No. 63, Enclosure 2. One of the abler officials in the Colonial Office, A. W. L. Hemming, had suggested two months earlier that the French might act. He assumed that they intended to stop at the Saloum River, but he proposed that British authority be established in Niumi. He wrote, "If we do not take steps to this end, the French will no doubt before long spread southwards into this territory." He also wanted to extend British sovereignty in other areas, if possible through a limited protectorate that would not saddle Britain with financial burdens significantly greater than those she had already assumed. Memo of 2 Mar. 1887, PRO, CO 87/130, No. 31.

to divide up Ma Bâ's patrimony.[i] Several days later, a treaty was signed "in order to put an end to the continual wars that devastate Saloum and Rip and to assure these countries the good administration indispensable to their prosperity."[32] All the signatories accepted the French protectorate, and agreed on the perpetual exclusion of Saër Maty. Power was to be hereditary in the families of the four chiefs in conformity with local rules of succession and subject to the approval of the French government. All tatas were to be destroyed within one month, and no new ones were to be built. The only tax on trade the chiefs could collect would be a 3 per cent export duty.[33]

The only tata left standing was Mamour N'Dari's fortress in Nioro. This was divided between Mamour N'Dari's family and the fifty-man garrison that the French left in the marabout capital. A small part of the wall of this structure still stands opposite the mosque in Nioro. It was the only physical remnant I could find of the bitter wars that once ravaged the area.

The Gambia Frontier

The British reaction to the sudden appearance of the French in the Gambia was one of shock and indignation. A. W. L. Hemming, a colonial official, wrote:

> This action is very serious and is a violation of the spirit, if not the letter, of the Treaties of Versailles (1783) and Paris by which Senegal was guaranteed to France and The Gambia to Great Britain. The understanding has always, so far as I know, been hitherto observed that neither country should interfere in the affairs of the native tribes bordering on the River [who are] under the influence of the other [country].[34]

Alfred Maloney in Bathurst and Sir Samuel Rowe in Freetown wrote indignant letters to London demanding diplomatic action, but the Colonial Office's legal experts did not support their posi-

[i] Unfortunately, Lieutenant Minet, the officer who divided the lands, was killed before he could get back to Dakar. There are no reports of his meetings with the chiefs and no indication of what considerations influenced his decisions. Earlier that year, Minet had been sent to Sine-Saloum to "organize" the new cercle before Librecht d'Albreca, the Administrator, arrived. There are also no reports on this mission and no indications of the political problems it dealt with. Minet had been entrusted by Genouille with a number of political missions.

tion. Britain's only claim to Badibu, they reasoned, was the long-standing alliance with Mamour N'Dari, but he had been deprived of recognition. Saër Maty, with whom the British had signed a treaty in February 1887, had attacked a country under French protection, and therefore the French were within their rights.[35]

On the other hand, the British were not going to let the French action jeopardize the existence of what had been a profitable possession. This time Hemming commented: "We cannot allow the French to come down to the banks of the Gambia. If we do, we had better arrange at once to hand over the settlement to them, as it will be impossible for us to carry it on."[j] While waiting for diplomatic action, Rowe tried to sign as many treaties as possible with friendly African chiefs.[36] In July 1887, he signed a treaty with Fodé Karamo Marone in Niombato. Later that year, both Administrator G. T. Carter and Governor Rowe made trips up the Gambia distributing British flags to any chiefs who would take them. The French response was to rush into the disputed area with French flags.[37] The Colonial Office also quickly realized that if Bathurst was to preserve its hinterland, the British would have to commit some resources to the pacification and control of that area.[38]

The French, who considered themselves within their rights, were angered by the British actions. Governor Clément-Thomas complained bitterly:

> [Accepting] the status quo makes us the dupes of the English, who violate it without the slightest scruple, and if this situation should last, we will see our influence completely shattered throughout this region.[39]

Clément-Thomas, like many of the men under him, thought that the logical course was to exchange some French possessions elsewhere for the Gambia.

The question was finally resolved in Europe to the satisfaction

---

[j] A. W. L. Hemming, comment on telegram announcing the defeat of Saër Maty, 5 May 1887, PRO, CO 87/130. The Gambia was not a lucrative colony, but until the peanut crisis of the middle 1880's, it operated in the black. Gouldsbury's expedition to the Sudan in 1881 was financed by the Gambian government surplus. Hargreaves, *Prelude to the Partition of West Africa*, p. 265.

of none of the officials in Africa. In 1889, London and Paris signed a treaty settling a number of territorial conflicts. The frontiers were drawn on a map without any acknowledgment of either ethnic boundaries or geographic realities. The treaty set up a fingerlike British colony, approximately six miles on either side of the Gambia River, jutting into the interior of Senegal, cutting across ethnic groups and traditional states, and separating the Gambia from its natural hinterland. The boundary line made the Gambia an economic backwater, whose second-most-important source of income was (and is still) the smuggling of low-price goods into high-tariff Senegal. The annoyance of the French officers of Nioro knew no bounds. The treaty deprived them of valuable frontage on the Gambia River, and created dissensions among the marabout chiefs, who saw their domains split in half.

In 1890 and 1891, the first of several border commissions went through the remapped area, though at the request of the British it did not undertake a complete mapping but merely measured the distances of key villages from the river.[40] Immediately disputes arose. J. H. Ozanne, the Traveling Commissioner of the North Bank Province, planted a British flag at Pantiang, on the French side of the border, and the French Administrator angrily tore it down. When Saloum chiefs collected taxes on the British side of the line, the British protested. The result of the disagreements was a special mission to measure the disputed villages in 1893.[41] Finally, in 1896, a third commission successfully mapped the frontier, or at least the part of it that touched Rip and Saloum. Ozanne was forced to return the tax money collected from several villages that proved to be on the French side of the frontier.[42]

The definitive mapping of the frontier did not make it any less a problem for the French, whose policies have always been somewhat limited by the existence of the Gambia. During the period up to and including World War I, local populations tended to move away from French areas into the Gambia, motivated either by the differences in taxes, by French recruitment policies, or simply by the fact that they were more likely to be left alone in the Gambia. At the same time, the French waged a continual battle to direct trade goods from Rip and eastern Saloum away from their natural transportation routes, the creeks that flow into the Gambia River, and to prevent the movement of low-price goods from the Gambia into Senegal. The people of the border areas have always moved freely from one area to the other, and a half century of efforts to make the frontier a real wall have had only a partial success. Perhaps the most unfortunate result of the border is that the cheapest transportation route between the western Sudan and the sea was never adequately developed because it crosses the Senegal-Gambia border. Instead, France directed the exports of the area via more expensive railroad routes to Dakar and Kaolack. This has limited the development of western Mali, eastern Senegal, and upper Guinea.

Pacification Problems

The conquest of Nioro did not complete the pacification of Sine-Saloum. There were still a few unresolved questions, and the most important concerned Sine. It was in Sine that peanut exports had grown most rapidly, but the five-year civil war had limited the development of the trade. The Bur Sine, M'Backé Deb N'Diaye, had won his throne in a heated battle with Alboury's stepson, Niokhorbaye Diouf, only shortly before French troops marched into Nioro.

Since the battle between M'Backé and Niokhorbaye gave no sign of ending the civil war, Genouille decided to use his troops to pacify Sine. The troops that had served in Rip were divided into two groups. One returned by boat. The other went overland to Fatick, where the Governor himself met the column and had a conference with M'Backé, who was recognized as Bur. Two French officers then proceeded to Diourbel in Baol, where they met with Niokhorbaye, the former Bur, and told him to lay down his arms, choose his village, and return to Sine. If he did so within twenty-five days, France would guarantee his safety, and perhaps his succession to the throne. Niokhorbaye bowed to the ultimatum.[43]

This agreement, however, did not stop the conflict between

M'Backé and Niokhorbaye. It merely changed the nature of the fight from open confrontation to raids and efforts to win French support. It was only by chance that M'Backé was on top when the victors of Goumbof set up camp in Fatick, but M'Backé was determined to use this chance to eliminate his rival. Some of the Commandants preferred Niokhorbaye, who still commanded much support, to the heavy-drinking M'Backé. J. Génébre, in 1888, was convinced that Niokhorbaye was the stronger, but that France should continue to back M'Backé because a switch would involve a loss of face, and because

> M'Backé, impotent as he is to resist Niokhorbaye if our aid is absent, will remain the plaything of the [French] government, which will be able to put through any reforms that it considers useful for his country, and [thus] at least assure more effective protection of the merchants who are established there.[44]

M'Backé took great care to avoid an overt confrontation with his rival, and to keep from alienating the French. In 1888, several of Niokhorbaye's supporters, sensing a change in the balance of power, came over to the Bur's side. This changed the odds by giving M'Backé more revenue and more warriors. Loss of revenue put greater pressure on Niokhorbaye to raid, and therefore to antagonize the French.[45] M'Backé kept the French informed of his rival's doings. In May 1888, the Governor gave M'Backé the right to attack Niokhorbaye, but the Bur did not feel strong enough to do so.[46] In 1890, when Niokhorbaye built a tata, M'Backé wanted to act, but this time the French told him to wait.

In 1891, Bur Saloum Guédel M'Bodj suddenly decided to go to St. Louis to pay his respects to the Governor. Guédel, who was having difficulties at home, felt that he should conciliate his distant overlords. M'Backé, equally dependent on the French, was not to be outdone. While Administrator Ernest Noirot was making plans for Guédel's visit, M'Backé gathered together five hundred horsemen and left for St. Louis.[47] It was with great difficulty that Noirot stopped M'Backé and arranged for both Burs to visit separately, each accompanied by ten men. M'Backé visited St. Louis in September, and two months later Guédel followed him. Both violated taboos against viewing the sea.

While in St. Louis, both signed protectorate treaties. These treaties committed the Burs to providing the land necessary for military posts, roads, telegraph lines, railroads, and other facilities for commerce and industry. The Burs were to submit part of their revenues to the Governor, and they guaranteed that no one would be reduced to slavery and no military expeditions would be undertaken without the Governor's approval. In return, the French promised that subject to the Governor's approval the two thrones would remain hereditary according to the rules of each country, and no changes would be made in the "habits, customs, and institutions of the country."[48] The French, of course, speedily violated their part of the bargain.

Shortly after M'Backé's return from St. Louis, Noirot let it be known that he would seize the property of any tyeddo joining Niokhorbaye on his raids. The treaty and Noirot's threat led to a further breakdown in Niokhorbaye's camp, and as M'Backé prepared to move, his rival fled. Niokhorbaye was arrested by a pro-French chief in Baol, and was shipped off to the French Congo.[49] M'Backé remained Bur Sine until his death in 1898, and proved to be a stronger ruler than many in the administration expected.

In Nioro, the biggest problem of the French was their own insecurity, an insecurity rooted in their fear of militant Islam and their suspicion of perfidious Albion. These fears made the French keep a close eye on Biram Cissé. After the invasion of Rip, Biram Cissé denied ever having signed a treaty with the British. However, there were reports that he had close ties with Bathurst. There were also many complaints of tyranny and of exactions by Cissé's men. Cissé's base of power, Kaymor, had been returned to Guédel, and Cissé had been given Sabakh-Sandial. At least two of the chiefs under him, Cissé's long-time ally, N'Deri Kani Touré, and a Mandinka chief, refused to accept orders from Cissé. N'Deri Kani, who possessed 350 warriors, seems to have had a power approximately equal to Cissé's.[50]

Information about Cissé's contacts with the British and rumors that he had threatened to chase the "toubab," i.e., the white man, from Nioro persuaded Lieutenant Maurel, the Commandant at Nioro, to have him removed. On a June day in 1888, when a large group gathered at Cissé's residence in Guidimar, Maurel sent a telegram to St. Louis informing his superiors of his decision.[51] Early one morning, several days later, Cissé was arrested by N'Deri Kani's men and speedily taken to Nioro.[52] From Nioro, he was escorted by three hundred of Guédel's tyeddo to a boat at Latmingué.[53] His eventual destination was exile in distant Gabon. The operation was handled smoothly, and apparently without bloodshed. N'Deri Kani replaced Cissé as chief, and though his authority was at first resented by several Mandinka villages,[54] he soon distinguished himself as a competent and dependable chief—that is, one who could always be counted on to do what the French wished. It is difficult, however, to say just who was whose agent in the deposition of Cissé. Maurel had strict orders never to leave his post, and was dependent on his chiefs for information. Much of the information on which Maurel acted came from the man who replaced Cissé. In later letters, Maurel spoke of a conspiracy to attack the post, but this was not evident in earlier reports.[55]

Biram Cissé in Rip and Niokhorbaye Diouf in Sine were both eliminated without any use of force on the part of the French. In effect, the 1887 campaign finally conquered and "pacified" the region, though no substantial obligations had yet been imposed on the chiefs or peasants. In effect, too, France had killed the possibility of any effective resistance by the Tijani league. Shortly after Saër Maty fled across the Gambia River, Mamadou Lamine was defeated by General Gallieni, and was killed while fleeing. Though many battles awaited the French elsewhere in Africa, Senegal was effectively under control. In order to prepare for future resistance, Alboury felt obliged to flee to the Sudan.

The campaign also ended a period in which French demands on the African rulers consisted primarily of the protection of trade, and began one in which France took upon itself the administration and economic development of an extensive African domain. In areas brought under French rule by Faidherbe, France's chief concern had been for a stable order, so that commerce might develop without interference. Now the French administration had to concern itself with making its authority accepted in a large conquered area, with constructing roads and improving agricultural methods, and with formulating educational policies and laws.

THE FOUNDIOUGNE PERIOD
1887–1898

The French Administrator

IN THE DECADE after the victory at Goumbof, the French presence in Sine-Saloum was minimal. There was a fifty-man garrison in Nioro under the lieutenant who commanded the cercle of Nioro. Small forces were left behind in Kaolack and Fatick, but not for long. In 1890 France was officially represented in the cercle of Sine-Saloum by one lone Administrator. But French military power was in the wings, always available though seldom visible.

The Administrator's presence there was more important, perhaps, than the military. Placed above the existing African political structures, the Administrator was the highest authority in the cercle. He had the power to veto and to otherwise control the actions of the African rulers, and to make new policy. For the first time, France had a literate representative on the spot, capable both of collecting information and of acting on it. His function in the earliest years was primarily to protect and encourage French political and commercial interests, but his role grew rapidly in importance.

The system was nowhere near being the direct administration that the French were later to claim. The Administrator was alone, a stranger who did not know the languages, who could not find his way from place to place without a guide, and who had to govern a territory of more than 20,000 square kilometers. To assist him, he had at most one clerk (usually a Senegalese from the Four Communes), an interpreter, and after 1892 he

had a handful of guards, almost all of them, like himself, foreigners. Under this small bureaucracy was the traditional African structure of power. All information on which to base decisions came from the chiefs, and all decisions were carried out by
them. Their power was, if anything, increased by the French desire for simple and clearly articulated structures of power.

During the first years, the effectiveness of French administration was very much limited by the rapid turnover in personnel.
In three years there were five Commandants in Foundiougne.
Changes in Nioro were also frequent, partly because of the
prevalence of disease. The first man who stayed long enough to
leave his mark was Ernest Noirot (1890–96). Noirot was a former
artist and onetime actor with the Folies-Bergère, who had no
exceptional qualifications for a colonial career except natural
intelligence. He had drifted into his life's work almost by accident when he took a position with Bayol's mission to Fouta
Djallon in 1881. He was impulsive and had a sharp tongue,
which alienated many of his colleagues. On the one hand, he
had great sympathy for the people he was governing, and he
made a more substantial effort than his successors did to understand the customs and traditions of his charges. On the other
hand, he was deeply committed to the ideal of assimilation, and
his dedication to controlled social change led him to make a
number of blunders in dealing with the chiefs. He pursued all
of his aims with great energy and a fertile imagination, and his
belief in the value of what he was doing was nearly unshakable.[1]
Within two weeks of his arrival, Noirot had submitted plans for
a mapping project, a bridge, and a school, all of which required
funds not provided for in the official budget, and had set up a
Moslem court at Foundiougne.[2]

During the early years of the new order, the French had no
interest either in changing the traditional political and social
structures or in really governing their new domain. Early Administrators were told that Sine-Saloum was not to become a
territory of direct administration, but was to remain a protectorate. The administration wanted only to extend the area within
which commerce could operate freely. Direct administration

was instituted only near the major factories. By agreement with the Bur Saloum, the area of Kaolack under direct administration was increased, and the island of Foundiougne was placed under French authority. In Sine, the Bur willingly ceded Fatick to the French, though he soon discovered to his surprise that he had also given the French several nearby villages.[3] The French hoped that these areas of direct administration would undergo a more intense economic development. This seems to have happened, though the strengthened economy induced a movement of Moslem immigrants to the island of Foundiougne that caused some difficulties.[a]

Areas of direct administration were ruled through village and canton chiefs appointed by the administration on the basis of loyalty and service to France. These Africans were usually former soldiers or interpreters, and were seldom part of the existing power structure. They depended for their power on the French, though power exercised over a period of time frequently legitimized itself, and some families established a claim to certain chiefships. This is most striking with the Sows of Kaolack, a family descended from a Fulbe trader who had become village chief in the 1870's.

The existence of two separate commands, Sine-Saloum looking to the Governor, and Nioro to the military authorities, caused conflict. In addition, there was a tendency for each Commandant to defend the interests of chiefs under his command in traditional conflicts with their neighbors. This was most evident in the struggle for Oualo, a strongly Moslem area claimed by the Bur Saloum though ruled for many years by Nioro. The Governor finally awarded it to the Bur because the land was part of Saloum's traditional domains.[4]

Problems with Chiefs

In Rip, the aged Mamour N'Dari was once again king in his own country, his power restored by French arms. He enjoyed this twilight of power briefly, and then in March 1889 he died.

[a] Administrator of Sine-Saloum to Governor of Senegal, 15 Dec. 1888, 5 Sept. 1890, ARS, unclassified. In 1890, six languages were being spoken in the area.

He left behind a large family, which adapted itself to the new order with speed and agility. Mamour N'Dari's oldest son, Mandiaye Bâ, succeeded automatically to the post of Eliman. Earlier Commandants had marked Mandiaye as hostile to French authority, but he quickly assured his superiors of his devotion. Mandiaye and his aides told the Governor: "We write you this letter to make known to you that we are in God's hands and yours. All that you order us to do, we will do without question."[5] Mandiaye, like his neighbor N'Deri Kani, consistently received praise from his French superiors—both of them carried out instructions quickly and efficiently—and yet a perusal of his personnel dossier reveals an enigmatic and secretive personality that no Commandant knew well: "Too soft for this difficult command . . . intelligent and active . . . a most reprehensible nonchalance . . . must be watched, but his management of Rip has been good."[6]

While always doing what he was told, Mandiaye shrewdly kept as much power in his own hands as possible. For instance, he took care to prevent his subjects from seeing the Commandant without his approval. The tirailleurs stationed in Nioro were not changed frequently. Many married Mandiaye Bâ's slaves, became part of local society, and were more loyal to the chief than to the Commandant. The invisible wall Mandiaye built around the post was discovered only by accident. A peasant with a problem had been trying to get in to see the Commandant. Unable to do so, he went to Foundiougne and presented his complaint to Noirot, who gave him a note and told him to hand it to the lieutenant when the lieutenant went out on a walk. When the peasant did so, the lieutenant, who either did not understand or did not want to understand, told the man to come see him in his office. The man never arrived. Apparently he had been persuaded to return to his village.[7]

The new frontier cut across a series of chiefships. The chiefs in Rip had to relinquish either the areas of their chiefships that lay on the British side of the line or the ones that lay on the French side. Diatta Selang, heir to the old Mandinka throne, became chief on the British side where most of the people were

Mandinka. The other major chiefs remained with the French. For N'Deri Kani Touré this meant moving his residence and losing a good half of his lands. The probable reason for this movement to the French side was French policy toward the chiefs. According to a report submitted by J. H. Ozanne, the first British Traveling Commissioner of the North Bank, the French Commandants supported the chiefs, confirmed their privileges, and guaranteed their right to their slaves and to a substantial income. Thus, the French had the support of the chiefs, but were detested by the general populace because of their taxes and labor levies.[b]

The French decided to compensate their two best chiefs, Mandiaye Bâ and N'Deri Kani Touré, for lands lost. Congheul was given to N'Deri Kani and part of Niani to Mandiaye. These were both areas that had been extensively ravaged during the marabout-soninke wars, and had been neither pacified nor organized. The French did not want to commit men and troops to the area, and they hoped that their favored chiefs would organize it for them. However, within both areas there were many Mandinka and pagan Wolof villages that hated their new chiefs and refused to pay taxes to them.[8]

The result was a high level of stability in Rip and continual reports of pillage in Niani and Congheul. The chiefs in Rip were ruling areas their families had long inhabited and had for a generation ruled. There were traditional ties of loyalty and traditional obligations. Time had determined who owed what to whom. In Niani, the chiefs were ruling strangers, often strangers who did not want their new marabout overlords. They had to tax to establish their authority, and they had to use force to see that their demands were met. Referring to one difficult Mandinka

[b] Traveling Commissioner's report, North Bank Province, 30 Jan. 1893, AG. Ozanne's report may be in error on certain particulars. He refers to a head tax, which if collected was for the chiefs. A head tax was not levied by the French regime until several years later, partly because of French insecurity, partly because of the tendency of the peasants to emigrate when financial burdens got heavy. Ozanne also describes an efficient organization within most Moslem chiefships. According to his report, a chief would maintain a man in each village, who lived off the village, levied taxes, and collected fines, much like the sakhsakh of Sine.

village in Niani, a French official wrote: "Their biggest complaint against Mandiaye is that he is a Wolof."[9] The same official commented that Mandiaye and N'Deri Kani were to be watched closely because "in every Wolof there is a tyeddo to whom it is best not to give too much liberty."[10] Both chiefs lost their eastern lands, but received compensation elsewhere.[c]

French relations with the two Serer rulers were somewhat more strained, partly because Noirot wanted to make major changes in the political and social organization of the Serer states, and partly because he was slow in coming to understand their political systems. Shortly after Niokhorbaye was deported, Noirot compared the two Serer rulers:

> Although a drunkard, M'Backé is more intelligent and has much more authority over his entourage than Guédel. That comes probably from the fact that the Bur Sine is an absolute ruler, while the Bur Saloum is chosen by the Slaves of the Crown, who can depose him. In these conditions, Guédel submits to the ascendancy of his Jaraf and Farba, which is not surprising, because he is not a man of energy capable of imposing his will on the resistance that he meets.[11]

Authority was absolute, yet collegial, in Sine. What made M'Backé seem stronger to the inexperienced Noirot was that once the conflict over the Burship was resolved, the Bur spoke for a political entity within which there was substantial consensus. This was no longer true in Saloum.

Noirot later came to see another important difference. When M'Backé did not want to do something the French requested, he said "Yes" and then did nothing. Guédel was more direct. When he meant "No," he said "No." A man with a strong sense of his rights, Guédel often said "No."[12] Guédel was intransigent when faced with attacks on his authority, but he showed himself

---

[c] N'Deri Kani received a part of Kaymor in 1896, and the diminutive canton of Dramé when its chief died in 1899. Mandiaye received Omar Khodia's canton when Omar died in 1898. (Lieutenant Chaudron, "Monograph on the cercle of Nioro du Rip" [1901], ARS, 1 G 283.) The Bur Saloum, who lost part of Kaymor, received Congheul. He was very unhappy about the exchange, but his protests were of little avail. (Administrator of Sine-Saloum to Governor-General, 14 Nov. 1896, ARS, 13 G 328.)

flexible in his efforts to reconcile the tensions that were splitting Saloum. His biggest problem was the heritage of hostility left by a generation of war.

The absence of good records for the period right after 1887 leaves us uncertain about Guédel's policy toward Moslem areas reconquered by French arms. There seems to have been a conflict between the tyeddo's desire to settle old accounts[13] and Guédel's desire to win back the loyalty of the Moslems of eastern Saloum. This explains both Guédel's effort to recognize Wack N'Diouka Bâ as his heir and his later conversion to Islam.

Wack N'Diouka was the son of Saër Maty by Guédel's cousin Diouka, who had been captured by the marabouts during a raid in 1885. Wack, as the son of a guelowar, was eligible to be elected Bur. After Saër Maty's flight to Bathurst, Diouka returned to Kahone and became Guédel's wife, but Saër Maty kept his son. The French, worried about the loyalties that young Wack N'Diouka might command, interceded in Guédel's behalf at Bathurst, but the British were not willing to deprive a man of his own son.[14]

The issue of Wack N'Diouka's custody remained alive for a long time, but since Wack never returned to Senegal, Guédel lost a chance of conciliating the two factions. In about 1891, Guédel became a Moslem, though we do not know whether it was for personal or political reasons. He was converted by Moulay Nasr, an itinerant Mauritanian marabout, not connected with Nioro. The conversion aroused much opposition among Guédel's pagan tyeddo, men who had battled Islam long and bitterly. We know little about reactions in eastern Saloum except that Guédel's men still could not collect taxes there.

Eastern Saloum was not the only area to resent the return of tyeddo rule under the Bur Saloum. The islands of Gandoul had once known the authority of the Bur Djilor, though the islanders had been only intermittent tributaries. The Mandinka-speaking southern islands and some of the larger villages of the Serer-speaking northern islands had allied themselves to Ma Bâ and converted to Islam. They did not willingly accept the return of tyeddo rule. Dionewar, the largest village of Gandoul, refused to pay taxes to Sambodj M'Bodj, the Bur Djilor. With the support of the French Administrator, Sambodj invaded Dionewar, collected all the guns he could find, took the village war drum, and imposed a fine. To back up the tyeddo, the Administrator slapped on an additional two-hundred-franc fine.[15]

Sambodj himself, however, soon became a problem. He had both the fortune and misfortune to be a neighbor of the Administrator. Although he had been backed by the French in Gandoul, he antagonized them by pillaging the mainland. When he marched into Foundiougne with forty armed warriors, the Administrator asked Guédel, who was a close relative of Sambodj, to remove him;[16] Guédel complied with the request. Several other chiefs were removed from their positions for similar actions, including a brother of M'Backé who pocketed money collected for the Administrator.[17]

Guédel had another serious problem, which concerned the ambitions of the Bumi, Semou Djimit Diouf. As Bumi, Semou was heir to the throne. Many members of Guédel's entourage were opposed to his succession, both because he was a member of the rival Kévé Bigué clan and because he had earlier been with the marabout forces. He was a natural wartime choice as Bumi, a key man in a "government of national unity," but with the end of the fighting, the old clan rivalry once more became evident. At the same time, Semou and his followers had cause for discontent. The Bumi in Saloum usually held a major income-giving chiefship, but Semou had only one village and was forced to farm the land himself.[18] He did, nevertheless, command substantial support, and Guédel apparently felt that he challenged his hold on the throne. The crisis was exacerbated by an incident that might have been insignificant if it had involved someone else.

Anthiou, a member of Semou's entourage, was having a love affair with a guelowar princess. Anthiou was related to Semou, but was a *tangann*—that is, one of the fishing-and-farming Serer of the coastal regions. Tangann social organization was completely egalitarian, and Anthiou was thus considered lowborn. In theory a guelowar princess could marry whomever she wished, but in practice her hand was sought by the wellborn, and her family arranged the best match possible. Semou advised Anthiou not to pursue the marriage he sought, but when Anthiou went ahead, Semou defended him and sent away the tyeddo who came to arrest him. "A guelowar," he said, "should not interfere with what happens in the hut of another guelowar."[19]

A year later, in November 1894, Guédel died suddenly at Korki. Only after Guédel's death did Noirot find out that he had been gathering forces for a showdown with Semou, that he had sworn not to return to Kahone until the conflict was decided, and that he had made plans to flee if the French intervened on Semou's side.[20] Almost two years after Guédel's death, Noirot wrote that Guédel had had an alliance with M'Backé and the Teigne Baol for the propagation of Islam. Guédel had married the Teigne's sister, and M'Backé his daughter, all without informing the Administrator. It is probable that Noirot exaggerated the extent of this alliance. M'Backé does seem to have become a Moslem, but his conversion did not have much effect on Sine.[21]

Guedél's sudden death placed his supporters in a difficult position. They could not continue the campaign against Semou because they did not have a strong candidate for the Burship. Semou immediately began to conciliate his rivals by confirming all chiefs in their titles, and to impress the French by promising a series of reforms that Noirot had been urging on Guédel. (The most important were the reduction of the tax on migrant farmers and the abolition of an ordeal the French considered barbaric.[d]) Semou accepted all of Guédel's debts, but he later removed some of Guédel's people, apparently at the request of the French on the grounds that they had been "pillaging."[22] Many members of Semou's family were Moslems, but he himself did not convert. The consolidation of Semou's power involved not so much the conciliation of rivals and enemies as the winning of French favor.

[d] The ordeal consisted of passing a hot blade over a man's tongue. (See p. 172.)

Difficult as relations with the Serer chiefs were, the problems they presented were easier to resolve than those of sparsely populated Niombato, an area of fourteen villages, most of them rather small. Niombato was made up of islands and the heavily forested strip of land in western Niumi that faced them. This area contains the only really dense forest in Senegal north of the Gambia. Dominated at times by Niumi and at other times by Saloum, the villages of Niombato participated in neither state, and resisted all efforts to impose an overlord. Noirot wrote in 1895: "We do not have in Niombato any chief capable of exercising the least authority there, or rather, as I have said, everyone is a chief."[23] And his successor wrote:

> They are hard workers and very eager for gain. Defiant at first, they are basically excellent people and return as soon as they feel themselves in the presence of people who wish them well. Harassed by the people of Saloum, with whom they were at war, they have remained for a long time under the direction of their own chiefs in a sort of independent republic. Very proud of their independence, which has cost them much blood, they wish to depend neither on Saloum nor on any native chief.[24]

When Ma Bâ invaded Djilor, he found in neighboring Niombato small groups of very willing allies. Marabouts in two of the larger villages became the political leaders. However, each village had its own chief, called the Alcati, and its own Almamy, who was both qadi and religious leader. Chief Fodé Karamo Marone signed a treaty with the British in 1887, but this treaty was ignored when the boundary was drawn, in spite of Fodé Karamo's wish to remain in British-controlled territory.[25]

The chiefs in Niombato were either unwilling or unable to carry out orders. Taxes were not collected until Noirot began sending an interpreter, Moussa Soumaré, to collect them. There is no information on the methods he used, but in 1896 Noirot was forced to ask Semou, the Bur Saloum, to assign a tyeddo escort to help Soumaré collect the taxes.[26] Niombato's determination to ignore the French was reinforced by its trade ties with Bathurst. The area was sparsely populated—the French could find only 4,575 people when they counted heads in 1891—but peanuts were being cultivated there. Noirot, though lacking information on which to base a close estimate, judged its peanut exports to be about a million kilos. All of these peanuts were transported to Bathurst by dugout canoes. Thus, to the degree that the French intensified their efforts to regulate movement across the Senegal-Gambia border, the inhabitants of Niombato increasingly resented French rule. Noirot wanted to place a Resident in Niombato and to start a school there, but St. Louis did not think that the area merited special attention.[27]

Financial Organization of the Protectorate

Until 1891, areas outside of the Four Communes were organized under a makeshift administrative system, which, because of limited funds, could not undertake more than the maintenance of order and the removal of some barriers to commercial development. The colonial administration found itself dependent for funds on two reluctant sources. The first, the French parliament, was loath to increase its colonial subsidies. The second, the Conseil Général, which controlled local revenues, was equally unwilling to give the colonial administration what it wanted, especially for investments outside the Four Communes. When the Conseil refused to provide for a School for the Sons of Chiefs and Interpreters, the administration decided to seek other funds. In opening the Conseil Général session of December 6, 1890, Governor Henri de Lamothe said:

> The functioning of representative institutions granted to the colony by the liberalism of the Metropolitan government has not exactly been favorable to the maintenance of peaceful and mutually tolerant relations between inhabitants of all faiths, of all origins, and of all functions and professions. To make freedom of movement respected, to stop pillage and wars between chief and chief—this must be the first objective of our policy. Later, when the people have become accustomed to a tranquil existence, of which the continual battles of preceding periods can scarcely permit them to know the satisfactions, new needs will come forth to the great advantage of com-

merce and of the development of French influence. Within this order of ideas, I am happy to announce to you that, without imposing any new charges on your budget, I have already obtained from several native chiefs in the areas of protectorate formal pledges for the creation of French language schools. . . . I have considered going further and creating, with the aid of funds or tribute furnished by the countries under protectorate, a kind of special budget, which would permit the execution of useful works in the interior of the country, and could even contribute to lightening to some degree the charges that the budget submitted to your deliberations bears under the title of political affairs.[28]

The following spring, Lamothe explained more clearly to Paris why he thought it was necessary to limit the expansion of self-governing institutions and to create sources of revenue over which the Conseil Général would have no control. He wrote:

The natives no longer correspond either with the Governor or with the Administrators of their cercles; they no longer obey orders coming from functionaries who have the right and the duty to give them; but they address themselves uniquely to diverse members of the local assembly and to certain influential persons from St. Louis, with whose opinions alone they comply.[e]

In December Lamothe issued the decree setting up regional budgets, each to be administered by the local Commandant du Cercle. Revenues were to come from a head tax, and from fines, ferry fees, patents, and other local sources. The most important source was the head tax, the exact amount of which was to be determined by agreements with individual chiefs. Of the funds collected, one-fourth was to be returned to St. Louis to be used for projects affecting all the protectorates. The rest was to be used to pay personnel assisting the Administrator and to finance schools and public works.[29]

At this time Noirot was seeking to regularize and control the

[e] Governor of Senegal to Minister, 6 Apr. 1891, ARS, unclassified. At this time, the politicians from the Four Communes had not yet begun to play an active role in the politics of Sine-Saloum.

traditional tax structure. He wanted a secure income for the chiefs that did not depend on their entourages, and a tax structure that would tie them more closely to the administration than to their aides. The head tax helped immeasurably. When St. Louis suggested a 50-centime tax, Noirot spoke to the chiefs, and then countered by proposing a one-franc tax, with half going to the chiefs.[f] A census had been conducted in 1891 with the head tax in mind, and although Noirot thought that the results underreported the population by one-quarter to one-third especially in eastern Saloum, the census provided a basis for taxation. Almost 60,000 francs went into the regional budget the first year, and twice that the following year, when the tax was doubled.

There were difficulties of course. Even in areas open to trade and to a money economy, villages often resisted taxation, but where no money economy existed, the tax was a heavy burden. It was necessary to permit payment in kind for several years, but this was only a temporary expedient.[30] A British administrator wrote that many peasants walked three days with loads on their heads to the nearest factory in the Gambia in order to get money to pay the tax.[31] Not surprisingly, many traders took advantage of the peasants' ignorance of the value of different coins. One of the results of the head tax was a steady migration of people from high-tax areas—to low-tax areas of Senegal and to the Gambia. In 1896, Semou complained that thirty villages in eastern Saloum had emigrated to flee taxes.[32] Two years before, the British administration had imposed not a head tax but a hut tax of one shilling (one shilling equaled 1.25 francs).[g] The British tax remained constant for many years, mostly because the British were not undertaking substantial administrative responsibilities or public works. The French gradually raised theirs, first

[f] Administrator to Governor of Senegal, 14 Jan. 1892, ARS, unclassified; Director of Political Affairs to Administrator of Sine-Saloum, 22 Jan. 1892, ARS, unclassified. The chiefs' share of the tax money was divided as follows: 25 per cent to the Bur, 10 per cent to the canton chief, and 15 per cent to the village chief.

[g] Administrator of Sine-Saloum to Director of Native Affairs, 3 Nov. 1896, ARS, 13 G 328. The nature of the tax led to a substantial reduction in the number of huts the second year it was levied.

in areas where money was available, much more slowly near
the Gambia and in areas with a purely subsistence economy.
Only after the establishment of the Gambian hut tax was a 75-
centime head tax introduced in the cercle of Nioro. Tax collection in Nioro proved easy because those living in surrounding
areas were already paying higher amounts. The second year the
tax was doubled, in part to prevent migrations from Saloum to
Nioro.[33]

When the village of Diohine, in Sine, refused to pay, M'Backé
asked for authority to send in his tyeddo. The Governor agreed:
"Let the Bur undertake whatever repression he judges useful.
... Do not accompany the Bur when he goes to Diohine to punish his subjects."[34] Diohine speedily submitted, though M'Backé
had to use force again the following year. In eastern Saloum, the
problem was hostility to tyeddo and a lack of money, which
resulted from a shortage of commercial outlets. Taxes were not
collected regularly there until after 1896.[35] The same was true of
Niombato.

As fast as Noirot found revenues for the Burs, he found ways
for spending them. He pressured the two Burs to spend part of
their new income for a secretary and an interpreter, with the
objective of creating at each court a small administration dependent on both the Bur and the Administrator. He also wished
to be able to correspond in French. In Sine, Noirot hired a former priest, Léopold Diouf, as secretary for the Bur, and a retired
spahi as the Bur's interpreter. Diouf was also to run a school for
the Bur's children.[36] Noirot was very disappointed when Diouf
became not an agent of French cultural penetration but a court-
ier as anxious to please the Bur as any tradition-bound tyeddo.

In acting as he did, Diouf was wiser than the Bur Saloum's
secretary, Isaac Konaré, who conformed more closely to Noirot's
wishes but aroused the hostility of Semou Djimit. Konaré accompanied the Bur and his tyeddo on a tax-collecting expedition to eastern Saloum in 1895, and described his painful pre-
dicament in a report. Konaré's authority was carefully limited
by the Bur, and Konaré was faced with a wall of hostility and
silence. Yet he was well aware that his presence restrained the

tyeddo. In one village, an old Moslem simply refused to pay. The tyeddo were enraged and would have killed the man, Konaré felt, had he not been there. Instead, Konaré was asked to send a telegram to the Administrator demanding permission to take hostages. It was given, but their increased authority did the tyeddo little good, for as they moved further east, they found only deserted villages.[37]

Establishment of the head tax was not Noirot's only step in reforming the tax structure of the Serer states. He also made changes in the amount of tax paid by traders and the manner in which it was collected. Traditionally the Serer states received most of their revenue from taxes on peasant villages and from the *coubeul,* an export tax set by treaty at 3 per cent. This tax was collected by an alcati, who usually received his post as a reward for service. He kept most of the coubeul for himself, and often made further demands that the commercial houses considered excessive.[38] In 1892, Noirot persuaded the Bur Sine to replace the coubeul with an annual patent fee of 50 francs, to be paid by the individual trader directly to the Bur's secretary. The Bur's announcement stated:

> In order to show my father the Governor that I want to conduct my country along the road that he has traced for me, the sum of 15 francs out of this 50 francs will be paid into the treasury of the administration of the cercle in order to be specially appropriated for the maintenance of French schools, which I would like to grant to my subjects.[39]

In the first year, 150 patents were sold, approximately doubling the revenue of the Bur.[40] Later that year, Guédel M'Bodj agreed to end the coubeul in Saloum.[41] No patent was required in the cercle of Nioro because the administration wanted to encourage traders to come into that neglected area.

Slavery

Few of the political problems faced by the conquerors of Africa were more politically sensitive than slavery. In their quest to sell the ideas of empire and *la mission civilisatrice,* the colonialists could ill afford to arouse the indignation of the abolitionists back home, but neither could they jeopardize their recent conquest by moving too speedily on an institution that was an integral part of African social life. Slavery was not important to all Senegambian peoples. The institution did not exist among peoples such as the Nones, the Diolas, and the Serer N'Diéghem, who had egalitarian social structures and simple political institutions. Slavery had, however, long been deeply rooted in the cultures of the Serer, the Wolof, and their other neighbors.

There were three kinds of slaves: trade slaves, domestic slaves, and the privileged slaves of the crown. The trade slaves were those taken in war or slave raids, or purchased from slave dealers. They had no rights and could be sold. The ending of the Atlantic slave trade did not end the trade in slaves within Africa, for slave trading remained the most effective way for an African leader to get the revenue he needed to buy ammunition, guns, and horses. There was a market for trade slaves in the Sudan and within most of the societies of Senegambia. Unlike the trade slave, the domestic slave became part of his owner's extended family and received land from his owner; with time, a relationship evolved in which the slave had both rights and obligations. The slave owed his master five mornings of labor a week and worked the rest of the time either at a trade or on land his master gave him for his own profit. The master had to feed the slave, clothe him, and provide a wife for him. The product of the slave's labor was his own, and he could and often did accumulate property. About one-third of the population of the region was made up of slaves, with the Moslems of Rip owning more slaves than the Serer peasants of Sine did.[42]

The importance of slavery in Senegambian society forced French officers, ambitious for empire, to compromise with it less than a decade after the seemingly clear-cut abolition of slavery in French possession in 1848. As French rule extended to the mainland, the abolition of slavery was held to apply only to areas that had been under the French flag in 1848. In 1857, Faidherbe, himself an abolitionist, decreed that any escaped slave who sought refuge in St. Louis or Gorée was to be expelled as an undesirable vagrant. The abolition of slavery was extended to Dakar only in 1877, and in 1879 to Rufisque.[43] In 1880, the aged dean of the French abolitionists, Victor Schoelcher, gave a carefully documented speech in the Senate denouncing not only the continued existence of slavery, but the active practice of the slave trade in areas under French sovereignty.[44] Although Governors and Ministers vehemently denied Schoelcher's allegations, his speech led to a change in policy. The courts in Senegal, over the opposition of Governors Brière de l'Isle and Canard, began freeing any slave who appeared in French territory; and in 1882, Governor René Servatius decreed that any slave setting foot on French soil could have a patent of liberty for the asking.[45]

The most striking result of the new policy was the massive migration of slave-owning Fulbe out of those areas near the Senegal River that were under direct administration. The number of Fulbe in the cercle of St. Louis dropped from 50,000 in 1880 to 30,000 in 1882 and to 10,000 by 1889.[46] Only the disannexation of these areas and the creation of a protectorate within them in 1889 stopped the outflow.[47] Knowledge of the new French policies created fears among France's African allies, and strengthened the determination of anti-French chiefs to resist a regime that threatened their power and the structure of their societies. However, within a very short time, the conquest had extended so far that these chiefs had no place to go.

While the administration was trying in its own limited way to introduce African leaders to certain new principles, the army was proving that "la mission civilisatrice" did not keep Frenchmen from learning African methods. After the invasion of Rip, the French officers gave female slaves to African soldiers as a reward for service. Coronnat vigorously defended his action and explained in this way what had been done:

> I take this occasion to state again: (1) that none of the women who came to St. Louis were led by force; all were slaves, but not of my troops; (2) that no man was authorized to take prisoners, or to carry off as much as a pin. The King of Saloum made war in his manner and took prisoners of both sexes. I

had nothing to do with it. . . . At Kaolack, after my departure, a certain number of women were put in the presence of a certain number of tirailleurs, drivers, and spahis, and after coming to terms, there resulted a certain number of unions in conformity with the customs of the country and under the jurisdiction of the King of Saloum, on whose territory the action took place. There was in that no violence of any sort. . . . I simply sought to reconcile the customs of this country with our own. . . . The measures taken at Kaolack constituted real progress from the humanitarian point of view, by comparison with what happened in previous years in the campaigns of the upper river and elsewhere.[48]

The incident became known when one of the spahis tried to sell his "wife" for 75 francs. In most such cases, a woman born far away would not have known what to do, but this one found her way to a lawyer. Judicial officials, aware of the political implications of her case, suspended action and contacted the Governor. Neither the Governor nor the Undersecretary of State for the Colonies, Eugene Etienne, felt that the case could be suppressed, but Etienne gave instructions that neither Coronnat nor his officers were to be mentioned. The case was to be handled simply as a criminal action against the spahi who had tried to sell the woman.[49]

The administration avoided a head-on confrontation with slavery, choosing rather to operate through pressure on the African chiefs. In December 1892, a convention was signed with the chiefs of the cercle of St. Louis guaranteeing freedom of movement for goods, establishing a head tax, and regulating slavery. All slaves were henceforth to be considered "domestic slaves, who are not slaves but servants, like those of whom it is spoken in Chapters 24 and 43 of the Book of God [the Koran]."[50] No slaves were to be sold within the cercle, though people were to be free to purchase slaves in areas where the sale was legal. The slave was to have the option of buying his freedom for five hundred francs, and if a man was fined, his slaves were not to be turned over to another in payment without their approval.

This convention was rapidly extended to other areas. In 1893, the Burs of Sine and Saloum signed. The issue had already been raised in the cercle by the creation of areas of direction administration. Here the law was explicit: "If this slave finds himself on French territory, he will be free under law. You should under no pretext assist the agents of the Bur Saloum in their efforts to recapture him."[51] The law said that French soil freed slaves, though Administrators were careful not to encourage runaways.[52] By 1892, it was evident that most slaves were an integral part of their communities and had no intention of seeking liberty. It is probable that the new regulations were enforced only when it was in the interest of a chief to do so. When a chief stopped a caravan and freed the slaves, or when he freed the slave of a cruel master, the freed man had no place to go. He often did not know where his home was, and in the eyes of his neighbors he remained a slave. While a freed slave had every right to return home, in many of the cases litigated he was housed and given land by the chief who freed him. He was thus freed from dependence on one man and made the dependent of another. The Bur Sine complained to Noirot that since few slave routes crossed Sine, he did not receive as many slaves as did Guédel in Saloum.[53]

The military men in Nioro were more reluctant than the administration in Sine-Saloum to act against slavery, but events in Saloum and the Gambia pressed them. Guédel was always willing to free slaves belonging to his longtime rivals, and Noirot generally backed him; this often resulted in bitter exchanges with the Commandant in Nioro. An especially vehement exchange of letters followed Noirot's liberation of a group of Mandiaye Bâ's slaves being sent to Cayor with the Commandant's approval. Noirot discovered what the lieutenant did not know, that the slaves had been taken in a recent raid.[54]

In the Gambia the freeing of the slaves was begun shortly after the appointment of the first Traveling Commissioners in 1893. All trade in slaves was outlawed, as was any kind of mistreatment of them. When the head of a family died, all of that family's slaves were to be freed.[55] The new law, while it did not immediately destroy slavery, made it possible for any slave who

crossed the border and charged his former owner with mistreatment to get his freedom. Among the slaves freed in 1894 was a
band being sent from Moussa Molo to the Bur Saloum.[56] One
harassed Commandant wrote that British policy was "to free the
slaves from our territory who flee to the Gambia, and not to free
those of their chiefs, but to claim them if they come to our territory."[57] The same man felt that the slaves were "less mishandled
than before, but still slaves, and our chiefs regard them as absolute property." Finally, in 1896, the chiefs of Rip were persuaded
to sign the convention that the chiefs of the St. Louis cercle had
signed. The question aroused a great deal of emotion, the Commandant wrote, but the chiefs accepted the convention.[58]

Although French policy did not threaten domestic slavery or
completely end the slave trade, it did limit the mistreatment of
the slaves and provide a sanctuary for any slave who wished to
escape his state. In 1903, the courts were instructed by Governor-General Ernest Roume not to recognize slavery at all henceforth. A subsequent study commented:

> In 1903, on the formal instructions of the Government Gen-
> eral, it was proclaimed throughout French West Africa that
> the distinction between free men and slaves would henceforth
> not exist for the French authorities; the legal consequences of
> this formal act were not slow in making themselves evident
> to interested natives. Slavery, even under its domestic form,
> is considered by all the Negroes, and by the captives them-
> selves, not as a kind of life imprisonment for an individual,
> but as the obligation of this individual to belong to the most
> vile of castes; this is for him social degradation rather than
> constraint.[59]

Slave-raiding had continued on a small scale throughout the
1890's and slaves continued to move north across the Gambia
River, coming mostly from Samory in the Sudan, and Fodé
Kabba in the Casamance.[60] The defeat of those two leaders and
the definitive pacification of West Africa greatly reduced the dimensions of the trade, and a 1905 decree forbade the constraint
of any person's liberty as well as the sale or movement of slaves.
However, slaves were still being sold in Sine-Saloum in 1904,

and as late as 1907 a highly rated chief in Saloum was removed for having permitted the trade in his canton. The laws of 1903 and 1905 definitely killed the slave trade within Senegal and checked harsh treatment of slaves, but slaves continued to exist, not so much as the property of others, but as a status group within a hierarchical social system. To the degree that slavery in this latter sense has since been destroyed, it has been destroyed by economic and social change.[61]

Chiefship

For the peoples of Sine-Saloum, the most important changes taking place were changes in political structure, in particular in the nature of chiefship. Traditionally, the strongest check on the chief's power lay in the insecurity of his position and the built-in possibility of conflict. But the French wanted clear-cut lines of authority, and after 1887, it was only the French administration that could and did remove living chiefs. The only outlet for a would-be rival was intrigue at the political center. The French policy of strengthening the chief was often barely conscious. Many Administrators did not like the chiefs and regarded them as drunkards and thieves. At the same time, the Administrator found himself dependent on the chiefs to get things done, so he delegated great power to the chiefs. Noirot saw clearly that the administration could act only through the chiefs and thus sought to give them a financial interest in carrying out French policies.[62]

However, it was difficult to get beyond a chief and check up on him. Noirot complained that he often could not protect those who protested against a chief's demands or get anyone to testify openly against a chief.[63] The French were unable to restrain a chief when he coerced his people, and they could not keep him from speaking in the name of French power when he dealt with uncooperative villagers. The Administrator usually lacked information about conflicts between village and chief, and either supported a chief or left him free to act as he pleased. One French official described the problem this way:

He is almost always accompanied by local chiefs, who are in turn escorted by troops of horsemen and footsoldiers naturally living on the country. A good guard is kept around him; only those who have the consent of the chief can approach him. Those who would do without this formality pay dearly for their audacity. . . . The chiefs and their entourages even make use of his presence to inflict, on the least pretext, fines and penalties that are often considerable; thus they ruin the populations they are charged with administering. All this is done, of course, in the name of the Europeans, who become, as a result, objects of terror in the minds of Negroes.[64]

Equally important in the transformation of chiefship was the separation of the Bur from the traditional instruments of his power, the tyeddo. The French detested the tyeddo, who did the Bur's will and lived by what they took from peasants and traders. "These courtiers, supported by Burs, who can no longer count on them, are our real adversaries," one Administrator wrote.[65] The French wanted to reduce the size of the Burs' entourages and make the tyeddo full-time farmers, though this was not something that could be done quickly. However, Noirot commented in 1896 that many tyeddo in the Kaolack area had already made the transition. Obviously, the existence of a good cash crop helped.

In the traditional system, a major chief was to some degree the instrument of his entourage. "In spite of all my efforts," Noirot wrote about M'Backé, "the Bur has no other will but that of his entourage, which is conservative to an extreme, and which only reluctantly sees the old ways disappear little by little."[66] In the new order, with power more effectively centralized, the entourage became much more the instrument of the chief's will. With the coming of the twentieth century, diatribes of Administrators against the entourages became more rare. This does not mean that the entourages no longer existed. One recently retired chief admitted that in the 1950's he had an entourage of 25 men.

A chief's entourage existed outside the legal power structure. No one lower than the chief of a canton received any income from the state. And yet the entourage, even though carefully circumscribed, remained important. Both Burs, for example, were told that they could use their own methods of collecting taxes. Thus the Administrator wrote the Bur Saloum: "Your colleagues are not so weak toward their subjects as you; either that will change or the kingdom of Saloum will change."[67] Still, though this traditional tyeddo role was preserved, only a small number of the tyeddo assisted in collecting taxes. The vast majority of them—perhaps a fourth of the total population—were rapidly submerged into the mass of the peasantry.

There were a number of other changes, and one of the most important was an attack on some of the symbols and rituals of chiefship. In 1891, the two Burs left their native region for the first time and visited St. Louis, violating a time-honored taboo against viewing the sea. Earlier the same year, Noirot invited Guédel to a conference at Kaolack. When Guédel arrived, accompanied by more than 250 tyeddo, Noirot invited him to come on the boat. Guédel refused, and after lengthy negotiations, camped by the side of the boat. Noirot left the next morning, and Guédel addressed a painful letter to the Governor explaining that as a Bur, he could not board a boat. "The two things that I fear in life," he wrote, "are first to offend the Governor, second to board a boat."[68] The Governor branded Guédel's refusal as absurd, and several months later Guédel finally boarded the Governor's boat to pay his respects.[69]

The administration was not yet prepared to set up a hierarchy of courts independent of the traditional political structure, but Noirot was interested in bringing about certain reforms, in particular the elimination of the practice of testing a man's innocence by passing a hot blade over his tongue. (It was thought that if a man were innocent, the blade would not burn him.) In 1892, Noirot proposed to M'Backé that the ordeal be eliminated and that the following reforms be made: first, that only the guilty party—not his family—be punished; second, that existing criminal penalties—fines, hot irons, loss of limb—be replaced by confinement to forced labor; and third, that he establish a monthly court at Diakhao, over which the Bur and the Administrator would preside.[70] The suggestions left M'Backé completely dumbfounded, and Noirot dropped the question for a while. It was only after several years of thought that he came upon an alternative to the ordeal. He proposed to Semou Djimit Diouf that an oath on the *N'Doug,* a very powerful fetish, be substituted for the hot blade.

"But the N'Doug kills," Semou answered. In fact, it was generally believed that N'Doug killed both the man who committed an evil act and his family.[71] The response to the suggestion was an emotional and disturbed meeting, at which Noirot's proposal eventually prevailed. In time, the use of fetishes for oaths before tribunals in pagan areas became general practice. Noirot's suggestion of a prison produced an equally shocked response from M'Backé: "If we can no longer eat the family of a criminal, how will my Burs, *dialigués,* and sakh-sakhs find themselves a living?" he asked.[h]

The problem of succession to the chiefship proved more amenable to change than the judicial system. In the first years, the French accepted the traditional power structure intact. They interfered only to demand the removal of chiefs like Sambodj M'Bodj, who threatened French commercial interests. When Guédel M'Bodj died, Semou Djimit Diouf succeeded him, and was automatically confirmed by the French. This confirmation probably prevented a civil war, since many of the Diogop Bigué were passionately opposed to a Kévé Bigué Bur. In Sine during the same year, the Bumi died, and Noirot announced that no new Bumi would be chosen. He insisted that the heir to Sine know French, and demanded that the two leading candidates, Coumba Djimbi N'Diaye and Coumba N'Doffène Diouf, go to school.[72] When M'Backé died in 1898, there was still no Bumi, and Coumba N'Doffène, the Thilas, was technically the heir.

[h] Administrator of Sine-Saloum to Governor of Senegal, 14 Aug. 1893, ARS, unclassified. The term "eat" refers to the expropriation of all or part of the criminal's property. The "Burs" mentioned were a small number of Burs less important than the Bur Sine.

SOCIAL AND ECONOMIC CHANGE

1887–1914

State and Commerce

THE FLAG FOLLOWED COMMERCE into Sine and Saloum, and those who planted it there considered the protection and extension of commerce their primary goals. Nevertheless, the alliance between commerce and the administration was not always a blissful one, largely because economic conditions were poor at times and they made the administration's political tasks more difficult. The economic crisis that began in the early 1880's continued into the 1890's and was probably aggravated by the worldwide depression of this period. During the first years of French administration, the establishment of peace and the introduction of taxation counteracted the effect of low peanut prices (15 francs per 100 kilos in 1893), and acted to stimulate peanut cultivation. Exports from Sine-Saloum rose from 5,000 tons in 1890 to 11,000 tons in 1893. Then, as the price dropped further, exports went down in the two succeeding years, to 10,000 tons, then to 8,000. This was especially distressing to Noirot, who saw the development of peasant agriculture as a prerequisite to the social changes he sought. Knowing that there was a large markup, Noirot begged the local commercial houses to pay the peasants a higher price, and urged the government to give some kind of aid. He also started a model farm, and began investigating the possibility of introducing other export crops, in particular cotton and the castor oil plant. In 1896, he was on tour when he heard that the commercial houses had started paying only 7.50 per kilo. He immediately returned to Foundiougne and wrote the Governor reporting the anguished pleas of peasant and chief:

I beg of you, please make our merchants understand that in wanting to obtain industrial products at too low a price, they expose themselves to the possible desertion of their shops. . . . Our influence over these peoples is not yet sufficiently establishd to enable them to do without our commercial activity. The needs that we are trying to encourage in the natives are not yet so imperious as to force them to produce in spite of everything. We have in the east of Saloum 40,000 people who have little or no contact with our commerce, and who are capable of living and of clothing themselves. . . . If he [the peasant] were not obliged to get money in order to pay his tax, he would make no effort to seek out European commerce.[1]

Noirot asked the Governor to establish a minimum price and to require that commerce use money instead of barter. The administration flatly rejected both requests: "Such measures, contrary to all of our principles of commercial liberty, would not fail to arouse the protests of the merchants."[2]

Noirot remained hostile to the commercial syndicate, a combination of the four largest commercial houses,[3] and opposed their desire to force prices down, but at the same time he and his successors destroyed the only possible response that local societies had to the unity of the merchants. This was the laff, a prohibition on the sale of peanuts imposed by the Bur. The laff had been used in the early 1860's when Coumba N'Doffène I tried to stop the cultivation of peanuts in the hope that the French would go away. In 1889, both Burs imposed the laff, and no sales were made for a month, until they received generous gifts. Administrator Génébre explained:

Today, the cultivator possesses sufficient reserves of millet for his own food and would like to sell his peanuts at a higher price than the commercial houses want to pay. In these circumstances, he is largely supported by his king, whose coubeul will be that much higher if the products of his country are sold at a higher price. On different occasions, the houses have complained to me of this state of affairs and have demanded my intervention with Guédel.[4]

Génébre presented the claims of the commercial houses, but with little effect. The laff was usually withdrawn only when generous gifts had been given to the rulers; the Serer continued to hold out, and in 1892 Noirot addressed a vigorous protest to Guédel:

> Remember that as Bur Saloum you do not have the right to impede commerce and to stop the cultivators from selling their products. On the contrary, in your position as chief of Saloum, all of your efforts should tend to protect commerce, to aid it, and to develop it. The purchase price is not your business; it is the business of the merchants and the cultivators. . . . Stop the laff immediately if you do not wish to see yourself replaced in Saloum.[5]

Guédel did not scare easily. He immediately wrote the Governor:

> Me, I am not a cultivator, but I am eager to see my people sell their peanuts because I have debts that I can only pay when the peanut trade goes well; I have nothing but the coubeul for my expenses. Knowing that I have only that, what makes you say that I impede the peanut trade?[6]

Prices kept going down, and the chances of breaking the laff seemed to diminish. At the end of 1893, M'Backé addressed a plea to the Director of Political Affairs: "The Sine-Sine, after having cultivated peanuts in order to pay his tax, is forced, because the price of the nuts is so low, to go look for work in the Gambia in order to provide what the peanuts cannot get for him."[7] Efforts to impose the laff continued to draw warnings and threats.[8] With time the laff became a futile gesture, and it was used less and less.[a]

There is a certain irony in Noirot's vigorous attack on the laff, because he was one of the few Administrators who defended

---

[a] A similar effort in the North Bank Province of the Gambia to resist the imposition by the commercial syndicate of a larger bushel was broken after a three-month suspension of trade. In early March, a number of peasants gave in. Some of them wanted to marry, and marriages could not be negotiated until peanuts were sold, and they had money and goods. (Annual Report, Traveling Commissioner, North Bank Province, June 1894, AG.)

peasant interests. He was firmly convinced that, given a decent price and a nearby shop with desirable goods, the peasant would produce whatever the traders were willing to buy. Noirot was continually pushing the commercial houses to extend their operations, to use money rather than barter, and to experiment with new crops.[b] When Noirot found that peasants and Fulbe were forbidden to buy such luxury goods as mosquito nets and imported cloth, he put pressure on the chiefs to end such restrictions.[9] He also gave the commercial houses a lecture on merchandising:

> It is true under all latitudes that the woman motivates commerce; it is she who must be interested, it is necessary to arouse her coquetry, awaken her taste. . . . But we must not create illusions for ourselves and await the client behind the counter; if he does not come to us, we must go to him.[10]

The commercial houses, however, remained conservative in their merchandising practices, and preferred to rely on administrative action to make commercial expansion possible in Senegal. To do this, the administration put an end to taxes like the coubeul and the *namou*, both of which restrained trade, and imposed a head tax, which stimulated trade by making the Africans work for money to pay the tax. The *namou* was a tax on the seasonal farmers—called *navetanes* in Senegal, "strange farmers" in the Gambia. They were first noticed in the Gambia as early as 1848, a little more than a decade after the first purchases of peanuts at Bathurst. The Governor's Annual Report of that year described them thus:

> The Sera Woollies [Sarakollé] and Tilli-bunkas [Mandinka and perhaps Bambara; the word means "people of the east"]

---

[b] Administrator of Sine-Saloum to Governor of Senegal, 1 Mar. 1895, ARS, unclassified; Administrator to M. Laborde, Kaolack representative of Maurel Frères, 11 Mar. 1895, ARS, 13 G 32. The idea that the African peasant would respond to economic incentives was expressed earlier by Faidherbe. Though it seems self-evident to modern students of Africa, Noirot's belief that Africans would labor willingly for European goods was not always shared by his contemporaries. Commercial houses were conservative, and Administrators often found that using force was the easiest way to produce short-term results.

often visit the countries near the Gambia, frequently coming not less than 500 or 600 miles from the interior; and after paying a small custom to the chief of the country in which they settle, they are permitted to cultivate the ground under his protection for one or more years, according to their agreement, and to sell the produce to the European merchant or trader. The greater portion of the groundnuts exported is raised in this manner by parties who have no permanent connection with the soil they cultivate.

It is difficult to estimate the effect of the marabout-soninke wars on these migrations. The conflicts probably put a brake on the size of the migrations, but they seem to have continued, perhaps encouraged by the marabout leaders, who were interested in commerce. Noirot counted six to seven hundred strangers in 1892, mostly Mandinka.[11] They settled near the factories, worked land during the rainy season, and left when the harvest was in. In 1893, Ozanne counted almost a thousand in the North Bank Province, many from Saloum.[12] These were probably men from the east, who came down to the river to earn money for their head tax.

The navetanes in Saloum, even those who came from eastern Saloum and temporarily took land in the west, had to pay a twenty-franc tax to the Bur Saloum. The rights to collect the namou were farmed out, and in many cases the migrant found himself faced with demands that made the trip unprofitable. In some cases, men left in the middle of the season. Even when nothing else was demanded, the twenty-franc tax made it difficult for a migrant to clear much profit.[13] The French wanted the navetanes there, however, and Noirot battled for several years to reduce the namou. Finally, in 1895, Semou Djimit reduced the tax in Saloum to five francs, and provided that the tax would be collected by an Administrator or a delegate, who would give it to the Bur.[14] In 1896, M'Backé reduced the namou in Sine to six francs.[c]

[c] Administrator of Sine-Saloum to Madiouf Diouf, 30 Dec. 1896, ARS, 13 G 326. One incidental result of this labor migration is a scattering of Bambara villages in Sine-Saloum. Of the many who came to work, a few stayed.

During France's first decade in Sine-Saloum, commerce benefited from an active program of public works construction. Dredging operations in the Saloum River made it possible for an oceangoing vessel, the *Richelieu,* to pick up a load of peanuts at Kaolack in 1896. A year or two earlier, Noirot had organized the construction of a telegraph line to Fatick, and then in 1896 he had it extended to Kaolack and to M'Baye-M'Baye in eastern Saloum. Soon afterward, the line was extended even further—to Sedhiou in the Casamance. Both Noirot and his counterparts in Nioro undertook active road construction programs. By 1898, Sine-Saloum had 555 kilometers (344 miles) of dirt road, and Nioro had 150 kilometers (93 miles). Lacking substantial financial resources, the Administrators depended primarily on labor corvées for most of these projects. Villages that refused to work on a given project were usually fined.[a]

It was in the cercle of Nioro that road construction was most important. This is a fertile area with more than adequate rainfall. And yet the products grown there were not moving to Kaolack and Foundiougne, but were being transported down two creeks, the Miniminian Bolon (Swarracunda Creek to the British) and the Bao Bolon, to the Gambia River. Commercial policy within the cercle was designed primarily to break this tie with Bathurst and to increase peanut production. Prices of goods in Nioro tended to be about two or three times as high as prices in the Saloum factories, which were at a safe distance from the Gambian frontier.[15] In 1898 a road was opened from Kaolack to Medina Saback, N'Deri Kani's village, near the Gambia frontier, but as we will see later, the construction of the road and the intiation of other measures to encourage the expansion of commerce in Nioro met with little success.

One of the advantages of the new order to the commercial houses was the reinforcement of the credit system. Though cred-

[a] Administrator of Sine-Saloum to Governor-General, 28 Mar. 1896, ARS, 13 G 325; E. Noirot, "Aperçu Général: Travaux Publics," ARS, 13 G 327; Administrator to Governor-General, 10 Feb. 1898, ARS, 13 G 330; *Journal Officiel,* 14 Apr. 1898. For several years after Noirot's departure, his successors were hard-pressed to maintain the roads he had built.

it had been given to peasants, chiefs, and subtraders before the French conquest, this had been done at great risk. In 1892, Noirot wrote that almost all of the subtraders in Sine—150 at that time—operated with goods advanced to them by the commercial houses. Those who could not pay back these advances generally remained in Sine, thinking themselves out of reach of French justice. This time, however, Noirot wrote to M'Backé, demanding that he seize the goods of eight traders.[16] In this particular case, M'Backé was reluctant to act, but obviously the time had come when the subtrader could no longer run out on his debts. The involvement of the administration did not help the peasant, for interest rates continued to remain exorbitantly high; and since many peasants found themselves imprisoned in a cycle of debts, traders were still able to demand high rates of interest. From time to time the administration also made or guaranteed loans. In 1887, the Gorée Chamber of Commerce advanced seed to many peasants, and in 1894 the administration guaranteed a loan of 11,000 francs worth of rice and millet to Guédel during a famine.[17]

A number of French officials were worried about the peasants' indebtedness. A peasant would go into debt sometimes because bad planning or a natural calamity had caused a shortage of food or seed, sometimes because he desired to make a good marriage. Once in debt, he had to pay interest rates so high he was likely to stay in debt. Several times the administration helped out during famines, but only to the extent of guaranteeing loans by the commercial houses; usually these loans were for seed and were repayable in kind at a moderate rate of interest.

Savings societies had been introduced successfully by the French in North Africa and Indochina, but had not been tried in black Africa. In 1907, after a famine, many of the Saloum peasants had eaten their seed reserves. The central administration transmitted a credit of 20,000 francs to Amédée Charles Lefilliâtre, Administrator of Sine-Saloum, and he offered the peasants in the Kaolack area advances of seed at a 5 per cent rate of interest. For every 100 kilos given out, 105 kilos were to be returned. There was a good harvest that year, but when the returns were piled up and weighed, the seed reserves were found to be only a little larger than at the beginning. Lefilliâtre convened a council of chiefs and proposed the formation of a savings society, a *société de prévoyance*. Members were to pay five francs in seed to become members, and were to return 30 per cent above what they had been advanced until a good reserve was piled up. In 1910, a section was set up in Fatick; and the next year, a decree authorized the creation of similar societies elsewhere in French West Africa. After the war, membership was made compulsory.[18]

These savings societies were never permitted to become more than the germs of cooperatives, nor were they ever more than a very limited and bureaucratic way of dealing with a serious problem. The primary purpose of the societies was the maintenance of seed reserves, though they were authorized to make advances for food in famine years. The Administrator was president, and he maintained tight control over operations. Either because of the influence of the commercial houses or because of their own philosophies, officials were not willing to permit Africans to participate in decision making, or to create institutions within which Africans could regain some control over their own affairs.

A similar *dirigisme* influenced the policy of sending local peanut crops on long routes north to Saloum instead of transporting them through the Gambia. This was by far the most important subject of correspondence from Nioro in the 1890's. Roads were built, a short-lived free cart service carrying goods to Kaolack was begun, and chiefs were pressured to see that the peanuts were sent north. The chiefs made promises, but the peanuts kept following the shortest route to the market. Finally, the chiefs of border cantons were given the right to collect a 10 per cent export duty and a 12 per cent import duty. This did little more than produce bitter protests from French commercial houses with Bathurst branches.[19]

In 1903 and 1904, customs stations were set up, though the administration did not spend enough to create an effective cus-

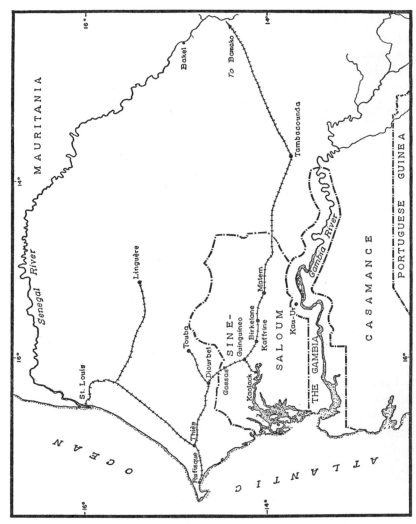

The Senegal-Gambia Border, the Dakar-Niger Railroad, and the Cercle of Sine-Saloum

toms wall. Lefilliâtre had suggested that for eastern Saloum alone thirteen customs posts were necessary.[20] Five posts were set up, run at first by village chiefs, but they were taken over soon afterward by customs officers from outside. They never brought in much revenue and were regularly bypassed. In 1912, 95 per cent of customs revenues in the cercle still came from the post at Foundiougne.[21] However, the new posts did hinder movement across the border, and along with the new roads and higher prices in Senegal, they undoubtedly contributed to a partial shift to routes through Saloum.[22] In 1903, Nioro reported that peanuts from Sabakh-Sandial were still moving south, but that 1,300 tons had moved north from the cantons of Rip and Niom.[23] The wall has never, however, been completely effective, and up to the present the movement of goods in border areas has been influenced mostly by differences in prices.

The desire to cut the amount of exports transported through the Gambia influenced the route selected for the Thiès-Kayes railroad, the final link in the system planned in 1880. The route for the railroad, designed to connect Dakar to Bamako and the Niger River, was planned so that it would not compete with existing transport routes, but would serve areas relatively untapped, or tapped only by the Gambia River. The route went directly west into the peanut-growing regions of Baol, and then turned south through part of Sine and a fertile but lightly inhabited sector of eastern Saloum, always keeping within an area where rainfall was adequate for agricultural development.

Construction began in 1908, the railroad entered Sine in 1909, and it passed through Saloum in 1912. The development of eastern Saloum had long been held back by the lack of transportation and by a low water table, which severely limited settlement. The construction of the railroad was paralleled by a well-digging program. At one station, Birkelane, it was necessary to go down 63 meters (over 200 feet) to find water. In July 1912, a trunk line connecting Guinguineo and Kaolack was completed, and the following year the Baol peanut crop, hitherto transported to Rufisque, went to Kaolack. The full impact of the railroad was not felt until after the First World War, when Kaolack became for a while the second port of French West Africa; but the five years before the war saw rapidly increasing commercial activity and the large-scale movement of people into areas opened up by the railroad.

Organization of the Trade

The French conquest did not radically change the economic organization of Sine-Saloum. Production remained primarily in the hands of peasant cultivators, ownership remained in the extended families, and the economy continued to be dominated by the peanut crop. Although concessions of land were given to commercial houses, these were usually parcels of unclaimed and often unusable land. Until 1904, only three agricultural concessions had been given to outsiders, and nothing seems to have been done with two of them. The third concession belonged to a Gorean, who engaged in commercial agriculture and grew cotton experimentally for a number of years.[24] The hopes of Noirot and several of his successors that cotton might replace the peanut as the region's staple crop were never realized, though several commercial houses made periodic purchases of cotton grown on model farms.[e]

The chief reason that the peanut remained king was a rise in prices.[f] The peanut trade benefited both from world prosperity and from the increased use of margarine made from peanut oil. Germany and the Netherlands became significant purchasers of Senegalese peanuts in the years before the First World War, and peanut production rose steadily throughout this period. Sine-Saloum, which had exported only 8,000 tons in 1895, exported

[e] Administrator of Sine-Saloum to Director of Native Affairs, 16 Oct. 1905, ARS, 13 G 346. At the request of the administration, a number of chiefs planted fields of cotton.

[f] Reports submitted by the Administrators did not contain accurate information on prices in Kaolack and Foundiougne between 1896 and 1908. In 1908, the price dropped once again, this time to twelve and a half francs per one hundred kilos. Just as in earlier crises, peasants refused to sell, and the administration brought pressure on the chiefs not to interfere with the free operation of the market. After this drop, the price shot up to over twenty per hundred and remained at this level until the beginning of the war. Of course, the further one got from oceangoing vessels, the lower the prices paid. Governor-General to Minister, 22 Feb. 1909, ARS, 2 G 8/10.

17,000 tons in 1903, 40,000 in 1909; and then, responding to the price stimulus, exported 100,000 tons in 1914. Foundiougne remained the most important port until 1914, when for the first time Kaolack surpassed it. Kaolack, which had handled only 3,000 tons in 1891, exported over 41,000 in 1914.[25]

In spite of this rapid growth, commerce remained conservative—reluctant to take risks or to enter unproved regions. The increase in production took place not in new areas but in areas that already had substantial acreage in peanuts. Until 1904, the administration could not persuade any commercial house to go into Niombato, though in the decade that followed, the Djilor-Niombato area experienced a large immigration and the most rapid increase in production in Sine-Saloum. In the same way, when the railroad was built in eastern Saloum, groups of peasants immediately moved there, sometimes before the stations opened. The commercial houses came afterward.

The commercial system had a neat hierarchical structure. At the top were the major commercial houses, many of which had their central offices in Europe. These houses had representatives in all of the major settlements and some of the minor ones. Maurel Frères, the largest, had nineteen posts in Sine-Saloum in 1912, and six other houses had more than eight apiece. These houses, operating as a syndicate, determined the price and monopolized imports and exports. They were usually in close contact with Europe on prices, and their major branches were usually, though not always, directed by Europeans. The large houses generally did not give credit directly to the peasants.

Below the big houses was a group of small entrepreneurs—in 1912, 21 of the 35 French-directed commercial enterprises were run by one man with two or three employees. These men, who were generally former employees of the big houses, bought directly from peasant producers and gave credit where necessary to peasants and to African subtraders. It was the subtraders, operating on credit extended by the commercial houses and by the smaller operators, who carried trade goods into the countryside and brought back the peanuts, although some of the peasants—those who had horses or mules—brought their own crops into the *escales,* hoping to get a higher price there. (In 1912, there were 64 *escales, i.e.* points of trade recognized by the government, and at 30 of them there were no permanent establishments.)[26] Some of the African subtraders also invested in land, hiring navetanes to clear and work it, but it is not clear how long this had been taking place or how widespread it was.

Social Change and Population Movement

The new roads and the railroad were the arteries of a new economic structure that made important changes in the style of life of most peasants. To be sure, some had been involved in the market economy before the conquest. The head tax, however, forced peasants in all parts of Sine-Saloum to grow at least a limited amount of peanuts, and the development of transportation encouraged them to produce more, and thus to participate on a larger scale in the world market. By 1914 every canton of the cercle was involved in production for the world market, and was to some degree dependent on imported goods. This brought about the radical enlargement of the villager's world, and transformed subsistence cultivators into peasants.[27]

Economic change did not immediately produce radical social change. The introduction of money and of imported luxury goods did not, in the first generation, necessarily bring changes in the peasant's style of life. Some of the areas that saw the greatest boom in exports had the least social change, largely because both the French and the traditional chiefs wanted to minimize changes that might undermine the old order or cause dysfunctional stress within it. The possibility of getting income from the land did permit the rapid conversion of the tyeddo into peasants. The status distinctions that are meaningful in modern Serer and Wolof culture are between the peasants on one side, and the slaves and members of castes on the other.

The most striking result of political and economic change was a series of population movements into, out of, and within Sine-Saloum. Economic development brought Lebanese traders and Senegalese from other parts of Senegal to the trading settlements. The Senegalese were largely from the Four Communes, and they came as employees of the commercial houses. Many were also clerks, guards, and interpreters working for the French government. These people created a series of small commercial and administrative centers which were predominantly Wolof, which did not look to the traditional chiefs for leadership, and which identified with the Four Communes. The largest of these centers was Kaolack, with a population of about 12,000 in 1908.[28] The new town population was relatively mobile and well traveled, moving back and forth between Senegal's urban centers.

The small but enterprising group of Lebanese merchants in Sine-Saloum's commercial centers were part of a group that had been emigrating from Lebanon and Syria since 1860. The vast majority went to North or South America, but in the 1890's a small number began coming to West Africa.[29] Arriving with no resources, the Lebanese were enterprising traders who were willing to accept a low standard of living. The first immigrants to Senegal arrived in 1892, but in 1908 they still numbered under 300.[30] Yet they were successful enough to arouse the vehement hostility of both traders and Administrators. In 1905, Lefilliâtre slapped a prohibitive thirty-franc monthly tax on Lebanese who sold in the African markets, explaining:

> This very high tax is proposed with the object of chasing from the markets this sort of itinerant merchant who takes up the space with his numerous tables to the detriment of the native, who does not know how to display the necessary merchandise.[31]

Five years later, Paul Brocard, the Administrator of Sine-Saloum, expressed the feeling of many European competitors in these words:

> The Syrians, whom our protégés take to be Europeans, have nothing that generally induces native respect for the white race. They are unclean physically and morally. No work is repugnant to them, provided it assures them a certain profit; and the reputation that they have acquired of constantly deceiving their clients seems to be perfectly merited.[g]

---

[g] Administrator of Sine-Saloum to Lt. Governor, 8 Jan. 1910, ARS, unclassified. Several of the Administrators were also troubled about usury, though high interest rates had long been widespread in the area.

Brocard excepted from his criticism those who had made enough money to open up small shops. His real objection was that the Lebanese sold for less, and thus posed a threat to the small French-run commercial houses. This did not stop the larger houses from giving goods to the Lebanese or from buying their peanuts. The newcomer usually started out with a small advance from a relative who had preceded him, and the Lebanese as a group proved themselves good credit risks. With time they took over a sizable part of the commerce. In 1912, there were 58 Lebano-Syrian traders in Sine-Saloum, most of them itinerant merchants. A thrifty Lebanese had an advantage over his African competitor because the African's family obligations were more likely to absorb his surplus wealth, while the Lebanese could reinvest his profits. The African traders remained an important group, but they tended not to accumulate capital.

Not the least of the administration's worries were the brightly colored religious pictures that the Lebanese peddlers sold, among them pictures of the Caliph. Conscious that the Lebanese were subjects of a ruler allied to Germany, the French saw in these pictures an act of subversion.[32] However, the conduct of the Lebanese during the war proved their fears groundless.

The same economic changes that brought the Lebanese to Senegal caused a substantial amount of movement within Sine-Saloum. Before 1900, much of this movement was away from high-tax areas, but the difference in tax rates was seldom more than a franc from one area to the next, and by 1900 most peasants knew that tax increases would catch up with them. After 1900, the movement was in the other direction, toward areas near factories, where good land was available, even though these were high tax areas. Sine received few immigrants because it was already densely populated, but the Djilor-Niombato area, which had been decimated by the wars, had a great amount of free land, and both navetanes and permanent Wolof settlers moved in large numbers. Similarly, in the years just before the war, the opening of railroad stations and the discovery of better well-digging techniques were opening up fertile areas of eastern Saloum.

Though economic growth brought immigration, high taxes

and political conflicts led to a parallel emigration to the Gambia, which troubled the French administration. Every emigrant meant less tax revenue and fewer kilos of peanuts. People were generally permitted to leave, though crops were often confiscated.[33] Many wisely left at night, especially when they had not paid their taxes. Some villagers moved to the Gambia side of the border but continued to work lands in Senegal. To stop this, the Governor authorized local chiefs to collect a prohibitive 75-franc tax from the peasants who lived in the Gambia and worked land in Senegal.[34] It was generally believed that the soil was better in Senegal; so if they were forbidden to work their old lands, the migrants would return. In 1904, Lefilliâtre forced one group to return by denying them the use of a well on the French side of the line.[35] In spite of these efforts, there was a small but steady increase in the population of the North Bank Province of the Gambia until 1904. Then there followed a seven-year period in which the North Bank population decreased. It is likely that the higher prices paid for peanuts in Senegal attracted many earlier migrants back. In 1911, the pattern was reversed again, and the population of the North Bank increased from 49,232 in 1911 to 53,868 in 1914. The McCarthy Island district experienced a similar jump.[h] This increase in migrants to the Gambia was caused by forced recruitment for the army and for railroad construction in Senegal. Railroad workers were paid, but wages were so low that compulsion was necessary to provide an adequate work force. The migration was stepped up even further during the war, when France began dipping deeply into her "reservoir of men." Migration was a serious problem only in those areas close to the frontier, where it was almost a certainty that an unhappy chief or an alienated village would pack up and leave.

Education and Social Services

The development of schools was the result both of an ideological commitment and of economic and political necessity.

[h] Traveling Commissioner's reports, North Bank Province, Gambia Archives. It should be remembered that most censuses underreported, and that the migrants who went back and forth were hard to count.

Many French officials believed strongly that teaching Africans to speak and write French would make political and cultural domination easier to achieve, though few were willing to give first priority to educational expenses, or to go further than training a class of interpreters, clerks, and literate chiefs.

The French placed a high premium on knowledge of their language, but the government had done little for education outside the Four Communes, with the exception of authorizing Faidherbe's school for hostages, which was closed for lack of funds in 1871. The School for the Sons of Chiefs and Interpreters, founded in 1892, had as its primary goal the formation of a corps of French-speaking chiefs and functionaries.

French education in Sine-Saloum received its initial impetus from Ernest Noirot's strongly assimilationist ideology and his determination to make French culture available to the Africans. Noirot argued that "the propagation of our language would efficiently serve the extension of our influence."[36] Within two weeks of his arrival, he found a clerk at one of the commercial houses who was interested in teaching. Noirot's first plea for funds to start a school went unanswered, but some of the commercial houses in Foundiougne were induced to provide money to pay the teacher, and a carpenter offered his labor.[37] The school in Foundiougne was opened in 1892; one in Kaolack opened in 1893. When Noirot hired Léopold Diouf as secretary to the Bur Sine, it was on the condition that he teach a class. Diouf found little time for teaching, but funds for education were becoming more readily available, and before Noirot left, there was a school in Diakhao. Noirot also set up *écoles maternelles,* schools in which girls were taught domestic skills and French. By 1895, Noirot had 245 students in five schools.[38] More than half were girls in two écoles maternelles. Relatively little was done in the succeeding decade to build on this base. The écoles maternelles were closed either because of the expense or the difficulty of finding female teachers, and the Kaolack and Foundiougne schools had fewer students in 1904 than in 1895.[i] Lefilliâtre, who

---

[i] Administrator of Sine-Saloum to Governor-General, 14 Nov. 1904, ARS, 13 G 342. Only after 1909, when Governor-General William Ponty gave a new stim-

became Administrator several years after Noirot left office, was convinced that too much education would induce the young to leave the land in quest of better jobs, thereby reducing peanut production.

Noirot's convictions also brought him into conflict with the church schools at Joal and N'Gasobil, which taught in Wolof. Noirot, who wanted the church schools to provide him with teachers, could not see the point of teaching Serer students the Wolof language. To priests who said that Wolof would be Senegal's liturgical language, he could only respond that he "would rather have a French-speaking Moslem than a Wolof-speaking Christian."[39]

In Nioro the question of schools was closely related to the French desire to infiltrate the area's closed and antagonistic Moslem culture. The first two attempts to start a school failed for lack of students, but in 1896 a school that taught Arabic was started. This time, with the support of Mandiaye Bâ, it had some success, though one Commandant remarked that most of the students came from Mandiaye's large family.[40]

At the same time, the chiefs were asked to enroll one or more sons in the School for the Sons of Chiefs and Interpreters. With some of the chiefs, a minor cold war broke out on this issue. When M'Backé tried to replace his son Latgarand with a younger son, the Administrator wrote back that Latgarand's education was not complete, and that there was a place for the younger son.[41]

European medicine was also introduced into Sine-Saloum. The first doctor was assigned to the cercle in 1905, though there had been earlier vaccination campaigns. The doctor was stationed in Kaolack, and he made twice-monthly visits to Fatick and Foundiougne. Much of the concern of the medical service was with public health problems—in particular, epidemics of yellow fever or smallpox, which the service fought with mass vaccination and quarantines. By 1913, there was a clinic in each

ulus to education, did the enrollments rise. In 1911, enrollments rose to 337, and they were up to 481 in 1914, in addition to almost 200 attending adult education courses in Kaolack, Fatick, and Foundiougne.

of the five residencies;*j* and medical personnel included two doctors, four nurses, and four *aide-médecins*. Consultations were free. The resistance to Western medicine seems to have broken down fairly quickly, and medical facilities, though limited, were widely used.

Some of the changes occurring during this period contributed to a better life for the average peasant, but only at the expense of the African community's capacity to deal with its own problems. The colonial officer at his best was a paternalist. He cared for the people he ruled, and tried to improve their living conditions, but he also assumed that he knew best, and was therefore interested in destroying the ability of African communities to resist the imposition of his will. Thus, even in setting up the savings societies, the administration carefully limited the amount of initiative any African could take. A certain nineteenth-century economic liberalism pervaded the administration and influenced its policies, but economic freedom was the freedom of commercial houses to operate free from restraint, not the right of Africans to organize and act in their own behalf.[42]

j A residency was a town or village in which a Resident, a French official responsible to the Administrators, was stationed.

THE KAOLACK PERIOD

1898–1914

Reforms of 1898

MANY OF THE EARLY Administrators were assimilationists. They believed in French civilization and tried to justify their presence in Africa by attempting to transform the societies they ruled into ones conforming to the French ideal. They encouraged commerce and strengthened the authority of the administration in an effort to achieve this greater end. St. Louis frequently had to remind the Administrators and Commandants that it had neither the means nor the desire to preside over the speedy transformation of African societies. Nevertheless, both ends and means were frequently discussed in correspondence from the officials at Nioro and Foundiougne. As early as 1888, an Administrator wrote of the desirability of transforming the Burs, Beleups, and Bumis into canton chiefs chosen by the administration, dependent on it, and ready to do its will.[1] This attitude was shared by many of the military men in Nioro. In 1896 one eager Commandant suggested: "The best way to have devoted and useful men at the head of provinces is to make them functionaries named by us, chosen from among the most intelligent and most worthy, regardless of family and heredity."[2]

Both Noirot and his successor, Hippolyte Alsace, made more moderate, though fairly detailed, suggestions for reforms. Alsace, who shared Noirot's commitment to social change but did not have his sensitivity to the needs and interests of the chiefs and people concerned, created a difficult situation for himself by letting some of these ideas be known. In a letter to the Director of Native Affairs, he complained:

The Burs Sine and Saloum, feeling that I have been working to modify their social organization, have opposed me—the one with a disguised resistance, the other with open hostility. But since my duty is to help them—not by force but by persuasion —to transform themselves, I have been patiently continuing my task. . . .

The recalcitrant Bur Saloum has contested my right to receive and listen to the claims of his subjects who have not been to his residence . . . [and] he shows himself excessively jealous of his authority, which he would like to preserve intact.[3]

Alsace's superiors were critical of his haste, and one wrote in the margins:

The Administrator always has the right to listen to claimants, but he should not change on his own authority the terms of a treaty approved by the President of the Republic. If M. Alsace had not tried to humiliate the Bur before his own subjects, this situation would certainly not have come about.[a]

And yet several days after this, the sudden death of Bur Sine M'Backé N'Diaye provided the administration with the opportunity to make basic reforms.

During the conflict with Niokhorbaye, M'Backé had chosen Niokhorbaye's Bumi, Coumba N'Doffène Diouf, grandson of the victor of 1867, as Thilas. This conciliatory gesture made Coumba N'Doffène third in line, but when Bumi Goor Diop died in 1894, M'Backé started grooming his brother, Coumba Djimbi, to succeed him. In response to Noirot's ultimatum, both candidates briefly attended school, but never for longer than several weeks. When M'Backé died, the council of chiefs gathered, and the Grand Jaraf expressed the consensus of the group by tapping Coumba N'Doffène, who was thus enthroned before

[a] Administrator of Sine-Saloum to Director of Native Affairs, 12 Dec. 1897, ARS, 13 G 329. A key difference between indirect rule as practiced by Lugard in northern Nigeria and indirect rule as practiced during France's first decade in Sine-Saloum is that Lugard instructed his officers never to hear the complaints of peasants without either the chief or his representative present. However the difference should not be exaggerated. The wise Administrator did not undercut his chiefs, and one Administrator in Sine-Saloum even wanted to punish peasants who made unjustified complaints against chiefs.

Alsace was even notified of M'Backé's death. Alsace immediately dashed up to Diakhao and informed the chiefs that he could not recognize their choice. Letters to Coumba N'Doffène during the month that followed were addressed to "guelowar Coumba N'Doffène Diouf, charged provisionally with the kingdom of Sine."[4]

Coumba N'Doffène sought to assure the French of his loyalty, but his assurances apparently did not satisfy them. In early February, the chiefs of Sine met in Diakhao with Alsace, Governor-General Chaudié, and Farques, the Director of Native Affairs. After they announced that the title of Bur was to be suppressed and Sine divided into two provinces, Grand Jaraf Bandiougour Sène arose, expressed his gratitude and his devotion to the French, and then explained that the Sine-Sine were in agreement and wanted Coumba N'Doffène. His announcement was of little avail. Coumba N'Doffène became *chef supérieur* (head chief) of eastern Sine, Coumba Djimbi of western Sine. Each of these provinces was in turn divided into five cantons varying in size from 3,000 to 14,000 people. The canton chiefs were to be chosen from the major chiefly families, and there was to be one council of notables for the whole of Sine, to be presided over by the Resident. Each of the chiefs was to receive a salary. The new system also provided for a provincial budget, and for a new judicial system under which the French could supervise court proceedings.[5]

While Farques and Chaudié were at Diakhao, Bur Saloum Semou Djimit Diouf died. Farques immediately proceeded to Kahone to impose the same kind of reorganization. Once again the election of a new Bur had already taken place. The man chosen, N'Diémé Diémou N'Dao, was acceptable to the French and became chef supérieur of the province of western Saloum. In Saloum, the two provinces were to have six cantons each, and were to have separate councils in recognition of the fact that Saloum was no longer effectively a single unit. The canton boundaries largely followed the lines of the old traditional chiefships, with smaller jurisdictions being combined or added to the larger ones. For example, the solidly Moslem lands of the Alwali

N'Demen were added to Moslem Oualo. The islands of Gandoul, where the people were unhappy with Saloum's rule, were attached to the area of direct administration under the authority of the canton chief of Foundiougne.[6] Niombato remained outside this expanded area.

The chiefs of eastern Saloum were unable to agree on a chef supérieur, so the canton chiefs were left directly under the authority of the Resident until a chief could be found. The chiefs in the East were the men who had held the major chiefships under Semou Diouf, and in the case of Serigne Pakala Mandiack Cissé, under Saër Maty. In the new hierarchy of authority, chiefs had to be approved by the administration and were dependent on it for salaries. In April 1898, the capital of the cercle of Sine-Saloum was moved to its largest city, Kaolack.

The New Order

The 1898 reforms marked a radical transformation in the colonial political system. The traditional political structure, if not completely destroyed, was effectively combined with the new one, and the French accepted in practice the idea of exploiting the traditional chiefship instead of substituting a new and more expensive kind of administration. The traditional chief was deprived of much of his autonomy and placed in a new bureaucratic structure that supported him and confirmed his privileges while it restricted his freedom of action.

Nowhere are the changes in the system more clearly manifested than in the burgeoning administrative structure. In 1892, Noirot had with him one clerk and one interpreter. There was a military force that averaged over fifty men in Nioro, and the spahis could easily be called down from Dakar, but he had neither guards nor soldiers under his command at this time. Five years later, his successor, Hippolyte Alsace, had fourteen people on his payroll, all African; six of them were teachers and five of them guards. In 1902, Lefilliâtre's bureaucracy consisted of twenty-nine men, of whom seven were Europeans. He had a European assistant, two men concerned with native affairs, two Residents, and twenty-nine guards. This increase continued.

Customs guards followed shortly afterwards, as did French doctors, well-digging crews, agricultural experts, and railroad men. By 1914, there were forty guards distributed among the various residencies and trading towns.

The growth of this bureaucracy and the arrival in Africa of professional administrators trained at the Ecole Coloniale led to the downgrading of a group of African clerks and interpreters who had often been trusted with important missions. Moussa Soumaré, an illiterate interpreter, had been sent into Niombato many times to collect taxes and had been entrusted with important political missions to African chiefs. Isaac Konaré, first as secretary to Semou Djimit and then as the Administrator's clerk, had also performed major duties. The most important of these men was Abdoulaye Diaw, a clerk. Diaw had been Noirot's right-hand man, and was Acting Commandant when Noirot was on tour, which was often. His correspondence shows an intelligence and an understanding of problems equal to that of most of the better colonial officers. However, with the growth of the white bureaucracy, Diaw was moved over into the chiefly hierarchy. In this area, he failed completely. (Diaw's failure will be discussed later in this chapter.)[7]

After 1900 the interpreters and guards played a much more limited role, though some were made chiefs, and met with mixed success. Most of the guards were former spahis and tirailleurs, usually from outside the area, though many married there and became integrated in local society. In the early years, it was important to have men from outside because the loyalties of local people were not dependable. Also, there were few local people with enough education to be clerks or teachers. Increasingly, positions in the local bureaucracy were given to local men who had graduated from the School for the Sons of Chiefs and Interpreters in St. Louis, and who were destined for chiefly responsibilities.

The administrative reorganization of 1898 was followed within several months by the death of Alsace. During the three years that followed, the cercle suffered from a lack of continuity of policy and from frequent changes of Administrators. After four

Administrators had come and gone in three years, Lefilliâtre arrived in 1901, and the post achieved a certain stability. Lefilliâtre and his successor, Paul Brocard, filled the position for a period of almost twenty years between them, a period that saw Sine-Saloum become the most economically active cercle in Senegal. Both were "broussards," or "bush men," administrators best adapted to the roving commands and the isolation of colonial life. After he left Senegal, advancement came slowly to Lefilliâtre because many of his superiors felt that he was not suited for a desk job. Lefilliâtre was the first graduate of the Ecole Coloniale to command the cercle, and he was intelligent and competent, though his superiors often considered him too impulsive and self-confident. Although he was committed to economic change and a certain humane paternalism, he was nevertheless a striking contrast to Noirot; he was neither as articulate and imaginative, nor as sensitive to the desires and interests of the African societies as Noirot had been.[8] Brocard was different from both Noirot and Lefilliâtre. An energetic former army officer, he enjoyed power, and he used it in a cold and authoritarian manner. He was frequently called down by his superiors for being too harsh on those who dared to disagree with him, but he was highly appreciated for the undeniable economic advances the cercle made under his direction.[b]

At the time of the 1898 administrative reorganization, the African chiefs agreed to place judicial proceedings under French surveillance. This agreement was incorporated into a general circular, "On the Organization of Justice in the Protectorate Areas," issued by Governor-General Chaudié two months later. In the circular he noted that most Senegalese wished to be governed by Moslem law, and a large minority by their own traditional law, but he laid down these three principles: first, that all qadis and other judges must be invested by the French; second, that the qadis must receive fixed salaries so that they would

[b] Dossier 3026, ARS; personnel dossier, FOM. Brocard's career ended under a cloud of suspicion. It was discovered that he was involved in a private business venture, and a court case was begun against him. He died in 1920, and his name was cleared posthumously.

not be dependent on fines for income; third, that a record must be kept of all sentences. Fines were to be divided between the regional budget and the province chief, who controlled the provincial budget.

Two court systems were set up in Saloum: qadis for the Moslems, and canton chiefs for the pagans. (The pagans could appeal to a council of notables.) In Nioro there was to be a qadi for each canton and a qadi superieur, or chief qadi, for the cercle.[9] The qadis were expected to read and write Arabic, and to read, write, and speak French, although the latter requirement was never enforced. More important, the new system gave the Administrator control over the selection of judges in most of the courts,[c] and made him the court of final appeal. In Saloum, the Moslem court system developed slowly, largely because few marabouts met the administration's standards of learning and political acceptability. Abdou Kane became qadi in Kaolack in 1898, but he was for many years the only Moslem judge officially recognized.

The 1898 reorganization was not definitive. After 1898, there were frequent changes in the size and shape of the various circumscribed areas.[d] In several cases, it was necessary to create

[c] In 1904, there were six tribunals in Saloum operating above the level of canton courts. Four were provincial tribunals in Sine, eastern Saloum, western Saloum, and recently attached Nioro. A fifth court was in Djilor, whose residents would not go to Kahone to be judged, and a sixth in Niombato, whose residents would go to neither Djilor nor Nioro. (Report on administrative and judicial organization, ARS, 13 G 342.)

[d] After 1908, the five major circumscriptions in the cercle of Sine-Saloum were Sine, Nioro, lower Saloum (the area around Foundiougne), eastern Saloum, and western Saloum. The boundaries of Sine were subjected to only minor changes, and were essentially those of the present cercle of Fatick. Nioro, after its attachment to Sine-Saloum in 1904, was briefly under a Resident in Foundiougne (1906–08), but Lefilliâtre, the author of the change, soon decided to make a separate circumscription, Nioro, out of the canton of Rip and adjoining cantons, where a distinctive Moslem Wolof community lived.

With Nioro no longer in his jurisdiction, the Resident at Foundiougne found himself charged with the least populous of the major circumscriptions, but the one with perhaps the most diverse problems and population groups. Dakar and St. Louis had always found Niombato too small to merit a special representative, but it continued to demand much of the Resident's time. The residency also included Djilor, the islands of Gandoul, and Foundiougne, which continued to be under direct administration.

Eastern Saloum, after a brief experience with a Resident, had no direct repre-

separate cantons for small groups who had been placed under the authority of alien chiefs, but in general the tendency was toward larger cantons, where power and its rewards were in the hands of a small group of reliable chiefs. Power tended to be concentrated at two levels, that of the Administrator, who made policy and interpreted the directives of higher authority, and that of the canton chief, who executed policy. The Resident neither governed nor made policy decisions. He surveyed events in the cantons, gave the Administrator information, and saw to it that directives were carried out. In general, Residents were changed more frequently than Administrators, and seldom had the chance to know their jurisdictions really well.

The significant aspect of the 1898 reorganization was the imposition of the cantonal organization, with the French assuming the right to choose chiefs and to determine the extent of the canton. There was a continuing tendency to diminish somewhat the autonomy of the chiefs, but in general the Administrators supported their chiefs and carefully avoided eroding the chiefs' power over their subjects. The Administrators clearly recognized that the canton chief was the foundation stone upon which the administration rested.

The separation of Sine into two provinces was a short-lived one, mostly because it had no real rationale. It could be justified only as part of an effort to destroy the very real political community that existed in Sine. This community had chosen Coumba N'Doffène Diouf as Bur Sine. As Bur, Coumba N'Doffène had a

---

sentative of the administration until the arrival of the railroad in the years just before World War I. More than any other area, this was one in which the French presence was very limited and the authority of the chiefs relatively unrestrained. Kaymor was detached from eastern Saloum and placed under the Resident in Nioro in 1908.

The fifth circumscription, western Saloum, which was directly under the Administrator, was the one that saw the most striking economic, social, and political changes. The Oualo area, which had been awarded to the Burs after a lengthy dispute in the 1890's, was once again attached to Nioro. Like Kaymor, it was Moslem and physically closer to the old marabout capital. Administrator of Sine-Saloum to Director of Native Affairs, 25 Nov. 1902, ARS, 13 G 336; A. C. Lefilliâtre, monograph on the cercle of Sine-Saloum, ARS, 1 G 290; undated report on administrative organization, 1904, ARS, 13 G 342; Administrator of Sine-Saloum to Lt. Governor, 4 Apr. 1910, ARS, unclassified.

prestige that his rival, Coumba Djimbi, did not have, and had at
his command much larger forces than those of Coumba Djimbi,
forces that proved necessary to check the independence of the
Serer peasantry. The crisis that forced the French to recognize
the unworkability of the separation was the refusal of peasants
in four of Coumba Djimbi's five cantons to pay taxes. When
Resident Victor Valantin toured the area in March 1899 to support the canton chiefs' efforts to collect taxes, he was greeted
at many villages only by armed men, since women, children,
and flocks had been quickly moved into the woods. At one village, Valantin was forced to beat a hasty retreat. At another,
there was a conference that ended with a flat refusal to pay.

Valantin was convinced that the seizure of the chiefs would
not bring the villages to terms. Only a chief's relatives would
really care about him. Instead, he asked that a military force be
sent to confiscate herds and execute certain chiefs as examples.[10]
The Governor-General ordered instead a "peaceful demonstra-
tion" by 22 spahis, who would seize flocks only as a last resort.[11]
Some of the villages paid when faced with force. Others fled.
Chiefs in surrounding provinces had orders to seize whatever
they could lay their hands on, and it is impossible to say how
many sheep, cattle, and goats were confiscated. Many animals
were undoubtedly seized and never returned.[12]

During the military action, Coumba Djimbi either was unable
to provision the spahis or did not want to. Coumba N'Doffène
not only provided provisions, but told the Administrator that he
himself could collect taxes. As a result, Coumba N'Doffène was
charged provisionally with western Sine, and when Coumba
Djimbi objected, he was arrested and deported.[13] The plan was
to place a French-educated Serer chief—there were several in
school—in western Sine, but Coumba N'Doffène proved himself
so effective that succeeding Administrators decided to retain
him and preserve a modified form of the traditional organization
of Sine.

Lefilliâtre was at first antagonistic to Coumba N'Doffène. He
wrote to Léopold Diouf, the Bur's secretary, "There are no more
Burs."[14] To Coumba N'Doffène he wrote, "You are only a simple

chief and nothing more."[15] By the end of the rainy season, he had changed his mind as the following letter shows:

> Sine—at the head of which we have a chief who is well endowed, intelligent, and strongly devoted to the French cause—cannot be more calm. The Serer, a farmer par excellence, thinks only about his field, which he loves more than anything else; imbued with thoughts of farming and herding, he does not dream of doing wrong. . . .
>
> The Sine-Sine does not like to see his country divided; he wants one chief, chosen by him, whom he can love; the present chief fills all of these conditions and is ideal for the Serer. He will only accept a second with a great deal of difficulty; I even believe I can say that we could not obtain these results without force.[16]

At about the time Lefilliâtre was writing these words, St. Louis was proposing a young Serer interpreter as a candidate for chief of the province formerly ruled by Coumba Djimbi. Lefilliâtre reiterated his previous position, reminding St. Louis that Coumba N'Doffène had collected all of the taxes, and had carried through an efficient census. Besides, he commented, the interpreter in question was a tangann, and thus ranked low on the Serer social scale. Coumba N'Doffène, Lefilliâtre suggested, should be kept in Sine until his death or until he made a major error, at which time he could be replaced by chiefs educated in French schools.[17]

Lefilliâtre's recommendation was accepted. Thus three years later he was able to write that "Coumba N'Doffène, although called chef supérieur by us, is the real Bur, or king, of former times, holding Sine in his hand and making it his instrument."[e] Coumba N'Doffène remained Bur until his death in 1923.

---

[e] Administrator of Sine-Saloum to Director of Native Affairs, 27 Apr. 1904, ARS, 13 G 332. In 1907, Lt. Governor Camille Guy suggested that the administration should rest directly on the canton chief, eliminating the often extravagant province chiefs, who were in most cases the holders of important traditional titles. He made plans to reduce six of Senegal's seven remaining holders of traditional titles—among them Coumba N'Doffène—to positions near the level of canton chief. (Memorandum, ARS, 13 G 71.) Somehow these plans got sidetracked before they were put into effect in Sine.

The Bur's power remained very real. From 1901 on, Sine appears very little in the Administrator's correspondence. Only a few of the Resident's reports are available, but a reading of those few and of the Administrator's correspondence makes it evident that this French version of "indirect rule" worked very well. Coumba N'Doffène collected taxes, generally the highest taxes in the cercle, and he maintained order. In return, France permitted him to rule. He successfully blocked the establishment of a mission at Diohine in 1901, and kept the Church out of Sine.[18] Directives from Kaolack did not go directly to the canton chief as often happened in other areas, but through the Bur. When a canton chief died or retired, the Bur generally took over for the interim and had his retainers do the chief's work until a new chief was chosen. At one time, the Bur had three cantons in addition to his higher post. He was amply rewarded for his services. His salary in 1911 was four times as high as that of any other chief in the cercle; and when he had difficulty with his debts, the administration helped out.[†]

Symbolic of this compromise was the decision in 1901 to put the Resident for Sine at Fatick, far from the Bur's capital at Diakhao. This was recognition that the Resident could safely remain a discreet distance from the center of political affairs. The residency had briefly been at Niakhar, much closer to the Bur, and Diakhao itself was considered, but in 1901 the residency was moved to the commercial center of Sine, and the school followed it.

One of the results of allowing the Burs so much autonomy was that in 1963, when I visited Sine, Coumba N'Doffène's successor, Mahecor Diouf, though retired, was still Bur to much of Sine, and was perhaps the only traditional chief in Senegal who

---

[†] In 1902, he was receiving 12,000 francs a year plus a share of taxes. No other chief received more than 6,000. (Administrator of Sine-Saloum to Director of Native Affairs, October 1902, ARS, 13 G 336.) In 1911, he was still getting 12,000, while the next highest paid chief, N'Déné Diogop Diouf, chef supérieur of western Saloum, was receiving only 3,000. (*Journal du Poste*, Kaolack, 31 Jan. 1911, ARS, unclassified. On the aid given to Coumba N'Doffène for the payment of his debts, see Administrator of Sine-Saloum to Director of Native Affairs, 12 Feb. 1903, ARS, 13 G 336.)

possessed real power. No small part of this power is due to the astuteness and perception of Coumba N'Doffène and Mahecor Diouf, both of whom combined a commitment to the preservation of a way of life with an understanding of political realities. Their continuing power was also rooted in other factors. Economic change has entailed a minimum of social change in Sine. The peanut crop became part of the agricultural cycle, but the peasants did not become dependent on this cash crop, and they continued to grow the millet and rice their families needed. As a result, indebtedness was less common and migration was rarer in Sine than it was elsewhere. The Sine-Sine did not move. Instead, they worked their lands more intensively. Just as the pattern of the peasants' work remained much as it had been, so too did their political and religious life. The Bur Sine remained the focal point of their loyalties, and he continued to fulfill the Bur's traditional role, presiding over ceremonies and sacrifices designed to ensure good harvests and conciliate divine forces.[19]

The operation of the bureaucracy in Sine was very different from that in the rest of the cercle. In both Nioro and Saloum the canton system evolved naturally and proved effective. Province chiefs existed only briefly, since they were soon found to be unnecessary. In both areas, the canton chief soon became the cornerstone of the administration, and directives were either sent out directly from Kaolack or passed through the Resident. In Saloum, none of Semou Djimit Diouf's successors commanded very wide support. The nucleus of a canton system already existed in certain large chiefships like Djilor and N'Doukouman. Within each of these areas there were families that had traditional rights to command, had bands of retainers, and could command widespread loyalties. The French generally chose Burs and canton chiefs from these families. In Nioro, the situation was different, but the units created by Ma Bâ and his followers were the nuclei of cantons. Each marabout chief commanded a limited area, in most cases an area where his father and grandfather had been marabouts. These chiefs were capable, realistic men, revolutionaries who had won power by their talents and were determined to maintain it. They proved to be pragmatic, flexible, and adaptable.

The Diouma Affair

Not surprisingly, the only real revolt against French authority did not come from either the Moslem or pagan chiefs, but was instead the type of outburst of religious feeling the French always feared. The leader of the revolt was a recent convert, Diouma Sow, a Fulbe who had been preaching in Oualo and in the Diammas, a small group of Toucouleur villages that, like Oualo, were strongly Moslem and unhappy with a settlement that placed them under tyeddo chiefs. In April 1901, while Abdoulaye Diaw, the chef supérieur, was on his way to Kaolack with the tax receipts, he received word that his residence at Malem had been burned by a band of fanatic Moslem warriors who were heading toward Kaolack. While Administrator Victor Allys gathered guns, ammunition, and warriors for the defense of the city, Diaw returned to the East with an Assistant Administrator, ten guards, and fifty Saloum tyeddo. Before they made contact with Diouma, they received word that he had been killed and his bands scattered by the Beleup N'Doukouman, Ibrahima N'Dao.

Diouma's force had never been significant, but its existence aroused in Allys fears of Moslem fanaticism. An investigation was immediately begun in Saloum and in Nioro. It was discovered that Diouma and another recent convert, Nadia Bâ, had started preaching a holy war and the coming of a Mahdi—a Moslem messiah—early in 1900. Neither got extensive support, but early in 1901, they started moving east with a band of about ten men. Diouma stopped in Diamma, preached, and then after a short stay, moved on to Pakala, from which he launched his attack on Malem. His band at this time consisted of approximately fifty men, of whom only three were armed.

Neither Allys nor Lieutenant Chaudron in Nioro could believe that his chiefs were ignorant of this activity. In Nioro, Mandiaye Bâ was dismissed on charges of withholding information. In

Saloum, N'Diémé Diémou N'Dao, the chef supérieur, was removed when Allys heard that the Fulbe of Ganiek, in N'Dao's
canton, had been preparing to join Diouma. N'Dao protested
that he had been framed—the chief who investigated the case
was the man who succeeded to his post—but his protests were
unheard.[20] In trials at Nioro and Malem, at least fifteen culprits
were sentenced to death and at least 65 men were sentenced
to hard labor or had their property confiscated, mostly on
charges that they knew of Diouma's activity and did not inform
the Administrator.[21] Diamma Thioyen was burned and its people
were imprisoned. For having received Diouma hospitably, the
village of Malem was fined 15,000 francs, a sum that could not
possibly be paid by a village with a subsistence economy, and
all of its weapons were confiscated. Ganiek was also punished,
though the report did not say how.[22] The prisoners taken in the
Diammas were turned over to two canton chiefs in eastern Saloum. Abdoulaye Diaw received the following instructions:

> In order to remove from this country these parasitic mara-
> bouts who exploit the people and are always ready to secretly
> arouse them against us, you will give strict orders that any
> individual who asks charity is to be arrested.
>   The prisoners from the Diammas assembled in the villages
> of Ibrahima N'Daw and the Serigne Pakala should be freed
> only when a payment of 73,000 francs has been received. No
> one will be released before half of the sum has been received.
> ... If the payments are not made, the prisoners will be dis-
> persed and assigned to people who will feed them in exchange
> for their labor and will be charged with guarding them.[23]

Diaw was also told to take prisoners in Malem and treat them
in the same way if Malem's fines were not paid within a month.
St. Louis and Dakar were stunned by the severity of the penalties and perhaps by the idea of an Administrator's using enslavement as a criminal penalty. This may explain the speedy replacement of Allys by Lefilliâtre several weeks after these
punishments were dispensed. When Lefilliâtre tried to find the
prisoners, 149 of almost 200 were not to be found.[24] Lefilliâtre
granted an amnesty, and during the next several years devoted

much effort to coaxing back to their homes the villagers that had fled to the Gambia.

The Diouma revolt had a number of consequences. First, no Resident was sent to eastern Saloum until the coming of the railroad a decade later made one necessary. This gave the chiefs of the region a greater independence, and not surprisingly, the area was the site of most of the complaints (from subjects and rivals) about "exactions." Second, in order to persuade the refugees from the Diammas to return, Lefilliâtre set up a special canton made up of the three Toucouleur villages under a Toucouleur chief. Third, and most interesting, a struggle for power between Beleup N'Doukouman Ibrahima N'Dao and the chef supérieur, Abdoulaye Diaw, followed the revolt.

N'Dao had been an interpreter and had served with the French in Guinea. He was also a Moslem and a member of the ruling family of N'Doukouman. He became Beleup N'Doukouman in 1898, and later the same year, when the Bumi Mandack died, he became chief of that canton also. A confident and sure-minded chief, he was, from the first, one of the strongest personalities in Saloum. French gratitude for his success against Diouma undoubtedly saved him from punishment on several occasions when he was accused of pillaging. Diaw was a very different sort. Born in St. Louis, he had been a clerk, had always received the praise of his superiors, and under Noirot had frequently been Acting Administrator. In 1896, he was named Resident in eastern Saloum; he was called back to Kaolack briefly in 1898, but in the following year was chosen as chef supérieur. To his superiors, he seemed to have all of the qualifications: he was intelligent, he knew the area—and he was a Moslem. But Abdoulaye Diaw knew what his superiors did not know—that as a chief he had to assert his power, build up an entourage, place his men in key posts, and support them. He had to have more power than his canton chiefs; but the canton chiefs—in particular N'Dao and Mandiack Cissé, the Serigne Pakala—had hereditary claims to their titles and could count on the loyalty of large areas.

At first, Diaw received high praise from Lefilliâtre, and he won his first battle. Either because of N'Dao's exactions or because of the head tax, there had been a large migration from Mandack to the Gambia—at one time, Diaw reported that half the population of the canton had left. When Lefilliâtre visited eastern Saloum in 1902, there were many complaints about N'Dao's exactions. Lefilliâtre later said that these complaints had been paid for by Diaw. N'Dao was stripped of the Mandack command as punishment for the exactions, but he was allowed to retain N'Doukouman, probably because of his role in the Diouma affair.[25]

Diaw successfully placed a friend, Samba Atta, as Chief of Congheul, and tried unsuccessfully to install his nephew as Bumi Mandack.[26] There were a number of complaints against Samba Atta, but when Lefilliâtre tried to investigate, he found a wall of silence in many villages. However, during the investigation, Samba Atta fled to the Gambia, and Lefilliâtre began to get complaints about Diaw.[27] Finally, in January 1903, Lefilliâtre, convinced that the charges against Diaw were legitimate, removed him. The letter explaining the action listed the following among Diaw's misdeeds: (1) he had illegally detached a number of villages from Congheul and placed them under his own authority so as to reap a share of the tax revenues; (2) he had stopped a slave caravan, and, instead of freeing the slaves, sold them; (3) he had not reported Samba Atta's raids, and had received part of the profits. To Lefilliâtre, the most shocking fact was that all of this had been done by a French-educated chief:

> He is more guilty than another chief who might have acted like him because we have given him instruction, raised him, made him what he is; in return, he repays us with ingratitude, dreaming only of the accumulation of property, the only goal toward which he moves, not retreating from any action in order to obtain it; he is guilty of the pillage of several villages and of traffic in human flesh, to cite only the most grave incidents. Not being from the area, he could not assume its interests. We should only have as chiefs men trained by us [serving] in their own area.[28]

Diaw returned to the bureaucracy and was sent to the Casamance, where he received praise for his integrity and his ability as financial officer.[29] Diaw had failed because he could not compete successfully against men with traditional claims to power.

Changes in the Chiefship

The experience with Diaw was one of a series of unsatisfactory attempts to impose chiefs from outside the area they ruled. The ideal for many French Administrators was the chief who was chosen for his talents and his loyalty to the French, the chief who commanded not by hereditary right, but because the French chose him. This idea was generally rejected rather quickly by the French officials on the spot, somewhat more slowly by those in St. Louis, who were not as close to day-to-day problems of government. Gradually, upper-level officers became aware of the realities, and in 1909 their awareness was articulated by Governor-General William Ponty in a circular setting forth his idea of a *politique des races*, which he addressed to the Lieutenant Governors of the various territories. France, he wrote, had too often imposed one people on another in the interest of neat, logical units. He explained further:

> We do not have the right to, in effect, sacrifice the future of one race to the future of another; each population group should preserve its autonomy with regard to its neighbors. . . . By letting each race evolve within its own particular mentality and by conserving as much as possible the particularism of the tribe, we promote . . . individual effort, with each group completely free from the political or religious influence of its neighbor.[30]

Outsider chiefs did best in stateless areas and in areas where the community was new. Moussa Soumaré, a retired interpreter, was generally praised for his work as chief in Fatick. Some outsiders were successfully moved into the chiefly hierarchy. Moussa's son, Silman Soumaré, became first an interpreter, then canton chief; and Alioune Sow became chief of Laghem. Others, like Abdoulaye Diaw and Samba Atta, found it necessary to use force to conquer the societies they commanded. I am inclined to think that the great number of complaints against outsider chiefs resulted not from the venality of the outsiders or the sense of responsibility of the legitimate chiefs, but rather from the fact that the peasants were more willing to yield to the demands of a legitimate chief.

Samba Atta's canton, Congheul, was an especially difficult one because a chief representing a predominant ethnic group could not be found, simply because there was no predominant group there. An old Mandinka state, Congheul had seen a large Wolof immigration and a buildup of hostilities during the religious conflicts. The Wolof were interspersed with the Mandinka in such a way that a line between the two groups could not be drawn. The first chief had been the Bur Congheul, but complaints from Wolof villages led to his removal. It was the Mandinka who complained most bitterly against Samba Atta, a Wolof. Unable to get any agreement on chiefs, Lefilliâtre imposed one of his guards, Biram Dior, as chief. While Lefilliâtre was at Kaolack, Dior got good ratings, but after Dior died, Brocard wrote that he had been as much a thief as his predecessor, only a more efficient one.[31] Sidi N'Diaye, a French-educated chief from Djoloff, was brought in, but this aroused the old tensions between Mandinka and Wolof, and there was a resultant migration to the Gambia.[32]

Ponty's phrase, "politique des races," moved into the bureaucratic vocabulary and was frequently used to justify decisions made in the cercle, but it did not become a universal rule. French administration was always very pragmatic in spite of the Cartesian principles that motivated many administrators. The administrator, though often hostile to the chiefs and to traditional society, generally chose men who could carry out his directives. The administrators tried to choose men who would be followed; then they used both threats and appeals to self-interest to tie these men to France, and let them do the hard work of executing policy. Mistakes were made and hard lessons often had to be relearned simply because the French officials who made the key decisions remained outside and above the societies they governed.

The acceptance of hereditary and indigenous chiefs did not constitute rejection of the bureaucratic ideal of chiefship, nor did it involve easing up on other policies designed to transform the chiefly class into a group more attuned to French ideals and practices—for example, the policy of training French-speaking chiefs. From the first, the French encouraged chiefs to learn French and forced them to send their children to school. This policy backfired in some cases, in none more flagrantly than that of Insa Bâ.

A younger son of Mamour N'Dari, Insa Bâ had been taken as a hostage after the conquest of Rip. He was then almost twenty years old and, like his brothers, literate in Arabic. He proved himself an adept student of French, and in 1889 was sent to a lycée in Algiers, where he displayed his verbal talents with pleas for money in two languages to his brother and to various administrators.[33] Mandiaye, who was expected to meet his brother's living expenses, may well have been reluctant to see a potential rival get a French education. Words came easier than living expenses, but Insa Bâ received his *baccalauréat* in 1895 and returned to Senegal, where he became a teacher. The opportunities open to a *bachelier africain* were very limited, and Insa Bâ was not the man to make the most of them.

The Commandant who dismissed Mandiaye Bâ was Lieutenant Chaudron, an extremely authoritarian officer who was continually slapping fines on village or canton chiefs for disobeying orders or for being slow in carrying them out. In one month, Mandiaye received three fines totaling 120 francs, including one for letting his animals stray onto the road.[34] While still a teacher, Insa Bâ wrote the Governor-General a very pointed letter protesting Chaudron's severity and defending his family's interests. This did not prevent his being chosen as chief after his brother's dismissal. Insa Bâ's response to Chaudron's continued severity was to sit down once again and write a letter to one of Chaudron's superiors.[35] There is no clear evidence that this caused Chaudron's departure, but he left soon afterward. It may have been the last time Insa Bâ acted resolutely.

From the first, Chaudron's successors were critical of Insa Bâ's performance. He was too timid, many complained, and he lacked authority. Furthermore, he was dependent on his brothers, and permitted them free rein in the villages. Mandiaye was still very powerful and so was Ousmane, a tamsir[g] who was highly respected in the area for his knowledge of the Koran, and long Mandiaye's strongest rival. Many of the Commandants considered Ousmane's influence dangerous, and one asked that he be deported.[36] Ousmane was a brother of Insa by the same mother, and he seems to have given his younger brother financial help during those hard years in Algiers. He had much stronger personality, and dominated the timid Insa. What the Commandants did not see was that Insa needed Ousmane. The French were conquerors in Nioro, and were still, a generation after the conquest, probably more unwelcome there than in other parts of the cercle. Insa's French education, far from giving him prestige, cut him off from his father's followers.

In spite of his ineptness, Insa Bâ was not removed until 1907. He was replaced by the man who had been a candidate for deportation in 1902, Ousmane Bâ. The choice proved a wise one. Ousmane spoke seven languages, including French, and had great prestige, both because of his earlier deeds on the battlefield and because of his reputation for learning. As one Assistant Administrator wrote:

> He has a great deal of authority in his province, as much through his title of chief as through that of tamsir. His reputation for probity permits him to be authoritarian toward his people without any complaints being formulated against him.[37]

After his removal, Insa Bâ served briefly on the staff of one of his former classmates, Lt. Governor Van Vollenhoven, and

[g] *Tamsir* is a Fulbe word meaning "one learned in the law." It comes from the Arabic *tafsir*, meaning commentator, and has been borrowed by the Wolof. Trimingham, *Islam in West Africa*, p. 247.

then returned to teaching. He obviously had no interest in teaching, and his personnel dossier contains a collection of consistently unfavorable reports.[38] Insa Bâ's failure pointed up serious flaws in French policy. He was obviously a bright young man, for he had received his "bac"—no small accomplishment—eight years after first being exposed to the French language. Yet when he returned to Senegal, he found that his options were few: he could be a chief, a lackey in the bureaucracy, or a teacher in a small African trading town.

Insa Bâ was not typical, however. His experience and his accomplishments cut him off from his own society at a time when French penetration was very limited. In later years, the French did not make the mistake of sending promising Senegalese to Algeria or France. Instead, they educated them in Senegal, training the elite at the School for the Sons of Chiefs and Interpreters during the prewar years. Often great pressure had to be put on chiefs to get them to enroll their children, but within a decade it became standard practice. Upon graduation, many of these men went into the army or were made minor officials, such as clerks or interpreters. Thus, by World War I, France had in Senegal a pool of potential chiefs who were literate in French and trained for the bureaucracy, and who also had traditional rights to rule.

In effect, this latter group, the group that began to take over chiefships in the years just before World War I, was the third of three important generations of chiefs. The first was the generation that was conquered. It was made up of men who recognized French military power, but were determined to maintain their traditional political systems and their control over the people. In the early period, the French had little information on which to base any interference in the selection of chiefs. By 1898, they had the information, though the chiefs were able to manipulate the administration somewhat by controlling the amount of information given the French. The chiefs of 1898 were largely men who had survived a process of weeding out, who knew the French, and knew what a chief could do and what he could not. They had worked out a modus vivendi with the conqueror, and efficiently carried out his will. Many spoke French, but few could read it. The third group was made up of men literate in French, trained in French schools, and promoted from the bureaucracy. Having worked as bureaucrats, they had an attitude different from that of the older chiefs, and were generally men who could exploit the traditional power of chiefship while operating in a bureaucratic system.

The evolution of chiefship reflected the increasing autocracy of the political structure. In the words of Jean Suret-Canale: "The despotism of the lesser officials was limited only by the despotism of their superiors."[39] The development of the French administration brought about the breakdown of limitations on the autocratic power of the chief and the Administrator—to the point where the most important check on the misuse of power was the ignorance of the man exercising it. There were a few men, like Lieutenant Chaudron in Nioro and Paul Brocard in Kaolack, whose ignorance only made their exercise of power more irrational. Brocard regarded the least expression of opinion as subversive of his authority, and even requested the dismissal of the pro-French qadi Abdou Kane when he signed a petition requesting a change in certain regulations.[h]

Checks on French Authority

In the early years of the twentieth century, two checks on arbitrary power did develop. We might speak of them as the intrusion of literacy and the development of political consciousness. A class of letter writers, literate young men who could handle the complaints of the illiterate, had developed around the turn of the century, and by 1910 the administration was receiving a significant number of letters from peasants. The letter writer not only wrote what the peasant wanted, but framed the peasant's case and presented it to the proper authorities. Obviously, the Administrators did not like this interference. Brocard wrote the Lieutenant Governor that justice was impossible

[h] Administrator of Sine-Saloum to Lt. Governor, 6 Sept. 1910, ARS, unclassified. Brocard considered Kane the instigator of a petition requesting changes in the regulation of Koranic schools. In other cases, Brocard asked criminal action against a peasant who complained about his canton chief and against a former clerk who had written a letter criticizing one of the Administrator's judicial decisions. Administrator to Lt. Governor, 26 Aug. 1909, ARS, unclassified.

under these conditions.[40] In fact, it meant that the exercise of
authority was more exposed. At every level, the man who exercised authority knew that he might be called on to justify his
actions.

The letter writers had more freedom of action when they were
from the Four Communes. In dealing with subjects, the Administrator had the right to impose jail sentences of up to fifteen
days without any judicial proceedings for a variety of charges,
among which was "any disrespectful act or remark insulting to a
representative or an agent of the Government."[41] Men from the
Four Communes were citizens and were not subject to this arbitrary treatment.

The most striking case involved Brocard and Mody M'Baye,
a former schoolteacher, who was accused of being an agitator
and was dismissed; subsequently he became a very active poli-
tician and public writer. In December 1912, M'Baye wrote Brocard presenting certain claims for a client. When Brocard did
not act favorably, M'Baye published his letter in *Le Petit Sénégalais,* a St. Louis newspaper. Shortly thereafter, when M'Baye
appeared in Kaolack on other business, he was arrested and sentenced to fifteen days in jail for having written an "insulting
letter." M'Baye immediately dashed off a telegram to the Governor-General and was freed within twenty-four hours, much to
Brocard's frequently restated displeasure.[42] Ponty feared any
incident that could be picked up by the Paris press and might
damage the administration's influence.

Another such incident took place when the Resident for Sine
set up camp on a peasant's fields, destroying the man's crops. The
Resident defended himself by saying that the village chief chose
the site. This was probably true, and the peasant was probably
a man who had given the chief trouble. However, the peasant's
case was presented by Galandou Diouf, who ran a shop for one
of the commercial houses in Nianing. The Resident was repri-
manded, and the peasant probably received some kind of compensation.[43] Diouf, who was then a member of the Conseil
Général, was associated for many years with Blaise Diagne, and
succeeded Diagne as Senegal's deputy in Paris.

Most of the citoyens were not interested in taking on the problems of the subjects, and insisted only on exercising their right to organize their own social groups. Brocard, who regarded any group not under his direct control as subversive, tried to break up the most important of these groups and arrest its leader. The group turned out to be merely a mutual aid society organized to help needy members and to pay for certain religious festivals. Brocard constantly protested what he considered the arrogance of the members and the illegal activities of the leader, who set himself up as an informal chief of the citoyens; but he was never able to prove anything, and citoyens were exempt from his arbitrary authority.[44]

The existence of this small but vociferous body of public opinion was a check on the arbitrary power of the Administrator. Until this time, only the commercial houses could go over the Administrator's head and exert pressure on him. The Burs had written letters, generally in badly translated and possibly inaccurate Arabic, but they had neither a friend at court nor a knowledge of how to frame their claims. The citoyens from the Four Communes had a Conseil Général with some control over local finances and a representative in the Chamber of Deputies. The increasing assertiveness of the citoyens in Kaolack was part of the same developing self-consciousness that led to the election in 1914 of the first African deputy, Blaise Diagne.[45]

The Reservoir of Men

The existence of a body of literate and politically self-conscious citizens served as a check on arbitrary actions, but it did not change the autocratic nature of the bureaucracy. It is possible that the literate citizens made the administration more effective by toning down its excesses. The mature system as it existed in 1910 was an efficient and effective one. In 1912 it endured a test that was a dry run for the stresses of the war. The test, which tried the administration as it had not been tried since the imposition of the head tax in the early 1890's, was the beginning of recruitment.

There was nothing new about recruitment. It was a largely African army that conquered the interior of Africa for France.

And France had often called on African allies to help with military operations elsewhere. The tyeddo of Sine and Saloum took part in the Djoloff campaign of 1890. In 1892, there was recruitment for a campaign in Dahomey, and in 1895 for one in Madagascar, with limited results in both cases. Noirot wrote after the Madagascar recruitment:

> The only way to get volunteers is to make them leave, and in using force, though I am very respectful of individual liberty, I do not believe that I am attacking it, because they have no conception of that liberty and the only way to make it known is to give our protégés an education in conformity with our spirit and our sentiments.[46]

In 1904, the recruiting of reserves was begun, though at Lefilliâtre's suggestion no effort was made to demand reserves from Niombato, Rip, and eastern Saloum. The first training camp found itself in difficulty because none of the cadres sent down to train the Sine tyeddo spoke Serer.[47] Lefilliâtre also had difficulty persuading the military authorities not to hold camp during the rainy season. He warned them that no one would show up.[48]

The serious difficulties began after France, motivated by rising tensions in Europe, decided to introduce conscription. For a generation, a number of French military men, disturbed about the declining French birth rate and the increasing disproportion between the populations of France and Germany, had been talking about French West Africa as a "reservoir of men" that could restore the balance of numbers in Europe. A decree proclaimed on October 25, 1912, first instituted "recruitment." The military authorities were to notify the administration of their needs, and the administration was to set up quotas of approximately one recruit for every thousand people. They were to be chosen from physically fit men aged 20 to 28. Exemptions were granted to criminals, the insane, and those needed to support a family or to work in the local administration. The Commandant divided his quota among the canton chiefs, and each canton chief used the most appropriate methods for getting men in his area.[49] From that date to the war, there was scarcely a report that did not mention some incident—a village that refused or a village that fled rather than turn over its young men—and to every such report, Brocard attached assurances that these demonstrations did not reflect the true sentiments of the population. No other period shows a correspondence with so many reports of trouble and of chiefs' protestations of devotion.

The area that resisted the draft most passionately was Niombato. This area was being swamped by immigrants, but it still preserved its autonomy and its hostility to the French. Until 1904, the only contact with the French administration was the unpleasant annual visit from the tax collector. When a customs station was being built, the workers were bombarded with stones, and soldiers had to be called in to protect them.[50] The same year Lefilliâtre decided to make a tour of the area. Somehow the word got out that the Europeans were coming, and the people of Djemack and a neighboring village immediately assumed that it was the British Governor coming to take possession. In order that he might find his way, they built a road through the forest from Djemack to Kong, the nearest village on the British side of the border.[51]

Niombato's hostility continued to manifest itself intermittently. The customs men had to go to Bathurst for supplies because the local people would not sell them food.[52] But taxes were collected, nearby Sokone showed a rapid commercial development, and things seemed to be getting better until the recruiting crisis. At first, Fodé Karamo, the canton chief, refused to provide recruits. When threatened with loss of his job, he agreed to try, but when faced with the opposition of his own people, he refused again. No local chief would carry out the administration's will, so Diogou Bâ was brought in from Nioro. Within several months, he was chased from the area by the local people, recruiting was suspended, and one of the Resident's guards was installed as acting chief.

THE TRIUMPH OF ISLAM

IN THE GENERATION that followed the breach of Saër Maty's tata at Goumbof, a small army of humble and unarmed marabouts won the final victory that had eluded Ma Bâ's proud warriors. Where force had failed, a network of itinerant marabouts succeeded. Some traveled from place to place. Others settled down, sometimes in their home villages, and combined farming with part-time teaching. The more successful set up schools and lived off their fees and the labor of their talibés, though often these schools had fewer than five talibés.

The most striking victory for Islam during this period was the conversion of Saloum, an accomplishment closely related to the decline of the traditional political system. There were several reasons why the Serer state in Saloum, which had functioned so well when threatened on the battlefield, suddenly lost its vitality. First, none of Semou Djimit Diouf's successors was able to make himself indispensable as an intermediary between the colonial regimes and the local units. Second, when the French deposed several of Saloum's Burs, the mystique of the Burship dissipated. Third, Saloum underwent more social change than Sine; and fourth, it already contained subsidiary chiefships approximately the size of cantons, which could be readily subsumed into the political system devised by the French.

Nevertheless, Islamization was both the most important cause and the most important effect of the decline of the traditional state.[1] In 1891 there were only a handful of Moslem villages in Serer areas. Bur Saloum Guédel M'Bodj became a Moslem at about this time, probably in order to win the loyalties of his very refractory Wolof subjects in eastern Saloum. In doing so, he

alienated many of his tyeddo, scarred warriors who had spent
most of their lives in a bitter war against Moslem militants.
Semou Djimit Diouf remained pagan, but by the time he died
in 1898 the tyeddo, once the major barrier to Islamization, were
rapidly ceasing to have any influence over the chiefs. Whether
by conviction or for practical political reasons, after 1898 most
Saloum chiefs—both Burs and canton chiefs—were Moslem.
Foundiougne and Kaolack also were predominantly Moslem. Increasingly, chiefs and traders carried the peasants with them,
and an ever greater number of villages included marabouts, men
who mixed teaching with agriculture and slowly established
local leadership positions. The Foundiougne-Niombato area was
swamped with Moslem immigrants, and was heavily Moslem by
World War I. The following statistics, supplied by Paul Marty,
show the numbers and the percentage of Moslems in the five
circumscriptions of Sine-Saloum in the period just before the
war. (The figures are probably for 1912–13.)[2]

	Total Population	No. of Moslems	Percentage of Moslems
Rip	20,850	19,301	93%
Eastern Saloum	13,284	10,742	81%
Lower Saloum (Foundiougne- Niombato)	19,508	15,419	80%
Western Saloum (Serer core area)	42,668	18,193	43%
Sine	86,616	12,697	15%

These figures reveal a high correlation between Islamization and
socioeconomic change. Lower Saloum and western Saloum—
central areas which had been heavily pagan in 1887 but where
large numbers had subsequently converted to Islam—experienced rapid change in the period between the conquest and the
war. (Moslems had made up less than 15 per cent of the population of western Saloum in 1887.) Significantly less change
occurred in eastern Saloum, which was already heavily Moslem
in 1887, and in Sine, which remained predominantly pagan.

The French tended to be very ambivalent toward Islam;
hence, their policies were often inconsistent. Faidherbe had

established, over Catholic objections, a policy of favoring Islam and using Moslem leaders who were willing to cooperate with the French government. In response to Faidherbe's policy, there had emerged in Senegalese Moslem communities a willingness to accept and even support the overlordship of Christians in return for jobs and freedom of religion. Not all of Faidherbe's successors saw the question as clearly as he did, but most were realistic enough to know that Islam had to be lived with, and some even saw it as a "civilizing" force. At the same time, there was often scorn for the low level of Moslem learning, contempt for the motives of the crusading marabouts, and fear of the force that Moslem religious feeling could and did manifest in opposition to the French.

Le Chatelier was one of those critical of the way many of the French encouraged Islam. He pointed to the rapid progress Islam had made in St. Louis and in Oualo under French rule. In St. Louis, the number of Moslem schools doubled between 1880 and 1890, and the market for Arabic books printed in Beirut or Smyrna was rapidly increasing. His study of Islam convinced him of the Moslems' growing power, and he concluded:

> Every day it becomes harder and harder to tear down the barrier that rises between us. They are conscious of their role as a part of the Moslem world, in opposition to Christian society. Without reaching the point of applying reformist formulas to us [*nous appliquer les formules réformistes*], many look forward to a political revolution that will eventually give their party hegemony in the country.[3]

And yet French efforts to control Islam or regulate its expansion were a resounding failure, none more so than the effort to regulate Koranic schools. In 1893, a regulation that required the licensing of all religious teachers was announced. It was ineffective in most of Senegal, and no effort was made to apply it in Sine-Saloum.[4] Instead, Noirot, who was antagonistic to these Koranic schools and wanted to make the study of French a condition of attendance, competed with them by introducing the study of Arabic into the French schools. The 1893 regulation was followed by new efforts, including a requirement that teachers of the Koran speak French. It immediately proved unenforceable.

In 1903, Lt. Governor Camille Guy decreed that no Koranic schools were to be opened without authorization. In order to open a school, the marabout was to be examined by a commission that included the Administrator and at least one person who knew Arabic. Most important, no school was to be open during the hours of the French school, and all students at the Koranic school were to attend the French school. This decree was also unenforceable. Paul Marty pointed out in a perceptive report ten years later that in most cercles the administration had no one to examine the marabouts, and even in places where it did, most of the applicants would not receive the authorization sought. To force the talibés to attend French schools would only destroy the Moslem schools without aiding French cultural policy.[5]

In fact, the Administrators seem to have realized that destruction of the Koranic schools would only have caused serious political problems. Nevertheless, some of the schools were closed. Lefilliâtre observed that none of the marabouts met the requirements of the law, but he insisted that one teacher in each of the major trading towns be permitted to keep a school open.[6] No real effort to enforce the regulations seems to have been made outside the areas of direct administration. In 1905, Lefilliâtre sent in a list of marabouts teaching in the villages, but commented that since there were no French schools, there was no reason to enforce the regulations.[7] Many important marabouts were, of course, in the villages at this time, and it is probable that one of the reactions to French efforts at regulation was that even more marabouts moved to the villages. By 1913, according to Marty, there were 131 marabouts in the five residencies of Sine-Saloum; these marabouts had 721 students, more than half of them in Kaolack.[8] Marty recognized that this was an underestimate. Even before Marty's study, local administrators dropped the effort to control Koranic schools and force the study of French. In spite of French efforts to slow the growth of the schools, they clearly enrolled more students than French schools in Senegal did until the end of World War II.[9]

Many of the charges the French leveled against the smaller Koranic schools were undoubtedly true. Most marabouts probably had a minimal understanding of Arabic and minimal knowledge of Moslem law and theology. There were marabouts who maintained a high level of learning, who had studied law and theology, and who were masters of the Arabic language, but they were few. And yet the village marabout's limitations were partly responsible for his success. In a nonliterate society, the barely literate man can be the carrier of literacy. The village marabout was in and of the village, and his literary skills made it possible for him to be an intermediary between the more learned Moslem communities and the peasantry. The quality of his learning was not as important as his effectiveness as a teacher and a proselytizer.

The ties binding village to town and region to region stretched across Senegal, and in some cases extended to the maraboutic tribes of Mauritania. Seen superficially, the new loyalties merely created new dimensions of conflict—for example, struggles between the major tariqas were superimposed on the old particularisms. But seen in broader perspective, Islam transcended those particularisms, for it involved the individual both in a tariqa, which was often international, and in the larger unity of Islam. After peace was established, these newer loyalties increasingly took precedence over the old.

Of the tariqas operating in Senegambia, two were of special importance, the Tijaniyya and the Mourides. These two were dominated by a small number of marabouts renowned for learning and for piety, who ran schools that maintained a high standard of learning. The most important within Sine-Saloum was Abdoulaye Niasse, a Wolof born in Djoloff. Niasse's father, descended from a line of blacksmiths, was a marabout who had migrated to Rip, probably at the time of Ma Bâ's retreat from Djoloff in 1865. The father, Mamadou, founded the village of Niacene, and Abdoulaye later founded Taiba Niacene. He was initiated into the Tijaniyya by a follower of Umar in about 1875.

Niasse had been associated with Saër Maty, but had remained in Rip after the latter's flight. While he did not cause any difficulties, Niasse had as little contact with the French as possible, and continued to run his school. According to one Commandant at Nioro,

> Abdoulaye is the leader of all the marabouts of Rip and of Saloum, and is superior to all of them—consequently, he enjoys a great authority over the masses.
>
> In appearance, he is not hostile to the French in spite of his antecedents. He does not seem, however, to have frankly rallied [to our side. He] avoids any relationship with the French authorities, but is careful not to make any errors.[10]

In 1890, Niasse made the pilgrimage to Mecca, stopping briefly at Fez, where Ahmad at-Tijani is buried. After his return, Niasse found himself faced with harassment by Mandiaye Bâ, probably because Bâ feared Niasse's influence and his large following. In 1900, a disagreement with Bâ forced Niasse to flee to the Gambia with the people of three villages, including most of his two hundred talibé. The villages were then burned and pillaged by Mandiaye's men.[11]

In 1910, after his return from a second visit to Fez, Niasse wrote the Governor:

> I have lived for a long time in perfect tranquillity, and spend my time cultivating my fields and teaching the Koran to young people who address themselves to me and who want to have themselves initiated by me into the study of the holy books.[12]

Niasse promised not to meddle in politics, and asked permission to return home. Later that year, he established himself just outside Kaolack. His reputation preceded him, and he was, almost from the day of his arrival, the most important religious personality in the cercle.[a]

---

[a] Niasse's son, Al Hajj Ibrahima Niasse, has built on his father's reputation, and today has a substantial following in Senegal and in other African countries, the largest being in northern Nigeria. Once a year Niasse's followers come to Medina, the Kaolack suburb where his mosque and school are located, to pay their respects. I am indebted to Al Hajj Ibrahima Niasse for information about

Abdoulaye Niasse's letter may have received more favorable consideration because it was written from the home of Al Hajj Malik Sy of Tivouane. The *Malikiyya* branch of the Tijaniyya benefited from official patronage because of Malik Sy's refusal to meddle in politics and his willingness to leave the secular and political domain to Caesar. Malik Sy's great influence with Senegalese Moslems, however, was due more to his reputation for piety and the high standards of learning at his school in Tivouane. The Malikiyya Tijaniyya differed from the more militant and military *Omariyya* branch in its attitude toward the French.[13] Malik Sy had a large following throughout Senegal, including talibé in at least a dozen places in Sine-Saloum. The most important of these was Abdou Kane, Malik Sy's son-in-law. Kane was a Toucouleur, born and raised in St. Louis. Though he was brought to Kaolack by the French as a qadi, he opened a school that was the most popular in the direct administration area until the arrival of Niasse.

Kaolack has remained to this day predominantly Tijani, though there is a Mouride minority and the Mourides have important communities elsewhere in the cercle. Mouridism is a Senegalese and largely Wolof phenomenon, a breakaway from the Qadiriyya.[14] Its founder, Amadou Bamba M'Backé, was a member of a marabout family of Toucouleur origin, which had settled in eastern Baol and become Wolofized. ("M'Backé" is the Wolof form of "Bâ.") Amadou Bamba's father, Momar Anta Sali, had migrated to Rip, where he founded a school at Porokhane and taught Ma Bâ's children, including Saër Maty. Momar Anta Sali returned to Cayor as a qadi with Lat Dior, and Amadou Bamba later returned to the family home in Baol. Amadou Bamba studied the Koran in Mauritania and gained a sound foundation in Moslem learning. He early attracted a substantial following, and may well have had political ambitions, as Marty suggests; but if this is so, he was very careful to avoid open rebellion. There were, however, many incidents attributable to

his family and his own religious activities. Ibrahima Niasse is known for his mastery of Arabic and his efforts to raise educational standards. For sources on Niasse, see Note 12, p. 259.

Bamba's following, and his refusal to have anything to do with the new proconsuls aroused French fears. They watched him carefully throughout his career, deported him twice, and after permitting him to return, denied him permission to settle in Touba, his chosen religious center. Instead, he had to remain in Diourbel, the nearby administrative center, until his death in 1927.

Amadou Bamba's greatest success was with the tyeddo and peasants of Cayor and Baol, in particular those who had earlier resisted Islam. Marty describes Bamba's following thus:

> It consists mainly of rural elements, tyeddo or peasants, lords or serfs—the heirs of the old pre-1886 order. These are the men whose fathers embraced Islam between 1860 and 1885, seeking in religion a base for resistance. . . . For them, the marabouts have replaced the Braks, Burbas, Damels, and their feudal lords, and it is under the banner of the Qadiriyya that they find themselves today. It is around Amadou Bamba, founder of the Mouride branch of the Qadiriyya and former chaplain of the last Damels, Samba Laobé and Lat Dior, that this group is largely gathered.[15]

Amadou Bamba made a vigorous effort to convert the remaining pagan chiefs and succeeded with several, but not with the Bur Sine. Islam was most successful where the traditional state had begun to break down, and no longer effectively fused the religious, economic, and political spheres. In Sine, the state was still functioning, and Coumba N'Doffène Diouf carefully guarded his ritual role, a role that was incompatible with Islamization. The Bur encouraged the Mouride marabouts, was hospitable to them, and gave gifts to those who prayed for him, but he remained the Bur and did not convert.

Mouridism is characterized by a general militancy, by the importance of the marabout as an intermediary between God and the believer, and by a belief in the value of work. Even before World War I, Mourides had founded agricultural colonies, where communities of the faithful lived under the leadership of marabouts who monopolized and distributed the wealth pro-

duced by the land.[16] The coming of the railroad made eastern
Saloum a prime target for setting up these communities. Gossas,
just within Sine, was founded by a Mouride marabout, Khar
Kane, in 1907, and as the railroad moved further east every new
station was the site of fights for land between the Mourides and
other claimants, many of them prior inhabitants.

In early 1912, Brocard estimated the Mouride population in
the railroad zone to be about seven thousand. He was disturbed
by the Mourides' presence, largely because they started fights
both by claiming others' land and by trying to convert other
Moslems forcibly. Brocard reported to the Governor:

> In addition to the militants who form the backbone of this
> army, there are numerous converts, who are much more dan-
> gerous because they are new to the religion, and thus become
> fanatic more easily.
>
> The Mourides are good farmers; that much is undeniable.
> They bring to labor a zeal and a discipline that produce ex-
> cellent results. But where does the product of this labor go?
> The merchants who live among them complain that they sell
> very little merchandise [to the Mourides] considering the
> amount they pay out for peanuts.[17]

The Mourides tried to penetrate Nioro also, and isolated Mouride communities were established in other parts of the cercle,
but in general the Mourides remained strongest in the new lands
of eastern Saloum.

In part, this was because Islam was already well established
in Nioro and in the commercial centers. The largely Tijani urban
communities had long played a major role in the extension of
Islam. With the exception of the small Christian communities
on Gorée and the Petite Côte, the trading communities have
been Moslem for a long time. Le Chatelier complained that for
the traders of St. Louis, the study of law and religion was second
only to their professional concerns.[18] During the religious wars,
these Moslem traders provided Umar, Lat Dior, and Ma Bâ with
both moral and financial support, though many also served the
French as clerks and soldiers. When the wars ended, they gave

increasing attention to education and religious concerns. Urbanization led to both the conversion of pagan migrants and a deeper commitment to Islam in those who had already converted because old elites and old deities were meaningless in large towns like St. Louis and Kaolack. The process of urbanization involved not so much detribalization as the adaptation of the newcomer to a Moslem Wolof urban culture, in which the mosque was the center of social activity.

This meant that the marabout took over many of the roles once filled by the chief. The French unwittingly aided the process by transforming the nature of chiefship. In the traditional state the Bur was the center of different spheres of activity. He was judge, political authority, and conciliator of the gods, who could assure good harvests. The French made the chief a bureaucrat, a secular official deprived of any religious functions. Only in a few areas like Sine did he continue to play his traditional role. Everywhere else the chief was burdened with unpopular tasks such as recruiting soldiers and collecting taxes, so the marabout took over his social and religious functions. The marabout prayed for rain, handled death and marriage, and with help from the French, became the source of law. Furthermore, the most successful marabouts were not those like the Bâ family, who accepted French authority, but those who sought to avoid any association with the French. Amadou Bamba and Abdoulaye Niasse threatened the French not because they were revolutionaries, but because they wished to have nothing to do with the conqueror. In the long run, France had to deal with the Niasses and the Bambas because they and their followers were successful in fusing once again political and religious authority, though they did it primarily on the village level, where French power was not omnipresent. In 1915, Brocard commented on the replacement of the chiefs by the marabouts:

> In recent times, the marabout—under our protection and free from responsibility and from annoyances—makes fruitful collections, takes in a sort of ritual tax, and has his fields worked; in short, he monopolizes all of the privileges that custom ac-

cords the chiefs without accepting any burdens in exchange. And we watch this spectacle, in which the most respected chiefs present their homage to marabouts from whom they have the right to demand the most humble obedience.[19]

The French aided Islam in other ways as well. They often placed Moslem chiefs in pagan or half-pagan areas; and even in places where they carefully avoided this pitfall, French authority was represented by Moslem clerks, guards, and interpreters.

Le Chatelier's fear that Islamization would transform the Senegalese into an anti-Christian community was exaggerated, but Islamization did create a non-Christian urban culture that could serve as an effective alternative to assimilation with the French ideal. Although assimilation was more talked about than implemented, Senegal has had a longer and more intimate contact with French culture than has any other colony.

Thus, the Senegalese moving out of traditional societies have had a choice of cultures on which to model their norms, values, and patterns of behavior. In Christian or pagan areas of Africa, Europeans often became the most important reference group for Africans who came in contact with them. In other areas the Moslem elites provided the model for change. The two cultures were not necessarily in conflict. The Mourides, for example, pushed the value of work and production for market as vigorously as any modernizing administrator—and with greater effect. However, individualistic and competitive values, which are often associated with economic development and the growth of a market economy, were inhibited by the new marabout-dominated collectivities. Learning and piety increasingly became as important a source of prestige as valor and generosity had been. Once the wars had ended, the warriors had few opportunities to prove their valor, and they ceased to be a significant social group. Certain aspects of tyeddo culture linger on, but in general it has been replaced by Islam as a source of values.

CONCLUSION

I HAVE SAID very little in this study about the terms often used by writers on French colonialism: "direct rule" and "indirect rule," "assimilation" and "association." If these terms have any validity at all, they are oversimplifications of what existed. As far as direct and indirect rule are concerned, the French ideal was certainly direct rule. The French bureaucracy was motivated by a Cartesian zeal for logical structures, and sought to create a neat, logical system in which the lines of authority were simple, clear, and direct and in which power was effectively centralized.

The administration wanted to achieve control by making the chiefs instruments of French policy; but the Administrator, as the man on the spot, often had to be pragmatic if he wanted French authority to take root. In Sine, for example, some form of indirect rule was most effective for getting the Administrator's will done, and Lefilliâtre saw this. The classical French canton structure evolved most clearly where social and religious change had weakened the traditional structure and made the traditional lines of authority fuzzy. Even in these areas, the canton chief was never quite like a functionary in Toulouse. Ponty's "politique des races" was a recognition of the need to respect the ethnic ties and traditional political and social structures that made an African colony different from an overseas version of France.

In Senegal I often asked retired chiefs just what the canton chief's job consisted of. In all cases, the first two things the chiefs listed were recruitment and the collection of taxes. Only when pressed a little did several of them talk about the chief's role as an intermediary between the people and the administration. In the Gambia, I asked two chiefs the same question. Both mentioned first their judicial responsibilities—that is, they stressed their responsibilities to their own communities rather than to higher authorities. This pinpoints a very important difference between the British and the French—at least within the Senegambian area.[a] The British, though remaining more aloof from African society than the French, respected the African community and attached great importance to judicial proceedings. The French thought more in terms of order, obedience, and devotion, and the African chiefs quickly adapted to the official myth by continually protesting their devotion, even in routine correspondence. In such a system, the successful chiefs were of necessity good liars, but it is difficult to say how seriously the administration regarded the chiefs' protestations of love. At any rate, the administration took care to tie the chiefs' interests to its own.

The differences between the two systems should not be exaggerated, however. Both the French and the British governed indirectly inasmuch as they remained outside the societies they ruled, operating through and dependent on the chiefs. But both governed directly insofar as they kept real power in their own hands. The British Resident in Zaria or Kano had as much power as his French counterpart in Kaolack. The difference was not in the relationship between the chiefs and the colonial authority, but in the fact that the French incorporated the chiefs in their

[a] Of course, this may not be so much the chief's conception of his role as his conception of what he should say to a white interviewer. The difference is still instructive. However, the differences in political institutions within each colonial system were probably greater than the differences between them. For a model of chiefship very similar to that created by the French, see D. A. Low, "British East Africa: The Establishment of British Rule, 1895–1912," in Vincent Harlow and E. M. Chilver, *History of East Africa,* II (Oxford, 1965), 38–56.

For other comparisons, see M. G. Smith, *Government in Zassau* (London, 1960), chap. 6; and J. C. Anene, *Southern Nigeria in Transition, 1885–1906* (Cambridge, 1966). Smith describes the transformation of the Zaria fief-holders from feudal retainers into district heads, salaried officials with carefully specified administrative responsibilities. The transformation is similar to the change that took place in Sine-Saloum.

superstructure while the British in northern Nigeria preserved the emirates and tried to modernize them.[1] This difference was largely the result of the differing assumptions about government and administration that the two bureaucracies took to Africa. The French ideal was Napoleonic and Cartesian: rationality, centralization, and the imposition of equal-sized units. The British ideal—reinforced by Britain's experience in India—was the preservation of traditional status roles and institutions.

As for "assimilation" and "association," neither term was at all relevant. Ponty's "politique des races" can be viewed as an implementation of the theory of association, but the African societies were not actually associated with France.[2] They were subservient. The ideal of assimilation did have some effect on attitudes—for example, there was a universal belief in the value of French education—but it had little effect on French policy. The schools had a very limited and practical goal: the satisfaction of the administration's personnel needs. Thus, the French educated clerks and trained soldiers. Of the Administrators in Sine-Saloum, only Ernest Noirot was strongly influenced by an assimilationist ideal.

In fact, the earlier products of assimilationist ideas were, for the Administrators, bitter fruit. Even though the expansion of self-governing institutions created according to French models was checked, the Four Communes still had their deputy, their Conseil Général, and their municipal counselors. The abolition of these institutions was not possible under the Third Republic; and against the administration's will, they contributed to a political self-consciousness that was just beginning to become evident in the early twentieth century. They also forced the administration to be very cautious. It could not permit incidents that would be given sensational and embarrassing publicity in the Paris press. The politically conscious community was a small one, but it and the fortunes of history forced France in later years to make the ideal of assimilation more meaningful.

Though these four much-used terms give us only limited insights, we can make other, more useful, generalizations. Throughout the period studied, economic interests played a major role in determining policy. Protection of the trade that had begun in the 1840's was the most important reason for sending military forces into Sine-Saloum on four occasions, and the rapid expansion of that trade was the constant concern of the Administrator. In addition, the reluctance of the Chamber of Deputies to appropriate funds for the colonies forced the administration to find those funds in Africa. Between 1891 and 1912, the collection of the head tax was the single activity in the cercle that consumed the most time and paper.

In assessing the importance of the economic influence on colonial policies, we must consider both the nature of the Administrators and the pressures that could be brought to bear on them. Few Administrators came to Africa in quest of fortune. They were much more strongly influenced by psychological imperatives: a desire to command, a desire to act, and in many cases a desire to shape the societies they administered. Consequently there were disagreements among merchants and Administrators, such as the conflict between Noirot and the syndicate over peanut prices and the dissatisfaction of many merchants with forced recruitment. But, as Hubert Deschamps has pointed out, the merchants' interests were not often in conflict with the enlightened despotism of the Administrator. And when they were, the commercial houses could and did exert considerable influence on higher authorities, sometimes going so far as to get Administrators posted elsewhere.[3] Only in the years just before World War I was there an African group that could influence policy, and it had only one deputy.

There were, of course, other factors motivating policy. The colonies had their own political interests—order and security in particular. The colonial administration wanted to stay on good terms with influential groups in metropolitan France, and the individual bureaucrat was interested in his advancement. In fact, an important factor disturbing continuity in the cercles was the desire of each Administrator to leave his own mark on the district he commanded, and thus to make changes in what his predecessor had done. The most important political question, however, was the maintenance of good relations with the Chamber of Deputies—though the Chamber did not closely survey colonial affairs, and the administration had a great deal of leeway as long as there were no scandals. With the exception of the elected representatives of the Four Communes, the people to whom the Administrator was answerable were French. This does not mean that all French power was exploitative—French idealism, for example, stimulated the abolition of the slave trade. What it does mean is that Africa played no role in administering Africa, and African interests were reflected in administration policies only to the degree that was necessary to maintain peace and quiet, and to the degree that the administration was motivated by certain lofty ideals.

Though economic interests brought France to Africa, for Paris colonial economic interests always remained secondary to continental affairs that affected national security. In fact, to the degree that France was threatened there, events in Europe shaped policies in Africa. This is particularly true of the forced recruitment of an African army that helped save France from German conquest in World War I. The 1912 decision to undertake forced recruitment represents a recognition of the primacy of the military security of France over African interests and French commercial interests.

From the African point of view, events in the nineteenth century resulted in a radical change in the form and distribution of power in Africa, even though the process of change was not sudden but was rather a gradual buildup of pressure on the Africans to adapt to new circumstances. The fact of change was not new, but its magnitude was. The final result of the changes introduced by the Europeans was the inability of African states to defend themselves from external threats. Previous African history, like all history, had been a constant process of innovation and adaptation. Five centuries earlier, the revolutionary innovation had been the Mandinka state model brought by the guelowar invaders. Earlier yet, it had been iron tools and weapons. During the nineteenth century, African blacksmiths learned how to make guns and many African leaders succeeded in turning new weapons technology to their own purposes. For example, Al Hajj Umar Tall, skillfully used his one cannon to good advantage against his African enemies. And the oral tradition records that in a conversation the night before the battle of Pathébadiane, Ma Bâ said to Lat Dior: "You know the white men and their ways. Tell us how we should fight them." Lat Dior wisely chose a wooded depression where his men could make contact before the French cannon decimated their ranks.

However, the processes of adaptation were slow, as the failure of Umar's blacksmiths to set up a cannon foundry illustrates. Africa was technologically too backward and had too limited an industrial base to compete effectively with constantly evolving European military technology. At Goumbof, Coronnat's rifles had twice the range of Saër Maty's.

And the power available to European representatives was rapidly increasing. Improvements in ship construction made possible a greater exploitation of tropical products. Although tropical diseases still took a high toll, progress in medical science made it possible for European troops to function in tropical areas. The power of France in Sine-Saloum after 1887 was such that there was no meaningful threat to French authority, though the Diouma affair aroused the fears of certain Administrators. In certain areas, especially some strongly Moslem communities, Africans refused to have anything to do with the conquerors. However, until those hostile to French power could transcend the traditional and limited loyalties that divided them, there could be no political base for unity. Coumba N'Doffène knew nothing of Africa and little of Senegal. His loyalties were to Sine, and he could come to terms with St. Louis more easily than with Nioro. Bur Sine Mahecor Diouf said in opening a session on the oral history of Sine: "I, Mahecor Diouf, am the bearer of the traditions of Sine and the heir of Maïssa Waly Dione."

Many of the proud bearers of Serer tradition stood valiantly against the irresistible forces of change represented by both the French and the Moslem crusaders. Under Coumba N'Doffène I, Sine was able to bar the Moslem advance and to limit French domination. In Saloum, the traditional state was able to call forth the services of the M'Bodj brothers in its war against marabout invaders. But under Coumba N'Doffène's successors, the structural weaknesses of the state made Sine the pawn of outside forces; and Saloum's need for allies in the battle against Islam furthered its dependence on the French, who proved to be as destructive of the Serer state as the marabout armies of Ma Bâ's heirs. In waging war against the Serer, Ma Bâ was, of course, only trying to carry out the will of God as he understood it. However, Ma Bâ Diakhou's quest for a strong and unified Islam was to be accomplished not through his military victories but through the missionary fervor he inspired in the succeeding generation of marabouts. In fact, the military successes of the ruthless visionary acted to further French domination of Senegal.

The cannon that breached the stone wall at Goumbof made its point, for the French conquest was accepted by the communities of Sine-Saloum. This does not mean that the new rulers were loved. Many Frenchmen I spoke to in Senegal assured me that the older peasants, who knew about the days before the conquest, were loyal and devoted to the French because the French had brought peace. I have my doubts. To be sure, in large areas the conquest was welcomed, especially in those areas that had been most ravaged by earlier wars. But most of this sort of good will has long been exhausted. Taxes, which the French quickly imposed, were no more popular in Senegal than elsewhere, and both forced labor and forced recruitment aroused great hostility. Certainly there were good Administrators, but too often the brutality of an Allys or the cold authoritarianism of a Brocard canceled out the humanity of their more generous colleagues. The Africans' response to arbitrary rule was often not active but passive resistance, an avoidance of the white man and his ways, a refusal to send children to the white man's school.

In spite of this resistance and a certain peasant conservatism, the processes of economic and social change have been as constant as the processes of political change. Many of the less perceptive Administrators often assumed that they were ruling a static society, but static societies, if they exist at all, are rare. Other Administrators sought to channel the processes of change, but at least one of the important changes, the Islamization of Africa and the Africanization of Islam, was totally beyond the control of the administration. The French conquest unintentionally aided this process by sending Moslem intermediaries into pagan areas and by making possible the free movement of men; but it is difficult to see how the French could have avoided doing so, since the bureaucracy needed literate Africans, who were generally found in Moslem communities.

The development of a market economy was another important change. Henri Brunschwig correctly sees in the African demand for European products one of the most important motive forces in nineteenth- and twentieth-century African history.[4] During the years of the slave trade, the enjoyment of those products was restricted to limited groups. After 1840, when the European merchants became most interested in peanuts, a crop ideally suited for peasant cultivation, peanut growing expanded, and the merchants wanted to make the peasants consumers as well as producers. Thus they urged suppression of laws restricting the peasants' use of European products. The marabouts were more in sympathy with and better able to adapt to the market economy, and were, not surprisingly, more interested in protecting commerce than the traditional pagan societies were. Ironically, the Moslem revolution reached its peak before the economic revolution could offer a real alternative to the slave trade. When the marabout state was at the height of its power, slaves were still the most important form of wealth, partly because they could easily be traded for guns and horses. The Moslems became the biggest slave traders because they were the most successful on the field of battle.

Economic change did not at first bring about radical social change in the traditional societies, and many of the Administrators preferred it that way. In Sine, the peasant culture was capable of adapting to the market economy without too great a strain. Similarly, Sine's political structure was easily incorporated into the larger French superstructure. (This change was made speedily because of the ability of Coumba N'Doffène II to adjust to new circumstances.) These changes had relatively little effect on traditional life. Status distinctions, for example, remained important, and society preserved its hierarchical structure. Thus, although the slave trade had ended, slave status remained.

However, certain changes in status groups and in the role of the chief occurred in Sine just as they did in other parts of the cercle. The tyeddo ceased to be an independent and influential status group, and members of that group rapidly merged with the peasantry soon after being deprived of their functional distinction. New groups moved into the society—clerks, traders, teachers—groups that had no assigned places in the traditional society. Most importantly, when the traditional political systems were incorporated into the modern bureaucratic state, the nature of political authority changed. The dominant leaders of the old order were transformed into the bureaucratic cogs of the new. During and after World War I more intrusive factors made themselves felt in Sine: first, military service, Islam, and the migration of young men to the cities; later, modern nationalism and the radio.

However, adaptation worked in both directions in colonial Senegal, and in many respects colonial power was, in effect, Africanized. At the same time the administration was working to transform the chief's functions, it was exploiting—and thereby recognizing—his traditional authority. To bring about a complete transformation of traditional rule, the administration would have had to spend more funds than the French Chamber of Deputies was willing to approve. The granting of "wives" to the tirailleurs was simply a more extreme way of adapting to African realities—a bizarre footnote to the "mission civilisatrice."

New religious movements too were forced to find common ground with African cultures. Africanization has, in fact, been one of the strengths of African Islam. The itinerant marabout, often scorned by his more learned Catholic rivals, has been more successful because he is African; and the Koran is all the more widely accepted because it is taught with an African accent. In this, as in other things, the new Senegal, far from being totally shaped by outside forces, guards its continuity with its African past. Change is constant, and yesterday's revolution provides the basis for the dynamic processes of today.

NOTES

NOTES

From 1856 on, the colonial government in Senegal published an official gazette under various titles. From 1856–59, it was *Moniteur du Sénégal et Dépendances: Journal Officiel*; in 1860 it became *Feuille Officielle du Sénégal et Dépendances*; and in June 1864, it resumed its original title. There were several title changes after 1888 until, in 1906, it became simply *Journal Officiel du Sénégal*. In 1895, the *Journal Officiel de l'Afrique Occidentale Française* was founded and was published concurrently with the Senegal journal. (In the Notes, titles have been shortened to *Journal Officiel* for the Senegal publications and to *Journal Officiel de l'A.O.F.* for the federation journal.) All of these journals contained lists of awards, statistics, ships in port, and, occasionally, reports on government policies and military campaigns. The government also published a *Bulletin Administratif*, which contained only decrees and edicts.

Complete authors' names, titles, and publication data are given in the Bibliography, pp. 265–77. The following abbreviations are used throughout the notes. For a description of the archives, see p. 265.

AG	Archives of the Gambia.
ANP	Archives Nationales, Paris.
AOF	Afrique Occidentale Française.
ARS	Archives de la République du Sénégal, Dakar (formerly the archives of the French West African Federation).
BCEHS	*Bulletin du Comité d'Etudes Historiques et Scientifiques de l'Afrique Occidentale Française.*
BIFAN	*Bulletin de l'Institut Fondamental de l'Afrique Noire* (1966–). *Bulletin de l'Institut Français de l'Afrique Noire* (until 1966).
CSE	Archives de la Congrégation du Saint Esprit, Paris.
FOM	Archives de la Ministère de la France d'Outre-Mer, Paris.
PRO	Public Record Office, London.

Chapter One

1. Gamble, *Contributions*. See also Rousseau, "Les Pluies." Rousseau's statistics differ a bit from Gamble's but the idea is the same.

2. Pelissier, "Les Paysans Sérères." See also Gravrand, *Horizons*, no. 65, pp. 4–8; no. 67, pp. 15–16; and no. 68, pp. 10–16.

3. W. J. Pichl, "The Congin Group: A Language Group in Northern Senegal" (Pittsburgh, Pa., 1966). I am grateful to Professor Pichl for giving me information on the languages in this part of Senegal before his monograph was published.

4. E.g., see Gamble, *The Wolof*, p. 47. On the role of matrilineage in Serer society, see Diagne; Dulphy; and Geismar.

5. See the bibliography of works on traditional history in Brigaud. On medieval West Africa, see Mauny.

6. On the history of the Serer states, see Gravrand, *Visage*, pp. 19–24; Cros; Aujas, "Les Sérères"; Bourgeau; and Boulègue.

7. V. Monteil, "Lat Dyor."

8. Diagne, p. 153.

9. The best descriptions of Serer social structure are in Gravrand, *Horizons*; and Diagne. See also Aujas, "Les Sérères," pp. 298–99 and pp. 309–11; and Bourgeau, pp. 27–31. On the Wolof, see Gamble, *The Wolof*; Labouret, "Les Paysans," pp. 125–37; and Silla. On the Toucouleur, see Boutillier *et al.*

10. Father Gallais to Father Libermann, 18 Mar. 1849, CSE, 153 VI.

11. Diagne, p. 156.

12. Senghor, "L'Homme noir."

13. Noirot, "Aperçu général" (1896), ARS, 13 G 327.

14. The notion that struggle for control of a political institution can strengthen that institution has been suggested by Gluckman in "Rituals of Rebellion."

15. Aujas, "Les Sérères," pp. 324–29; Bourgeau, p. 24; and oral sources.

Chapter Two

1. Blake, pp. 80–86. See also de Barros, pp. 98–104.

2. For an account of one of the French companies, see A. Ly.

3. Moore, p. 28.

4. Instructions to Chevalier Boufflers, November 1785, ANP, Colonies C6 18. See also Schefer, I, 27, 51.

5. Moore, pp. 127–28.

6. *Ibid.*, pp. 65–66.

7. Marty, pp. 5–24.

8. For the Sine treaty, see ARS, 13 G 31; for Baol, see FOM, Sénégal IV 24 a.

9. "Etat en aperçu des esclaves qui peuvent retirer les nations de l'Europe de la côte occidentale de l'Afrique," ANP C6 18.

10. Barbot, p. 39; Geoffroy de Villeneuve, III, 79–80, 86; Labat, IV, 243; Boilat, pp. 98–99.

11. Moore, pp. 86–87.

12. Letter of Governor Le Brasseur, 14 Apr. 1776, ARS, 5 D 1.

13. Pasquier, "Villes du Sénégal," pp. 387–426; Hargreaves, "Assimilation," pp. 177–84; Jore.

14. Zuccarelli, "L'Entrepôt fictif," p. 264. The quotation is from ARS, 2 B 2.

15. Hardy, *La Mise en valeur*, pp. 1–252.

16. Zuccarelli, "L'Entrepôt fictif," p. 272.

17. I am indebted to Mr. George Brooks for unpublished information about the successful commercial activities of the Gorée coasters.

18. Sauvigny report, 21 June 1822, FOM, Sénégal III 2.

19. Minister to Governor, 5 Feb. 1823, ARS, 1 B 10.

20. Petition of Gorée merchants, 20 June 1837, FOM, Sénégal IV 21 a.

21. Minutes of meetings, Conseil d'arrondissement de Gorée, 18 Sept. 1841, FOM, Sénégal IV 24 B.

22. Commandant of Gorée to Minister, 4 Aug. 1838, FOM Sénégal IV 21 a.

23. Schnapper, *La Politique*, pp. 3–33.

24. *Ibid.* See also Brunschwig, *L'Avènement*, pp. 53–63.

25. Bouët-Willaumez, FOM, Sénégal IV 246.

26. Schnapper, *La Politique*, pp. 118–28, 165.

27. Guiraud, pp. 33–36; Fouquet. I have converted the figures supplied by Guiraud and Fouquet from kilos to tons.

28. Petition of 28 Aug. 1854, quoted in Capperon, "Protet," pp. 14–21.

29. For French imperialism, the most important revisionist work is Brunschwig, *Mythes et Réalités*; on the British, see Robinson and Gallagher. Two other valuable critiques are Stengers and Landes.

30. Governor to Minister, n.d., FOM, Sénégal I 46 a.

31. Circular to several post commanders, 18 Apr. 1865, ARS 3 B 89.

32. Commission des Comptoirs, pp. 5–6.

33. *Ibid.*, pp. 46–67.

34. Pinet-Laprade, *Journal Officiel*, X (1865), 132.

35. On the occupation of Cape Verde and the establishment of Dakar, see Faure, *Histoire*; and Charpy.

36. Governor to Minister, 13 Oct. 1859, FOM, Sénégal I 46 a.

Chapter Three

1. I have not found a copy of this treaty, but an analysis is in ARS, 13 G 311.

2. Commandant of Gorée to Governor, 31 Mar. 1850, ARS, 4 B 16.

3. Captain de Rulhières, "Note sur la rivière de Salum," 25 Feb. 1853, FOM, Sénégal IV 24 b.

4. Captain de Rulhières, letter, 9 Feb. 1853, FOM, Sénégal IV 24 b.

5. Commandant of Gorée to Governor, 21 Dec. 1853, ARS 4 B 18.

6. Gallais to Kobès, 7 Dec. 1849, CSE, Paris, 153 VII; Arragon to Schwindenhammer, 1 Jan. 1849, CSE 153 VI; Gallais, "Royaume de Sine," CSE, 154 A II.

7. Chevalier to Kobès, 18 Jan. 1851, CSE, 154 A I.

8. Commandant of Gorée to Governor, 5 Feb. 1853, ARS, 4 B 18.

9. Luiset to Duby, n.d., CSE, 155 B VI.

10. Oral sources, primarily Bur Sine Mahecor Diouf.

11. Arragon to Libermann, 27 Nov. 1847, CSE, 153 III.

12. Truffet to Archbishop of Chambéry, 30 Nov. 1847, CSE, 153 II.

13. Truffet to Libermann, 19 June 1847, CSE, 153 III.

14. Gallais to Bessieux, 31 Dec. 1848, CSE, 153 V.

15. Arragon to Libermann, 29 Apr. 1847, CSE, 153 III.

16. Gallais to Abbé Grégoire, n.d., CSE, 154 A IV.

17. Gallais to Bessieux, 31 Dec. 1848, CSE, 153 V.

18. Gallais, "Notes sur la mission de Joal," n. d., CSE, 154 V.

19. Gallais to Libermann, 1 Nov. 1848, CSE, 153 V.
20. Gallais to Bessieux, 31 Dec. 1848, CSE, 153 V.
21. *Ibid.*
22. Arragon to Libermann, 29 Apr. 1847, CSE, 153 III.
23. "Notes sur la mission de Joal," n.d., p. 36, CSE, 154 A V.
24. Gallais to Chevalier, 7 Dec. 1849, CSE, 153 VII.
25. October 28, 1849, CSE, 153 VII.
26. Luiset to Schwindenhammer, 27 Mar. 1852, CSE, 155 A II.
27. Gallais to Kobès, 17 Apr. 1850, CSE, 153 VI.
28. Gallais to Bessieux, 31 Dec. 1848, CSE, 153 V.
29. Chevalier to Kobès, 2 Apr. and 6 Apr. 1850, CSE, 154 A II; 23 Feb. 1850, CSE, 154 A I; Luiset to Boulanger, 31 Jan. 1851, CSE, 154 B I.
30. Kobès to Governor, 24 May 1851, CSE, 154 B II.
31. "Rapport sur Joal," CSE, 156 A V.
32. Kobès to Commandant of Gorée, 4 Sept. and 10 Dec. 1855, CSE, 156 A III.
33. Chevalier to Kobès, 24 Sept. 1850, CSE, 154 A IV.
34. Pinet-Laprade to Governor, 9 Aug. 1859, ARS, 13 G 300.
35. Correspondence between Governor of Gambia and Commandant of Gorée, FOM, Gorée IV 1 c.
36. Report to Minister of Algeria and the Colonies, 14 June 1859, FOM, Sénégal IV 50 a.
37. *Ibid.*
38. *Ibid.*
39. FOM, 13 G 318.
40. *Annales Sénégalaises*, p. 406.
41. Governor to Minister, 16 Oct. 1859, FOM, Sénégal I 46 a.
42. ARS, 13 G 318.
43. *Annales Sénégalaises*, p. 237.
44. Minutes of the meeting, Conseil d'Administration, 13 Oct. 1860, FOM, Sénégal IV 50 a.
45. FOM, 13 G 318.
46. Faidherbe, *Le Sénégal*, pp. 258–88.
47. Landes, p. 510.

Chapter Four

1. Semonin, pp. 42–59.
2. Trimingham, *Islam* (Clarendon), pp. 88–101; Gouilly, pp. 85–95; V. Monteil, *L'Islam Noir*, chap. 5; Froelich, chap. 11. For a good short discussion of Sufism, see Gibb, chaps. 8 and 9.
3. On the Moslem revolution, see Smith; Waldman; Gouilly, pp. 96–115; Froelich, chap. 10; and Trimingham, *ibid.*, pp. 94–100.
4. See Abun-Nasr.
5. Trimingham, *History* (Oxford), pp. 181–86; Monteil, *ibid.*, pp. 85–90; Gouilly, pp. 72–76. On Umar's relations with the French, see Saint-Martin.
6. Bâ, *BIFAN*, p. 572.
7. Carrère and Holle, p. 127. See also Boilat, p. 391. For a more recent view of the role of Islam in Toucouleur culture, see the fine novel of Cheikh Hamidou Kane, *L'Aventure ambiguë* (Paris, 1961).
8. Mollien, p. 23.

4. Interview with Masayer Sise, daughter of Biram Cissé, conducted at Yundum, outside Bathurst, the Gambia, November 1963.

5. Administrator of Gambia to Governor-in-Chief, 4 Dec. 1877, AG.

6. Commandant of Kaolack to Commandant of Gorée, 30 Dec. 1871, ARS, 4 B 48.

7. Commandant of Kaolack to Commandant of Gorée, 22 June and 1 July 1871, ARS, 13 G 306.

8. Commandant of Kaolack to Commandant of Gorée, 15 July 1871, ARS, unclassified.

9. Commandant of Kaolack to Commandant of Gorée, 11 Jan. 1872, ARS, unclassified.

10. Commandant of Kaolack to Commandant of Gorée, 29 Mar. 1873, ARS, 13 G 307.

11. Commandant of Joal to Commandant of Gorée, 29 Apr. 1869, ARS, 13 G 314; Commandant of Kaolack to Commandant of Gorée, 29 Apr. 1869, ARS, 13 G 320.

12. Commandant of Joal to Commandant of Gorée, 3 June and 16 June 1868, ARS, 13 G 314.

13. Undated in 1869 dossier, ARS, 13 G 318.

14. See assorted letters, ARS, 13 G 318.

15. Governor of Senegal to Bur Sine, 8 Jan. 1868. ARS, 3 B 89.

16. Commandant of Kaolack to Commandant of Gorée, 20 Feb. 1869, ARS, 13 G 320.

17. Governor of Senegal to Bur Sine, 9 May 1870, ARS, 3 B 95.

18. Commandant of Joal to Commandant of Gorée, 14 Sept. 1871, ARS, unclassified.

19. Commandant of Gorée to Governor of Senegal, 30 Dec. 1871, ARS, 4 B 48; Commandant of Joal to Commandant of Gorée, 12 Oct. 1871, ARS, unclassified.

20. The "Governor's letter" is Governor of Senegal to Bur Sine, 27 Oct. 1871, ARS, 13 G 318. Sanoumon's payments are documented in Bur Sine to Commandant of Gorée, received 26 Oct. 1871, ARS, 13 G 318; and Commandant of Gorée to Governor of Senegal, 30 Oct. 1871, ARS, 4 B 48.

21. "Annales Religieuses de St. Joseph de N'Gasobil." See also Commandant of Joal to Director of Political Affairs, 23 Feb. 1875, ARS, unclassified.

22. Received 26 Feb. 1876, ARS, 13 G 318.

23. Governor of Senegal to Minister, 7 Apr. 1877, ARS, 13 G 311.

24. Commandant of Joal to Commandant of Dakar, 22 Jan. 1878, ARS, unclassified.

25. Commandant of Dakar to Governor of Senegal, 1 May 1877, ARS, 4 B 48.

26. Received 31 May 1877, ARS, 13 G 311.

27. *Annales Sénégalaises,* pp. 412–13.

28. Commandant of Dakar to Governor of Senegal, 1 Jan. 1878, ARS, 13 G 307; on the complaints, see Commandant of Dakar to Governor of Senegal, 14 Dec. 1877, ARS, 4 B 64.

29. Commandant of Dakar to Governor of Senegal, 8 Dec. 1877, ARS, 13 G 318.

30. Commandant of Dakar to Bur Sine, 8 Dec. 1877, ARS, 13 G 318.

31. Governor of Senegal to Minister, 22 Feb. 1878, ARS, "Situation politique."

32. Oral tradition.

33. Commandant of Joal to Commandant of Dakar, 17 Mar. 1878, ARS, unclassified.

34. Governor of Senegal to Minister, 21 Apr. 1878, ARS, "Situation politique."

35. For an account of the trader's claim, see Commandant of Dakar to Governor of Senegal, 6 June 1881, ARS, 4 B 64. For Semou Mack's suicide, see Commandant of Joal to Commandant of Dakar, 16 Jan. 1882, ARS, unclassified.

36. Oral sources: Bur Sine Mahecor Diouf and Latgarand N'Diaye, chef d'arrondissement at Sokone.

37. Governor of Senegal to Minister, 20 May 1882, ARS, "Situation politique."

38. Lt. Governor of Rivières du Sud to Governor of Senegal, 6 Mar. 1885, ARS, 4 B 74.

39. Administrator of Sine-Saloum to Governor of Senegal, 30 Aug. 1888, ARS, unclassified.

40. Commandant of Thiès to Governor of Senegal, 5 Sept. 1887, ARS, 1 D 52.

41. Governor of Senegal to Minister, 12 Nov. 1885, FOM, Sénégal, I 73 a.

Chapter Six

1. For examples of the French officers' justifications, see "Notes sur les contrées des côtes occidentales d'Afrique" (1867), ARS, 3 B 89; Governor of Senegal to Minister, 2 Apr. 1868, FOM, Sénégal, I 54 a. On Rufisque's growth, see Pasquier, "Villes du Sénégal," p. 405.

2. Corre, "Journal," pp. 1–70.

3. Commandant of Dakar to M. Pellen, merchant at Nianing, 14 Jan. 1879, ARS, unclassified.

4. Dessertine, "Un port sécondaire," II, 12.

5. Commandant of Gorée to Governor of Senegal, 30 Dec. 1871, ARS, 4 B 48.

6. Commandant of Kaolack to Commandant of Gorée, Mar. 1872, ARS, unclassified.

7. On the early evolution of the Communes, see Hargreaves, "Assimilation"; Johnson, chaps. 2–5.

8. Brooks, chap. 4. On the importance of steam navigation to the British settlements, see McPhee, pp. 69–105.

9. Charbonneau.

10. Fouquet, pp. 59–60; Adam, pp. 130–31.

11. Adam, p. 106.

12. Commandant of Dakar to Governor of Senegal, 9 August 1879, ARS, 4 B 64.

13. *Procés Verbal du Conseil Général*, 23 Feb. 1882, ARS.

14. Commandant of Dakar to Governor of Senegal, 12 Dec. 1881, ARS, 4 B 64.

15. Governor of Senegal to Minister, 9 Dec. 1876, FOM, Sénégal, I 61 c.

16. Gray, p. 461.

17. Hargreaves, *Prelude*, chaps. 3 and 4; Gailey, chap. 5; Catala.

18. "Annales Religieuses de St. Joseph de N'Gasobil"; Ciss.

19. Gravrand, *Visage*, pp. 55–56.

20. "Annales Religieuses de St. Joseph de N'Gasobil."

Chapter Seven

1. Ganier.

2. Governor of Senegal to Minister, 30 May 1890, ARS, unclassified.

3. Admininstrator of Gambia to Governor-in-Chief, 28 May 1879 (Enclosure 6 to No. 60), PRO, CO 87/113.

4. Administrator of Gambia to Governor-in-Chief, 29 Aug. 1879 (Enclosure 1 to No. 66), PRO, CO 87/114.

5. Governor-in-Chief to Administrator of Gambia, PRO, CO 87/114, No. 66.

6. Administrator of Gambia to Governor-in-Chief, 18 Nov. 1879, PRO, CO 87/115, No. 34.

7. Administrator of Gambia to Governor-in-Chief, 29 Aug. 1879, PRO, CO 87/114, No. 66.

8. *Ibid.*

9. Administrator of Gambia to Governor-in-Chief, 18 Nov. 1879, PRO, CO 87/115, No. 34.

10. Biram Cissé to Queen Victoria, 12 Sept. 1880, PRO, CO 87/116, No. 80.

11. Administrator of Gambia to Governor-in-Chief, 18 Nov. 1879, PRO CO 87/115.

12. Lt. Governor of Rivières du Sud to Governor of Senegal, 21 May 1884, FOM, Sénégal IV 104 a.

13. Lt. Governor of Rivières du Sud to Governor of Senegal, 24 May 1884, Papers of Victor Ballot, ANP, No. 175; Lt. Governor of Rivières du Sud to Governor of Senegal, 19 May 1884, ARS 4 B 74.

14. Administrator of Gambia to Governor-in-Chief, 3 June 1885, PRO, CO 87/124, No. 62; Lt. Governor of Rivières du Sud to Governor of Senegal, 8 July 1885, ARS, 4 B 74.

15. Administrator of Gambia to Governor-in-Chief, 29 June 1885, PRO, CO 87/125, No. 77; Administrator of Gambia to Governor-in-Chief, 11 June 1885, PRO, CO 87/124, No. 63.

16. Lt. Governor of Rivières du Sud to Governor of Senegal, 8 July 1885, ARS, 4 B 74.

17. Administrator of Gambia to Governor-in-Chief, 29 Aug. 1885, PRO, CO 87/125.

18. Governor of Senegal to Minister, 12 Mar. 1886, ARS, "Situation politique."

19. Administrator of Gambia to Governor-in-Chief, 5 Dec. 1877, AG.

20. Governor of Senegal to Minister, c. 1887, FOM Sénégal IV 105 a.

21. Administrator of Gambia to Governor-in-Chief, 11 June 1885, PRO, CO 87/124, No. 63.

22. Administrator of Gambia to Governor-in-Chief, 29 June 1885, PRO, CO 87/125, No. 77.

23. Administrator of Gambia to Governor-in-Chief, 15 July 1884, PRO, CO 87/122; 3 June 1885, PRO, CO 87/124, No. 62; 27 Apr. 1886, PRO, CO 87/128, No. 95.

24. Governor of Senegal to Minister, 15 Nov. 1886, ARS, "Situation politique."

25. *Collection of Treaties with Native Chiefs on the West Coast of Africa*, AG.

26. Governor of Senegal to Minister, undated, FOM Sénégal IV 105 a.

27. Instructions to Colonel Coronnat, FOM, Sénégal IV 105 a.

28. Colonel Coronnat to Saër Maty, 16 Apr. 1887, ARS, 1 D 52.

29. Coronnat; Denisart; Colonel Coronnat to Governor of Senegal, 8 June 1887, FOM, Sénégal IV 105 a ; assorted reports and telegrams, ARS, 1 D 52.

30. Biram Cissé to Administrator of Gambia, sent in dispatch of 25 Apr. 1887, PRO, CO 87/130, No. 63, Enclosure 1.

31. Undersecretary of State to Governor of Senegal, 25 Mar. 1887, FOM, Sénégal I 76 b.

32. *Journal Officiel*, 30 Jan. 1890.

33. *Ibid.*

34. A. W. L. Hemming, comment on telegram announcing the defeat of Saër Maty, 5 May 1887, PRO, CO 87/130.

35. Colonial Office to Governor-in-Chief, undated, PRO, CO 87/131.

36. Commandant of Nioro to Governor of Senegal, 2 Nov. 1888, ARS, 13 G 322.

37. Commandant of Nioro to Colonel Coronnat, 21 May 1888, ARS, 13 G 322; Governor of Senegal to Minister, 6 Jan. 1888, ARS, "Situation politique."

38. Memorandum, 14 June 1887, PRO, CO 87/130.

39. Governor of Senegal to Minister, 6 Jan. 1889, FOM, Sénégal I 80 b.

40. Captain Pineau to Governor of Senegal, 10 June 1891, ARS, 1 F 16.

41. Official correspondence, ARS, 1 F 17.

42. Official report, 6 Jan. 1896; Farques to Governor-General, 2 Feb. 1896, ARS, 1 F 19. For a more extended discussion of the boundary question, see Gailey, chap. 6.

43. Villiers, report on journey back to Dakar, undated, FOM, Sénégal IV 105 a.

44. Administrator of Sine-Saloum to Governor of Senegal, 30 Aug. 1888, ARS, unclassified.

45. Administrator of Sine-Saloum to Governor of Senegal, 17 Aug. 1889, ARS, 13 G 321.

46. Governor of Senegal to Bur Sine, 5 May 1888, ARS, unclassifiied.

47. Administrator of Sine-Saloum to Director of Political Affairs, 31 Aug. 1891, ARS, unclassified.

48. "Treaty with Sine," 1891, FOM, Sénégal IV 104 c.

49. Administrator of Sine-Saloum to Governor of Senegal, 23 Oct. 1891, ARS, unclassified; Governor of Senegal to Minister, 18 Nov. 1891, ARS, "Situation politique."

50. Governor of Senegal to Minister, 6 Jan. 1888, ARS, "Situation politique."

51. Commandant of Nioro to Governor of Senegal, June 1888, ARS, 13 G 322.

52. *Ibid.*, 30 June 1888.

53. *Ibid.*, 18 July 1888.

54. *Ibid.*, 5 Sept. 1888.

55. Mandiaye Bâ to Governor of Senegal, 18 Mar. 1889, ARS, 2 D 8/4.

Chapter Eight

1. Personnel dossier No. 3006, ARS. See also Debien.

2. Administrator of Sine-Saloum to Governor of Senegal, 5 Apr. 1890, ARS, unclassified.

3. Administrator of Sine-Saloum to Governor of Senegal, 1 Jan. 1888, ARS, 13 G 321; Bur Sine to Administrator, 8 Mar. 1889, ARS, unclassified.

4. Administrator of Sine-Saloum to Bur Saloum, 4 Mar. 1896, ARS, 13 G 326; Administrator to Governor of Senegal, 10 Mar. 1896, ARS, 13 G 327; Administrator to Director of Native Affairs, 15 Nov. 1896, ARS, 13 G 328; Commandant of Nioro to Commandant Supérieur, August 1895, ARS, unclassified; Administrator to Governor-General, 30 Sept. 1897, ARS, 13 G 329.

5. Telegram, Mandiaye Bâ to Governor of Senegal, 18 Mar. 1889, ARS, 2 D 8/4.

6. Personnel dossier, Mandiaye Bâ, ARS, 13 G 53.

7. Lieutenant Obissier, monograph on the cercle of Nioro du Rip, ARS, 1 G 217.

8. Report to Director of Political Affairs, ARS, 13 G 322.

9. Director of Political Affairs to Commandant of Nioro, 13 Nov. 1893, ARS, 13 G 322.

10. *Ibid.*

11. Administrator of Sine-Saloum to Governor cf Senegal, 17 Dec. 1891, ARS, unclassified.

12. Administrator of Sine-Saloum to Governor of Senegal, December 1893, ARS, unclassified.

13. Administrator of Sine-Saloum to Governor of Senegal, 31 Jan. 1893, ARS, unclassified.

14. Administrator of Gambia to Governor of Senegal, 31 July 1888, ARS, unclassified; Administrator of Sine-Saloum to Governor of Senegal, 9 Aug. 1896, ARS, 13 G 327; Administrator of Sine-Saloum to Director of Native Affairs, 3 Nov. 1896, ARS, 13 G 328.

15. Administrator of Sine-Saloum to Director of Political Affairs, 14 Jan. 1888, ARS, unclassified; Governor of Senegal to Minister, 23 Mar. 1888, ARS, "Situation politique."

16. Governor of Senegal to Minister, 23 May 1888, ARS, "Situation politique."

17. Administrator of Sine-Saloum to Governor of Senegal, December 1893, ARS, unclassified.

18. *Ibid.*

19. *Ibid.*

20. Administrator of Sine-Saloum to Governor of Senegal, 1 Mar. 1895, ARS, 13 G 326.

21. Administrator of Sine-Saloum to Governor of Senegal, ARS, 13 G 326; Administrator to Governor, 9 Aug. 1896, ARS, 13 G 327.

22. For acceptance of debts, see Noirot, "Aperçu général" (1896), ARS, 13 G 327; for the French request, see Administrator of Sine-Saloum to Governor of Senegal, 9 Aug. 1896, ARS, 13 G 327.

23. Administrator of Sine-Saloum to Governor-General, 3 Nov. 1895, ARS, 13 G 325.

24. Administrator of Sine-Saloum to Governor-General, 10 Dec. 1896, ARS, 13 G 327.

25. Administrator of Sine-Saloum to Governor of Senegal, 8 Nov. 1897 and December 1893, ARS, unclassified.

26. Administrator of Sine-Saloum to Bur Saloum, 18 Mar. 1896, ARS, 13 G 326; Administrator to Director of Political Affairs, 7 Apr. 1895, ARS, 13 G 325.

27. Noirot, *Notice,* pp. 12–19.

28. FOM, Sénégal VII 17 c.

29. *Bulletin Administratif, Sénégal et Dépendences* (Dakar, 1891), pp. 513–20.

30. Administrator of Sine-Saloum to Governor of Senegal, 15 Apr. 1895, ARS, 13 G 325.

31. Traveling Commissioner's Report, North Bank Province, 1897–98, AG; Commandant of Nioro to Governor of Senegal, 1 Mar. 1897, ARS, unclassified.

32. Bur Saloum to Governor-General, 27 Aug. 1896, ARS, unclassified.

33. Commandant of Nioro to Commandant Supérieur, 2 May and 1 July 1895, ARS, unclassified; Governor-General to Commandant of Nioro, 20 Oct. 1896, ARS, unclassified.

34. Penciled response on letter, Administrator of Sine-Saloum to Director of Political Affairs, 24 June 1892, ARS, unclassified.

35. Administrator of Sine-Saloum to Governor-General, 25 May 1892, ARS, unclassified.

36. Administrator of Sine-Saloum to Governor of Senegal, 25 May 1892, ARS, unclassified.

37. I. Konaré to Administrator of Sine-Saloum, 3 May 1895, ARS, unclassified.

38. Administrator of Sine-Saloum to Governor of Senegal, 18 Oct. and 21 Nov. 1892, ARS, unclassified.

39. *Journal Officiel*, 4 June 1892.

40. Administrator of Sine-Saloum to Director of Political Affairs, 18 Oct. 1892, ARS, unclassified.

41. Administrator of Sine-Saloum to Governor of Senegal, 20 Dec. 1892, ARS, unclassified.

42. Administrator of Sine-Saloum to Director of Political Affairs, 26 Jan. 1904; Police Sergeant at Foundiougne to Director of Political Affairs, 30 May 1904, ARS, K 18.

43. Deherme, monograph on slavery, ARS, K 25; Poulet, "Rapport sur le captivité" (1905), ARS, K 17; Canard to Governor of Senegal, 19 Feb. 1880, ARS, 4 B 64.

44. Schoelcher. This contains both Schoelcher's speech and Jauréguibéry's answer.

45. Director of Political Affairs to Governor of Senegal, 16 May 1884, ARS, K 12; Minister to Governor of Senegal, 2 May 1882, ARS, K 12.

46. Deherme, monograph on slavery, ARS, K 25.

47. For a discussion of the idea of a protectorate as applied to Africa, see Anene, chap. 3.

48. Commandant Supérieur to Governor of Senegal, 13 July 1887, ARS, unclassified.

49. Undersecretary of State to Minister, n.d., ARS, K 12.

50. Convention of 12 Dec. 1892, ARS, K 12.

51. Director of Political Affairs to Administrator of Sine-Saloum, 26 July 1889, ARS, 13 G 321; Director of Political Affairs to Administrator, 19 Jan. 1892, ARS, unclassified.

52. Administrator of Sine-Saloum to Governor of Senegal, 12 Aug. 1893, ARS, K 13.

53. Administrator of Sine-Saloum to Governor of Senegal, 27 Sept. 1893, ARS, K 13; Deherme, *L'Afrique Occidentale*, p. 109.

54. Commandant of Nioro to Commandant Supérieur, 5 Nov. 1895, ARS, 13 G 322; Administrator of Sine-Saloum to Governor-General, October 1895, ARS, 13 G 325.

55. Traveling Commissioner, North Bank Province, to Administrator of Gambia, 6 Jan. 1894, AG.

56. Annual Report, North Bank Province, June 1894, AG.

57. Commandant of Nioro to Commandant Supérieur, November 1895, ARS, unclassified.

58. Commandant of Nioro to Governor-General, 13 Nov. 1896, ARS, unclassified.

59. "Note à M. le Gouverneur Général sur la captivité en Afrique Occidentale Française" (1909), ARS, K 27. See also Guèye.

60. Commandant of Nioro to Governor of Senegal, 17 Nov. 1892, ARS, 13 G 322; Traveling Commissioner, North Bank Province, to Administrator of Gambia, 30 Jan. 1893, AG.

61. For one of the few really good descriptions of slavery in West Africa, see Keita.

62. Administrator of Sine-Saloum to Governor of Senegal, 14 Jan. 1892, ARS, unclassified.

63. Administrator of Sine-Saloum to Governor of Senegal, 23 Sept. 1895, ARS, 13 G 325.

64. Director of Political Affairs, Report on the Boundary Commission, 2 Feb. 1896, ARS, 1 F 19.

65. Noirot, "Aperçu général," ARS, 13 G 327.

66. Administrator of Sine-Saloum to Governor of Senegal, December 1893, ARS, unclassified.

67. Administrator of Sine-Saloum to Bur Saloum, 6 Mar. 1896, ARS, 13 G 326.

68. Bur Saloum to Governor of Senegal, received 20 Mar. 1891, ARS, unclassified; Administrator of Sine-Saloum to Governor of Senegal, 7 Mar. 1891, ARS, unclassified.

69. Commandant of the *Ardent* to Governor of Senegal, 11 Apr. 1891, ARS, unclassified; Governor of Senegal to Bur Saloum, 23 Mar. 1891, ARS, unclassified.

70. Administrator of Sine-Saloum to Governor of Senegal, 30, May 1892, ARS, unclassified.

71. Administrator of Sine-Saloum to Governor of Senegal, 1 Mar. 1895, ARS, 13 G 326.

72. Commandant of Nioro to Governor of Senegal, n.d., 1895, ARS, 13 G 326; "Aperçu général," pp. 2–3, ARS, 13 G 327.

Chapter Nine

1. Administrator of Sine-Saloum to Governor-General, 14 Feb. 1896, ARS, unclassified.

2. Director of Political Affairs to Administrator of Sine-Saloum, 19 Mar. 1896, ARS, unclassified.

3. Administrator of Sine-Saloum to Governor of Senegal, March 1889, ARS, 13 G 321.

4. Administrator of Sine-Saloum to Governor of Senegal, 17 Jan. 1889, ARS, 13 G 321.

5. Administrator of Sine-Saloum to Bur Saloum, 23 Jan. 1892, ARS, unclassified.

6. Bur Saloum to Governor of Senegal, 26 Jan. 1892, ARS, unclassified.

7. Bur Sine to Director of Political Affairs, 10 May 1893, ARS, unclassified.

8. Administrator of Sine-Saloum to Bur Sine, 14 Dec. 1896, ARS, 13 G 326; Administrator to Director of Native Affairs, 4 Dec. 1897, ARS, 13 G 329; Administrator to Bur Sine, 4 Dec. 1897, ARS, 13 G 329; Administrator to Bur Saloum, 4 Dec. 1897, ARS, 13 G 329.

9. Administrator of Sine-Saloum to Governor of Senegal, 1 Mar. 1895, ARS, 13 G 326.

10. Administrator of Sine-Saloum to Governor of Senegal, 2 July 1890, ARS, unclassified.

11. *Journal Officiel*, 3 Dec. 1892.

12. Traveling Commissioner, North Bank Province, to Administrator of Gambia, 6 Jan. 1894, AG.

13. Administrator of Sine-Saloum to Director of Political Affairs, 25 July 1895, ARS, 13 G 325; Administrator to Governor-General, 1 Mar. 1896, ARS, 13 G 326.

14. June 21, 1895, ARS, unclassified.

15. *Moniteur du Sénégal*, 31 Dec. 1897.

16. Report on the letter to M'Backé in Administrator of Sine-Saloum to Governor of Senegal, 27 Mar. 1892, ARS, unclassified.

17. Governor of Senegal to Minister, 20 May 1887, FOM, Sénégal I 76 a; Buhan and Teissière to Director of Native Affairs, 28 Dec. 1895, ARS, unclassified.

18. Lefilliâtre; Boyer; Clignet.

19. Agent Consulaire, Bathurst, to Commandant of Nioro, 4 Jan. 1902; Commandant of Nioro to Agent Consulaire, Bathurst, 15 Jan. 1902; Chambre de Commerce, Rufisque, to Administrator, 17 May 1910, ARS, unclassified.

20. Administrator of Sine-Saloum to Lt. Governor, 7 Jan. 1903, ARS, 13 G 336.

21. Monthly reports, Sine-Saloum, 1912, ARS, unclassified.

22. Traveling Commissioner's reports, 1909–14, AG.

23. Monthly reports, Sine-Saloum, January and March, 1903, ARS, unclassified.

24. Administrator of Sine-Saloum to Director of Native Affairs, 5 Aug. 1904, ARS, 13 G 342.

25. Brocard; Dessertine, "Un Port Secondaire," II, 18.

26. Batude, pp. 47–52; Lagrillière-Beauclerc; Administrator of Sine-Saloum to Lt. Governor, December 1912, ARS, unclassified.

27. On the definition of "peasant," see Fallers, pp. 108–10.

28. Dessertine, "Un Port Secondaire," II, 19.

29. Desbordes, pp. 9–13.

30. *Ibid.*

31. Administrator of Sine-Saloum to Director of Native Affairs, 3 Dec. 1905, ARS, 13 G 346.

32. Monthly report, Sine-Saloum, May 1912, ARS, unclassified.

33. Administrator of Sine-Saloum to Commandant of Nioro, 8 July and 7 Aug. 1895, ARS, unclassified.

34. Governor of Senegal to Commandant of Nioro, 24 June 1895, ARS, unclassified.

35. Administrator of Sine-Saloum to Duchemin, Chief of Frontier Mission, 15 Mar. 1904, ARS, 13 G 341.

36. Administrator of Sine-Saloum to Governor of Senegal, 5 Apr. 1892, ARS, unclassified.

37. Administrator of Sine-Saloum to Director of Political Affairs, 30 June 1890, ARS, unclassified.

38. Administrator of Sine-Saloum to Governor of Senegal, 1 Mar. 1895, ARS, 13 G 326; Noirot, "Aperçu général: Ecoles," ARS, 13 G 327.

39. "Aperçu général: Ecoles," *ibid.*; Administrator of Sine-Saloum to Guy Grand, 1 Apr. 1895, ARS, 13 G 325.

40. *Journal Officiel,* 26 May 1898.

41. Administrator of Sine-Saloum to Governor of Senegal, 29 Oct. 1893, ARS, unclassified; Bur Sine to Director of Native Affairs, 2 Nov. 1897, ARS, 13 G 329; Administrator to Bur Sine, 15 Dec. 1897, ARS, unclassified.

42. For a comment on the results of paternalism in Uganda, see Cyril Ehrlich, "Some Social and Economic Implications of Paternalism in Uganda," *Journal of African History,* IV (1963), 275–85.

Chapter Ten

1. Administrator of Sine-Saloum to Governor of Senegal, undated 1888, ARS, 13 G 321.

2. Administrator of Sine-Saloum to Governor-General, 10 Apr. 1896, ARS, 13 G 326.

3. Administrator of Sine-Saloum to Director of Native Affairs, 12 Dec. 1897, ARS, 13 G 329.

4. ARS, 13 G 329.

5. Director of Native Affairs to Administrator of Sine-Saloum, 25 Jan. 1898, FOM, Sénégal IV 128 c; Report on Governor-General's tour, *Journal Officiel de l'A.O.F.*, 17 Feb. 1898.

6. Administrator of Sine-Saloum to Director of Native Affairs, 10 Feb. 1898, ARS, 13 G 330; Director of Native Affairs to Governor-General, 18 Feb. 1898, FOM, Sénégal IV 128 c.

7. This increasing restriction of able Africans was characteristic of many European colonies. See David Kimble, *A Political History of Ghana, 1850–1928* (Oxford, 1963), chap. 2.

8. Personnel dossier, FOM.

9. *Journal Officiel de l'A.O.F.*, 21 Apr. 1898.

10. Resident for Sine to Administrator of Sine-Saloum, 26 Mar. and 6 Apr. 1899, ARS, unclassified.

11. Governor-General to Administrator of Sine-Saloum, 17 Apr. 1899, ARS, unclassified.

12. Administrator of Sine-Saloum to Director of Native Affairs, 25 and 27 Apr. 1899, ARS, unclassified.

13. Administrator of Sine-Saloum to Governor-General, 28 May 1899, ARS, unclassified.

14. Administrator of Sine-Saloum to Léopold Diouf, 12 May 1901, ARS, 13 G 331.

15. Administrator of Sine-Saloum to Bur Sine, 3 July 1901, ARS, unclassified.

16. Administrator of Sine-Saloum to Director of Native Affairs, 3 Oct. 1901, ARS, 13 G 332.

17. Administrator of Sine-Saloum to Director of Native Affairs, 9 Oct. 1901, ARS, 13 G 332.

18. Bur Sine to Administrator of Sine-Saloum, 6 Mar. 1901; Administrator of Sine-Saloum to Director of Native Affairs, 8 Mar. 1901, ARS, unclassified.

19. On rituals practiced in Sine and Saloum, see a series of short articles by Momar Ciss N'Doye that appeared in *Notes Africaines* during 1947 and 1948.

20. *Journal du Poste*, Kaolack, 1901, ARS, unclassified.

21. Commandant of Nioro to Governor-General, 4 May 1901; A. Diaw to Administrator of Sine-Saloum, 28 Apr. 1901, ARS, unclassified.

22. J. Rocaché to Administrator of Sine-Saloum, 13 May 1901, ARS, unclassified.

23. J. Rocaché to A. Diaw, 5 May 1901, ARS, unclassified.

24. *Ibid.*, note in margin by Lefilliâtre.

25. Administrator of Sine-Saloum to Director of Native Affairs, 27 July 1902, ARS, unclassified; Administrator to Director of Native Affairs, 11 Mar. 1902, ARS, 13 G 324.

26. Administrator of Sine-Saloum to Director of Native Affairs, 3 July 1903, ARS, 13 G 335.

27. Administrator of Sine-Saloum to Director of Native Affairs, 2 July and 31 July 1902, ARS, 13 G 335.

28. Administrator of Sine-Saloum to Secretary-General, 3 Jan. 1903, ARS, unclassified.

29. Personnel dossier no. 1666, ARS.

30. Governor-General to all Lt. Governors, 22 Sept. 1909, ARS, 13 G 72.

31. Lt. Governor to Governor-General, "Rapport d'Ensemble," 1910, ARS, 2 G 10/12.

32. Report of Inspector of Administrative Affairs, 9 Apr. 1913, ARS, unclassified.

33. There is a series of these letters, mostly written in 1893, in folders marked "Nioro" in the unclassified collection.

34. Extract from punishment register, Nioro, 1900, ARS, unclassified.

35. Insa Bâ to Director of Native Affairs, 29 Aug. 1901, ARS, unclassified.

36. Commandant of Nioro to Lt. Governor, 19 June 1902, ARS, unclassified.

37. Remark dated 9 June 1910, in personnel dossier no. 1866, ARS.

38. Personnel dossiers nos. 765, 3198, and 3761, ARS.

39. Suret-Canale, II (1964), 94.

40. Administrator of Sine-Saloum to Lt. Governor, 23 Nov. 1910, 25 Jan. and 2 Mar. 1911, ARS, unclassified.

41. Roux, pp. 160–66.

42. Dossier on Mody M'Baye case, ARS, 13 G 77.

43. Resident for Sine to Lt. Governor, 7 Sept. 1912, ARS, unclassified.

44. Administrator of Sine-Saloum to Procureur de la République, 30 Jan. 1912; Governor of Senegal to Administrator, 4 May 1912, ARS, unclassified.

45. I am indebted to Professor G. Wesley Johnson of Stanford and Professor H. O. Idowu of Lagos for information on politics in the Four Communes. (See Johnson, "Emergence.") Johnson's work and Idowu's forthcoming study of the Conseil Général will contribute immeasurably to our understanding of the development of African political consciousness in this key area.

46. Administrator of Sine-Saloum to Governor of Senegal, 27 Feb. 1895, ARS, unclassified.

47. Telegram, 15 May 1904, ARS, unclassified.

48. Administrator of Sine-Saloum to Lt. Governor, 27 Apr. 1904, ARS, 13 G 341; Administrator to Lt. Governor, 30 Oct. 1905, ARS, 13 G 346.

49. *Journal Officiel de l'A.O.F.,* 7 Feb. 1912.

50. Administrator of Sine-Saloum to Director of Native Affairs, 1 Feb. 1904, ARS, 13 G 340.

51. Administrator of Sine-Saloum to Director of Native Affairs, 14 Jan. 1904, ARS, 13 G 340.

52. *Ibid.*

Chapter Eleven

1. For a discussion of the relationship between Islamization and the breakdown of traditional political units, see Cardaire.

2. Marty, *Etudes sur l'Islam,* I, 308.

3. Le Chatelier, p. 260.

4. Decree of 23 Nov. 1893, ARS, J 86.

5. "Rapport sur les écoles qoraniques du Sénégal," ARS, J 86.

6. Administrator of Sine-Saloum to Lt. Governor, 23 Jan. 1904, ARS, 13 G 340; Administrator to Lt. Governor, 18 Apr. 1904, ARS, 13 G 341.

7. Administrator of Sine-Saloum to Lt. Governor, 18 May 1905, ARS, 13 G 344.

8. Paul Marty to Lt. Governor, 20 Nov. 1913, ARS, J 86.

9. Ollivon.

10. Commandant of Nioro, 12 May 1898, ARS, unclassified.

11. Commandant of Nioro to Director of Native Affairs, 29 Oct. 1901, ARS, unclassified.

12. A. Niasse to Governor-General, 24 Jan. 1911, ARS, unclassified. For a discussion of Niasse's importance as a religious personality, see Marty, I, 136–39. For accounts of the achievements of his son, Al Hajj Ibrahima Niasse, see V. Monteil, *L'Islam Noir*, pp. 132–33; Abun-Nasr, p. 146; and Froelich, pp. 236–38.

13. Marty, I, 203.

14. *Ibid.*, pp. 221–332; see also V. Monteil, "Les Mourides"; Bourlon, pp. 53–64; and Cheikh Tidiane Sy. The forthcoming work of Lucy Behrman should contribute further to our knowledge of Mouride history.

15. Paul Marty, Report of 20 Nov. 1913, ARS, J 86. This report contains much information later included in his book, *Etudes sur l'Islam au Sénégal.*

16. Duran, pp. 40–42.

17. Administrator of Sine-Saloum to Governor of Senegal, 7 Jan. 1912, ARS, unclassified.

18. Le Chatelier, pp. 269–70.

19. Political report on Sine-Saloum, 1915, ARS, unclassified.

Chapter Twelve

1. Deschamps, "Et Maintenant, Lord Lugard?"
2. See Betts.
3. Deschamps, *The French Union*, pp. 35–38.
4. Brunschwig, *L'Avènement*, chap. 4.

GLOSSARY

Alcati. In Senegambia, an African ruler's representative at a factory; in some areas it has come to mean village chief.

Almamy. A politico-religious title used for the ruler in a number of African Moslem states; in some areas, such as Niombato, it is the title of a village religious leader.

Alwali. Title of an important Moslem chief in Saloum.

Badolo. Wolof word for peasant. See *Jambur.*

Beleup. Wolof political title. In eastern Saloum it is held by a number of chiefs of Djoloff origin.

Bissète. Member of the Bur's entourage who had the right to say whatever he wished to the Bur. The title was hereditary.

Brak. Title of the ruler of Oualo, a Wolof state near St. Louis.

Bumi. In Sine and Saloum, title of the heir apparent; in Saloum, title held also by two territorial chiefs, the Bumi Mandack and the Bumi Kaymor.

Bur. Wolof word for king, used also by the Serer; title of the rulers in Sine and in Saloum. The title is also held by a number of lesser chiefs who headed what once were independent states.

Burba. Title of the ruler of Djoloff.

Coubeul. Payments made to Sine and Saloum by foreign traders.

Damel. Title of the ruler of Cayor.

Denianke. Fulbe family that ruled the Toucouleur society of Fouta Toro for two centuries. It was pagan, or at least not orthodox Moslem, and was deposed by the torodbe, or cleric, class in 1776.

Dialigué. In Sine and Saloum, title held by certain chiefs chosen from among the tyeddo.

Diogop Bigué. One of the two guelowar lineages that contested the throne of Saloum for almost two centuries.

Eliman. From Mamour N'Dari Bâ on, the title used by the chiefs in Nioro; a political title in a number of West African languages.

Farba. Political title of Mandinka origin found in a number of West African political systems. In Sine and Saloum the *Grand Farba,* who was elected from the tyeddo, was chief of the slaves. The *Farba Birkeur* was similar to a royal chamberlain.

Griot. The French term for an African caste that includes musicians, historians, and praise-sayers.

Gris-gris. Amulets containing verses of the Koran.

Guelowar. The ruling family, of Mandinka origin, in Sine and Saloum.

Jambur. Literally, "free men" in Wolof. The term connotes a more dignified status than does badolo, even though most of the jambur were also badolo.

Jaraf. Wolof and Serer political title for village chiefs. The *Grand Jaraf,* who was the chief of the jambur, was second in importance only to the Bur.

Kévé Bigué. One of the two guelowar lineages that contested the throne of Saloum for almost two centuries.

Laff. Word used in Saloum for a sellers' strike.

Lam. A Serer and Poular political title held by a chief in Fouta Toro and one in Sine.

Linguère. In Sine and Saloum, chief of the women; usually the mother or sister of the Bur.

Malikyya. Branch of the Tijaniyya that formed around the religious leader Al Hajj Malik Sy of Tivouane (Cayor).

Mansa. Mandinka word for king.

Marabout. French term for a Moslem religious leader; from *murabit,* the Arabic term for a member of a type of monastic community found in North Africa. In Senegal, it came to refer to all members of the orthodox Moslem faction in the nineteenth-century religious wars.

Mouride. Disciple of a sufi religious leader. In Senegal, it designated members of the predominantly Wolof tariqa founded by Amadou Bamba.

Namou. A tax on the navetanes.

Navetanes. Seasonal migrant workers who settled near French factories during the growing season.

Poular. Language spoken by the Toucouleur and Fulbe.

Qadi. Arabic word for judge.

Qadiriyya. A tariqa founded in Baghdad in the twelfth century; long the most widespread in West Africa.

Sakh-sakh. In Sine, the Bur's representative in a village.

Saltigui. In Serer areas, a diviner; in Wolof areas, an assistant chief.

Sandigui N'Diob. Important title in Sine designating the ruler of the village of N'Diob near the Baol border.

Serigne. Wolof word for marabout; also a political title in some solidly Moslem areas.

Soninke. Literally, "a giver of libations"; in the Gambia, the traditionalist faction in the religious wars of the nineteenth century; in the upper Senegal River area, name for a people called the Sarakollé by the French, and the Serawullies by the British.

Sourga. Jambur who took service in the entourage of a powerful chief.

Spahi. Member of an irregular African cavalry unit in French service.

Sufism. Islamic mysticism.

Talibé. Student or disciple.

Tamsir. One learned in Islamic law.

Tangann. The Serer of the coastal regions, who lived by farming and fishing.

Tariqa. Literally, "the way" in Arabic; a sufi religious fraternity.

Tata. Masonry fortifications built by the marabouts.

Teigne. Title of the ruler of Baol.

Thilas. In Sine, title of the man who was second in line of succession to the Burship.

Tijaniyya. A sufi order founded in North Africa in the eighteenth century; in Senegal, the largest Moslem sect and the one most militantly opposed to French expansion in the nineteenth century.

Tong. Word used in the Gambia for a sellers' strike.

Torodbe. The cleric class in Toucouleur society. See *Denianke.*

Toubab. European.

Tyeddo. Warriors in the Bur's entourage who were chosen from the slave class; also known as "slaves of the crown."

BIBLIOGRAPHY

The Bibliography is divided into three parts. The first is a list of the archives in which many of the letters and other documents cited in the notes are deposited. The second is an alphabetical list of works consulted; it includes both published and unpublished sources and primary and secondary material. The third is a list of personal informants. For a list of abbreviations used, see p. 243.

Archives

Archives de la Congrégation du Saint Esprit, Paris. Correspondence from missionaries at Gorée, Dakar, and on the Petite Côte. 1846–63.

Archives de la Ministère de la France d'Outre-Mer, Paris. Correspondence dealing with Sine-Saloum, Gorée, and certain general problems from the archives of the former colonial ministry. 1815–90.

Archives Nationales, Paris. Papers of Ernest Noirot (AP 148) and assorted *mémoires* dealing with Senegal in the old colonial archives (series C 6). 1763–1815.

Archives de la République du Sénégal, Dakar. Correspondence dealing with Sine-Saloum and with general policy in the collections of the former French West African Federation and in those of the former territory of Senegal. The first is classified, and there is a printed *Repertoire* available. The collection of the former territory of Senegal has not been classified, but is arranged largely according to date and place of origin. Included in both groups of documents are registers, *journals du poste,* and other documents from the various posts and administrative centers. 1840–1914.

Archives of the Gambia. This term is used advisedly for assorted registers and bundles of documents to be found in various government offices in Bathurst. 1866–1914.

Public Record Office, London. Colonial Office documents relating to the Gambia. 1874–88.

Works Consulted

Abun-Nasr, Jamil M. The Tijaniyya. London: Oxford University Press, 1965.

Adam, Jean. L'Arachide. Paris: Challamel, 1908.

Adanson, Michel. A Voyage to Senegal, the Isle of Gorée, and the River Gambia. Translated from French. London: J. Nourse, 1759.

Ames, David. "Plural Marriage Among the Wolof in the Gambia." Unpublished dissertation, Dept. of Anthropology, Northwestern University, 1953.

Anene, J. C. Southern Nigeria in Transition, 1885–1906. Cambridge: Cambridge University Press, 1966.

"Annales Religieuses," typewritten manuscripts available for each of the older missions in Senegal, ARS.

Annales Sénégalaises de 1854 à 1885. Paris: Maisonneuve frères et C. Leclerc, 1885.

Auchapt, Maurice. "L'Immigration saisonière dans le Sine-Saloum." Paper submitted in fulfillment of degree requirements, Ecole National de la France d'Outre-Mer, Paris, 1947–48.

Aujas, L. "Funerailles royales et ordre de la succession au trône chez les Sérères du Sine," BCEHS, VII (1927), 501–9.

———. "La Région du Sine-Saloum: Le port du Kaolack," BCEHS, XII (1929), 99–132.

———. "Les Sérères du Sénégal (Moeurs et coutumes de droit privé)," BCEHS, XIV (1931), 293–333.

Bâ, Tamsir Ousman. "Essai historique sur le Rip," BIFAN, XIX (1957), 564–91.

Barbot, Jean. A Collection of Voyages and Travels. Vol. V, A Description of the Coasts of North and South Guinea. Ed., Awnsham Churchill. London: Churchill, 1732.

Barros, João de. Asia. Lisbon: H. Cidade, 1945.

Batude, Fernand. L'Arachide au Sénégal. Paris: Receuil Sirey, 1941.

de Beaufort. "Extraits des trois lettres à M. Jomard avec l'itinéraire de son voyage at la description des lieux qu'il a parcouru," Bulletin de la Société de Géographie, II (1824).

Bérenger-Feraud, L. J. B. Les peuplades de la Sénégambie. Paris: E. Leroux, 1879.

Betts, Raymond. Assimilation and Association in French Colonial Theory, 1890–1914. New York: Columbia University Press. 1961.

Blake, John W., ed. Europeans in West Africa. London: Hakluyt Society, 1942.

Blet, Henri. Histoire de la colonisation française. 3 vols. Paris: Arthaud, 1947–50.

Boilat, Abbé P.–D. Esquisses sénégalaises. Paris: F. Bertrand, 1853.

Boulègue, J. "Contribution à la chronologie du royaume de Saloum," BIFAN, XXVII (1966), 657–62.

Bour, Charles. Les Dépendances du Sénégal. Paris: Baudoin, 1865.

Bourgeau, J. "Notes sur la coutume des Sérères du Sine et du Saloum," BCEHS, XVI (1933), 1–62.

Bourlon, Abel. "Mourides et Mouridisme, 1953," in Notes et Etudes sur l'Islam en Afrique Noire. Paris: J. Peyronnet, 1962.

Boutillier, J.-L. et al., eds. La moyenne vallée du Senegal: Etude socio-économique, Paris: Presses Universitaires de France, 1962.

Boyer, Marcel. Les Sociétés de prévoyance, de secours, et de prets mutuels en Afrique occidentale française. Paris: Domat-Montchrestien, 1935.

Brigaud, Felix. Histoire traditionelle du Sénégal. No. 9 of Connaissance du Sénégal. St. Louis du Sénégal: Centre du Recherche et Documentation Sénégalaise, 1962.

Brocard, Paul. Note sur le développement de la culture de l'arachide au Sénégal. Paris: Challamel, 1918.

Brooks, George, "American Legitimate Trade with West Africa, 1789–1914." Unpublished dissertation, Boston University, 1962.

Brunschwig, Henri. L'Avènement de l'Afrique Noire. Paris: Colin, 1963.

———. French Colonialism. Trans., William G. Brown. New York: Praeger, 1966.

———. La Colonisation française. Paris: Calmann-Lévy, 1949.

———. Mythes et réalités de l'imperialisme colonial français, 1871–1914. Paris: Colin, 1960.

Cadamosto, Alvise. The Voyages of Cadamosto. Trans. and ed., G. R. Crone. London: Hakluyt Society, 1937.

Capperon, L. "Bouët-Willaumez en Afrique Occidentale et au Gabon (1836–1850)," Revue Maritime, 1953, pp. 1085–1103.

————. "Protet, Gouverneur du Sénégal," *Revue Maritime,* 1956, pp. 1415–36.

Cardaire, Marcel. L'Islam et le terroir africain. Bamako: I.F.A.N., 1954.

Carlus, J. "Les Sérères de la Sénégambie," *Revue de Géographie,* VI (1880), 409–20; VII (1880), 30–37, 98–105.

Carrère, Frederic, and Holle, Paul. De la Sénégambie française. Paris: Firmin Didot, 1855.

Catala, René. "La question de l'échange de la Gambie britannique contre les comptoir français du Golfe de Guinée de 1866 à 1876" Revue d'Histoire des Colonies, XXV (1948), 114–37.

Centre de Hautes Etudes Administratives sur l'Afrique et l'Asie Modernes. Notes et etudes sur l'Islam en Afrique Noire. Paris: Peyronnet, 1962.

Charbonneau, J. and R. Marchés et marchands d'Afrique Noire. Paris: La Colombe, 1961.

Charpy, Jacques. La fondation de Dakar. Paris: Larose, 1958.

Ciss, Abbé Joseph. "Fadiouth l'île aux coquillages," *Horizons Africains,* No. 151 (January 1964), pp. 18–20.

Clignet, Rémi. "Un Exemple d'économie coloniale: L'Arachide dans le Sine-Saloum." Paper submitted in fulfillment of degree requirements, Ecole Nationale de la France d'Outre-Mer, 1952–1953.

Coffinières de Nordeck. "Renseignements sur la Rivière Saloum," *Journal Officiel du Sénégal et ses Dépendances,* No. 246, 1885.

Comité d'Etudes Historiques et Scientifiques de l'Afrique Occidentale Française. Coutumiers juridiques de l'Afrique Occidentale Française. 3 vols. Paris: Larose, 1939.

Commission des Comptoirs et du Commerce des Côtes d'Afrique. Rapports. Paris: Imprimerie Nationale, 1851.

Coronnat, Colonel. La Guerre au Sénégal: La Colonne du Rip en 1887. Paris: Edmond Dubois, 1890.

Corre, A. "Journal du Docteur Corre en Pays Sérère (Decembre 1876–Janvier 1877.)" Ed., G. Debien. *BIFAN,* XXVI (1964), 1–70.

————. "Les Sérères de Joal et de Portudal," *Revue d'Ethnographie,* II (1883), 1–20.

Cros, Charles. Le Pays de Sine et de Saloum (Sénégal): L'Histoire et la légende. Paris: Chalvet, 1934.

Cultru, Prosper. Histoire du Sénégal du XVe siècle à 1870. Paris: Larose, 1910.

Curtin, Philip. The Image of Africa: British Ideas and Action, 1780–1850. Madison: University of Wisconsin Press, 1964.

Dapper, O. Description de l'Afrique. Translated from Flemish. Amsterdam: W. Waesberge, Boom, and Van Someren, 1667.

Debien, G. "Papiers Ernest Noirot," BIFAN, XXVI (1964), 676–78.

Deherme, Georges. L'Afrique Occidentale Française. Paris: Bloud, 1908.

Denisart, Lt. Les Colonnes du Rip, 1865–1887: Episodes de la conquête du Sénégal: St. Louis du Sénégal: Presse du Premier Regiment des Tirailleurs, 1905.

Desbordes, J. G. L'Immigration Libano–syrienne en Afrique Occidentale Française. Poitiers: Renault, 1938.

Deschamps, Hubert. "Et Maintenant, Lord Lugard?" Africa, XXXIII (1963), 293–306.

———. The French Union. Paris: Berger-Levrault, 1956.

———. Methodes et doctrines coloniales de la France. Paris: Colin, 1953.

———. Le Sénégal et la Gambie. Paris: Presses Universitaires de France, 1964.

Dessertine, André. "Naissance d'un port: Kaolack de origines a 1900," Annales Africaines, VII (1960), 225–59.

———. "Un Port secondaire de la côte occidentale d'Afrique, Kaolack: Etude historique, juridique, et economique des origines à 1958." Mémoire presented to the Faculty of Law, University of Dakar.

Diagne, Pathé. "The Serer Kingdoms," Présence Africaine, No. 54, 1965, pp. 146–76.

Diallo, Moctar. "L'Islam dans le Rip," Bulletin de l'Enseignement d'Afrique Occidentale Francaise (1916), No. 20, pp. 42–45; No. 21, pp. 83–88; No. 22, p. 136.

Diouf, Ibrahima. "Légende autour d'une dynastie," Sénégal, No. 64, 1944, pp. 177–83.

Duchène, Albert. Histoire des finances coloniale de la France. Paris: Payot, 1938.

———. La Politique coloniale de la France. Paris: Payot, 1928.

Dulphy, G. "Etude sur les coutumes sérères de la Petite Côte (Cercle de Thiès)," Ethnographie, New Series, No. 37, 1939, pp. 3–70.

Duran, Pierre. "Notes sur le Mouridisme." Paper submitted in fulfillment of degree requirements, Ecole Nationale de la France d'Outre-Mer, 1954.

Durand, J.-B. Léonard. Voyage au Sénégal. Paris: H. Agasse, 1802.

Faidherbe, L. L. C. Le Sénégal. Paris: Hachette, 1889.

Fallers, L. A. "Are African Cultivators to Be Called 'Peasants'?" *Current Anthropology*, II (1961), 108–10.

Faure, Claude. "Documents inédits sur l'histoire du Sénégal," *Bulletin de la Section de Géographie* (1914), pp. 1–47.

———. Histoire de la Presqu'île du Cap-Vert et des origines de Dakar. Paris: Larose, 1914.

Fernandes, Valentim. Description de la côte occidentale d'Afrique: Sénégal au Cap de Monte, Archipels. Eds., T. Monod, A. Texeira da Mota, and R. Mauny. Bissau: Centro de Estudos da Guinéa Portuguesa, 1951.

Fouquet, Joseph. "La Traite des arachides dans le pays de Kaolack et ses consequences économiques, sociales, et juridiques." Vol. VIII of Etudes sénégalaises. St. Louis du Senegal: I.F.A.N., 1958.

Froelich, J.-C. Les Musulmans d'Afrique noire. Paris: Orante, 1962.

Gaby, F. J. B. Relations de la Nigritie. Paris: Edme Couterot, 1689.

Gaden, Henri. "Légendes et coutumes Sénégalaises. Cahiers de Yoro Dyao," *Revue d'Ethnographie et de Sociologie*, III (1912), 119–57, 190–202.

Gailey, Harry. A History of the Gambia. London: Routledge and Kegan Paul, 1964.

Gamble, David P. "History of the Groundnut Trade," in Contributions to a Socio-Economic Survey of the Gambia. London: Colonial Office, 1949.

———. The Wolof of Senegambia. London: International African Institute, 1957.

Ganier, Germaine. "Lat Dyor et le chemin de fer de l'arachide (1876–1886)," *BIFAN*, XXVII (1965), 223–81.

Geismar, L. Recueil des coutumes civiles de races du Sénégal. St. Louis du Sénégal: Imprimerie du Gouvernement, 1933.

[Geoffroy de Villeneuve, René-Claude.] "R. G. V." L'Afrique ou histoire, moeurs, usages, et coutumes des Africains. 4 vols. Paris: Nepveu, 1814.

Gibb, H. A. R. Mohammedanism. London: Oxford University Press, 1849.

Girault, Arthur. Principes de colonisation et de legislation coloniale. Paris: Receuil Sirey, 1943.

Gluckman, Max. "Rituals of Rebellion in South-East Africa," in Order and Rebellion in Tribal Africa. New York: The Free Press, 1963.

Golberry, S. M. X. Fragments d'un voyage en Afrique. 2 vols. Paris: Treuttel and Würtz, 1802.

Gouilly, Alphonse. L'Islam dans l'Afrique Occidentale Française. Paris: Larose, 1952.

Gravrand, Henri. "Les Sérères (Etude)," *Horizons Africains* (1953), No. 65, pp. 4–8; No. 67, pp. 15–16; No. 68, pp. 10–16.

———. "Rites d'initiation et vie en société chez les Sérères du Sénégal," *Afrique Documents*, No. 52, 1960, pp. 129–44.

———. Visage africain de l'eglise. Paris: Orante, 1961.

Gray, J. M. A History of the Gambia. Cambridge: Cambridge University Press, 1940.

Greenberg, J. H. Studies in African Linguistic Classification. New Haven: Compass, 1955.

Guèye, M'Baye. "L'Affaire Chautemps et la suppression de l'esclavage de case au Sénégal," *BIFAN*, XXVII (1965), 543–59.

Guiraud, Xavier. L'Arachide sénégalaises. Paris: Libraire Technique et Economique, 1937.

Guy, Camille. "Le Sine-Saloum," *Le Géographie*, XVIII (1908), 297–314.

Hardy, Georges. La Mise en valeur du Sénégal de 1817 à 1854. Paris: Larose, 1921.

———. Faidherbe. Paris: Editions de l'Encyclopédie de l'Empire, 1947.

Hargreaves, John D. Prelude to the Partition of West Africa. London: Macmillan, 1963.

———. "Assimilation in Eighteenth Century Senegal," *Journal of African History*, VI (1965), 177–84.

Homburger, L. "Le Sérère-Peul," *Journal de la Société des Africanistes*, IX (1939), 85–102.

Jobson, Richard. The Golden Trade of the Moors. London: Nicholas Okes, 1623.

Johnson, G. Wesley. "The Ascendancy of Blaise Diagne and the Beginning of African Politics in Senegal," *Africa*, XXXVI (1966), 235–53.

———. "The Emergence of Modern African Politics in Senegal, 1848–1920." Unpublished dissertation, Columbia University, 1967.

Jore, Leonce. Les Etablissements français sur la côte occidentale d'Afrique de 1758 à 1809. Paris: Société Française d'Histoire d'Outre-Mer, 1965.

Keita, Cheikna. "Les survivances de l'esclavage et du servage en

Afrique noire." Paper submitted in fulfillment of degree requirements, Ecole Nationale de la France d'Outre-Mer, 1958–59.

Kersaint-Gilly, Felix de. "Les Guelowars: Leur origine, d'apres une
légende très en faveur dans le Saloum oriental," *BCEHS*, IV
(1920), 99–101.

Klein, Martin. "The Moslem Revolution in Nineteenth-Century Sene-
gambia," in Boston University Papers on Africa: History. Eds.,
Daniel McCall, Jeffrey Butler, and Norman Bennett. Vol. IV. New
York: Praeger, in prep.

Kobès, A. "Mission apostolique de la Guinée et la Sénégambie,"
Revue Coloniale (1856), pp. 535–50.

————. "Situation de la colonie agricole de St. Joseph de N'gazobil
(Sénégal)," *Revue Maritime et Coloniale*, XV (1865), 79–87.

Labat, Jean Baptiste. Nouvelle relation de l'Afrique Occidentale.
Paris: Guillaume Cavelier, 1728.

Labouret, Henri. "Féodaux d'Afrique: Les Royaumes Sérères," *Le
Monde Colonial Illustré*, No. 116 (April 1933), pp. 51–52.

————. Paysans d'Afrique Occidentale. Paris: Gallimard, 1941.

Lafont, F. "Le Gandoul et les Niominka," *BCEHS*, XXI (1938), 358–
458.

Lagrillière-Beauclerc, Eugene. Mission au Sénégal et au Soudan.
Paris: C. Taillandrer, 1898.

Landes, David. "The Nature of Economic Imperialism," *Journal of
Economic History*, XXI (1961), 469–512.

Lecard, T. "Notice sur les états Sérères et leurs productions," *Moniteur du Sénégal et Dependances*, Dakar, Aug. 21, 1866.

Le Chatelier, A. L'Islam dans l'Afrique Occidentale. Paris: Steinhell,
1899.

Lefilliâtre, A. C. "Fonctionnement d'une société indigène de crédit
agricole à Kaolack." Supplement to the *Journal Officiel de l'Afrique Occidentale Française*, May 1, 1909.

Le Mire, P. "Petite Chronique du Djilor," *BIFAN*, VIII (1946), 55–63.

————. "Le Tour Petj," *Sénégal*, No. 40, 1942, pp. 909–13.

Leray. "Le navetanat au Sénégal." Paper submitted in fulfillment of
degree requirements, Ecole Nationale de la France d'Outre-Mer,
1946–47.

Ly, Abdoulaye. La Compagnie du Sénégal. Paris: Présence Africaine,
1958.

Ly, Mamadou Hady. "Monographie du Cercle du Gossas." Paper

submitted in fulfillment of degree requirements, Ecole Nationale d'Administration Sénégalaise, 1962.

McPhee, Allan. The Economic Revolution in British West Africa. London: Routledge, 1926.

Marmol-Carvajal, Luys del. L'Afrique de Marmol. Trans., Nicholas Perrot, sieur d'Ablancourt. 3 vols. Paris: Louis Billaine, 1667.

Marty, Paul. Etudes sénégalaises (1785–1826), Paris: Leroux, 1920.

———. Etudes sur l'Islam au Sénégal. 2 vols. Paris: Leroux, 1917.

Masson, Paul. Marseille et la colonisation française. Marseille: Borlatier, 1906.

Mauny, Raymond. Tableau géographique de l'ouest africain au Moyen Age. Dakar: I.F.A.N., 1961.

Mollien, Gaspard. New Voyages and Travels. Vol. III, Travels in Africa. Trans., Sir Richard Phillips. London: R. Phillips, 1825.

Monteil, Charles. "Réflexions sur le problème des Peuls," Journal de la Société des Africanistes, XX (1950), 153–92.

Monteil, Vincent. "Une confrérie musulmane: Les Mourides du Sénégal," Archives de Sociologie des Religions, No. 14, 1962, pp. 77–101.

———. "Le Dyolof et Al-Bouri N'Diaye," BIFAN, XXVIII (1966), 595–636.

———. Esquisses Sénégalaises. Dakar: I.F.A.N., 1966.

———. L'Islam Noir. Paris: Seuil, 1964.

———. "Lat-Dior, Damel du Cayor et l'islamisation des Wolofs au XIXe siècle," Archives de Sociologie des Religions, No. 16, 1963, pp. 77–104.

Monteilhet, J. "Au Seuil d'un empire colonial: La Reprise de possession des établissements française d'Afrique," BCEHS, II (1918), 137–248.

Moore, Francis. Travels into the Inland Parts of Africa. London: E. Cave. 1738.

N'Diaye, Djiby. "Monographie du Cercle du Foundiougne." Paper submitted in fulfillment of degree requirements, Ecole Nationale d'Administration Sénégalaise.

Noël, Pere Bernard. "The Centenary of St. Joseph of Nagasobil: January 1863–January 1963," Bulletin Général, No. 707, 1963.

Noirot, Ernest. "Notice sur le Sine-Saloum, Journal Officiel du Senegal. Published serially, 1892.

Ollivon, Y. "L'Enseignement musulman dans les colonies françaises et specialement en A.O.F." Paper submitted in fulfillment of degree requirements, Ecole Nationale de la France d'Outre-Mer, 1944–45.

Park, Mungo. Travels into the Interior Districts of Africa. London: J. Murray, 1816.

Pasquier, Roger. "En marge de la guerre de sécession: Les Essais de culture au Sénégal," *Annales Africaines,* II (1955).

──────. "Villes du Sénégal au XIXe siècle," *La Revue Française de L'Histoire d'Outre-Mer,* XLVII (1960), 387–426.

Pelissier, Paul. "L'Arachide au Sénégal: Rationalisation et moderni-sation de sa culture." Vol. II of Etudes sénégalaises. St. Louis du Senegal: I.F.A.N., 1952.

──────. "Les Paysanes Sérères," *Les Cahiers d'Outre-Mer,* No. 22, 1953, pp. 105–27.

Peter, Georges. L'Effort français au Sénégal. Paris: Boccard, 1933.

Petite, Edouard. Organisation des colonies françaises de protectorat. Paris: Berger-Levrault, 1895.

Pichl, W. J. "The Cangin Group: A Language Group in Northern Senegal." Pittsburgh: Duquesne University Press, 1966. A mono-graph published for the Institute of African affairs, Duquesne University.

Pim, Sir Alan. The Financial and Economic History of the African Tropical Territories. Oxford: Clarendon, 1940.

Pinet-Laprade, J. M. E. "Notice sur les Sérères," *Revue Maritime et Coloniale,* XIII (1865), 479–92.

Piolet, J. B. Les Missions catholiques françaises au XIXe siècle. 6 vols. Paris: Colin, 1902.

Pruneau de Pommegorge, Antoine. Description de la Nigritie. Paris: Maradan, 1794.

Rancon, André. Dans la Haute Gambie. Paris: Société d'Editions Scientifiques, 1894.

Roberts, Stephen H. History of French Colonial Policy (1870–1925). 2 vols. London: P.S. King, 1929.

Robinson, Ronald, and Gallagher, John. Africa and the Victorians. London: Macmillan, 1963.

Roger, Jacques François. "Rapport sur un voyage par terre de Joal à St. Louis," in Annuaire et mémoires du Comité d'Etudes Histori-ques et Scientifique de l'A.O.F., 1916.

Rousseau, R. "Les Pluies au Sénégal, 1887 à 1927," *BCEHS,* XIV (1931), 157–82.

Roux, Emile. Manuel à l'usage des administrateurs et du personnel des affaires indigènes de la colonie du Sénégal. Paris: Challamel, 1911.

Sabatié, A. Le Sénégal. St. Louis du Sénégal: Imprimerie du Gouvernement, 1925.

Saint Lo, Père Alexis de. Relation du voyage du Cap Verd. Rouen: David Ferrand, 1637.

Saint Martin, Yves. "Les relations diplomatiques entre la France et l'Empire Toucouleur de 1860 à 1887," BIFAN, XXVII (1965), 183–222.

Sarr, Alioune. "Histoire du Sine-Saloum," Présence Africaine, No. 5, 1949, pp. 832–37.

Schefer, Christian. Instructions générales données de 1763 à 1870 aux gouverneurs et ordonnateurs des etablissements français en Afrique occidentale. 2 vols. Paris: Edouard Champion, 1921.

Schnapper, Bernard. "La Fin du régime de l'exclusif: Le Commerce étranger dans les possessions françaises d'Afrique tropicale (1817–1870)," Annales Africaines, VI (1959), 149–99.

———. La Politique et le commerce dans le Golfe de Guinée de 1838 à 1871. Paris: Mouton, 1961.

Schoelcher, Victor. L'Esclavage au Sénégal en 1880. Paris: Librairie Centrale des Publications Populaires, 1880.

Semonin, P. "The Almoravid Movement in the Western Sudan," Transactions of the Historical Society of Ghana, VII (1964), 42–59.

Senghor, Léopold Sédar. "Ce que l'homme noir apporte," in L'Homme de couleur. Ed., Cardinal Verdier. Paris: Plon, 1939.

———. Liberté I: Négritude et Humanisme. Paris: Le Seuil, 1964.

Shoberl, Frederick, ed. The World in Miniature: Africa. 4 vols. London: R. Ackermann, 1821.

Sidibé, Thiecouta. "Notes sur les transports et le developpement économique du Sénégal." Paper submitted in fulfillment of degree requirements, Ecole Nationale de la France d'Outre-Mer, 1958–59.

Silla, Ousmane. "Persistance des castes dans la société Wolof contemporaine," BIFAN, XXVIII (1966), 731–70.

Smith, H. F. C. "The Islamic Revolution of the 19th Century," Journal of the Historical Society of Nigeria, II (1961), 169–87.

Soh, Sire Abbas. Chroniques du Foûta Sénégalais. Trans. and ed., Maurice Delafosse and Henri Gaden. Paris: Leroux, 1913.

Stengers, Jean. "L'Imperialisme colonial de la fin du XIXe siècle:

Mythe ou réalité," *Journal of African History*, III (1962), 469–91.

Suret-Canale, Jean. Afrique noir occidentale et centrale. 2 vols. Paris: Editions Sociales, 1961 and 1964.

Sy, Cheikh Tidiane. "Traditionalisme Mouride et modernisation rurale au Sénégal." Unpublished dissertation, 6è Section, Ecole des Hautes Etudes, Université de Paris, 1965.

Trimingham, John Spencer. A History of Islam in West Africa. London: Oxford, 1962.

———. Islam in West Africa. Oxford: Clarendon, 1959.

Villard, André. Histoire du Sénégal. Dakar: M. Viale, 1943.

Waldman, Marilyn Robinson. "The Fulani *Jihad*: A Reassessment," *Journal of African History*, VI (1965), 333–56.

Witherell, Julian. "The Response of the Peoples of Cayor to French Penetration." Unpublished dissertation, University of Wisconsin, 1964.

Zuccarelli, François. "L'Entrepôt fictif de Gorée entre 1822 et 1852: Une Exception fictif au régime exclusif," *Annale Africaines*, VI (1959).

———. "Le Régime des engagés à temps au Sénégal (1817–48)," *Cahiers d'Etudes Africaines*, II (1962), 469–91.

Personal Informants

Abdou Boury Bâ, *chef d'arrondissement*; Birkelane, Senegal; Sept. 27, 1963 and Jan. 1964.

Al Hajj Lamine Bâ, Imam of Bathurst; the Gambia; Nov. 4, 1963.

Pierre Basse, student; University of Dakar, Senegal; Dec. 28–30, 1963.

Mustapha Cissay, student; Yundum College, the Gambia; Oct. 28, 1963.

Ibrahima Dem; Pikine, Senegal; Nov. 16, 1963.

Bur Saloum Fodé Diouf; Guinguineo, Senegal; Sept. 30, 1963.

Bur Sine Mahecor Diouf, Diakhao, Senegal; Aug. 13, 1963.

Mam Biram Diouf; Fatick, Senegal; Aug. 15, 1963.

Momadu Moctar Jeng, griot; Bathurst, the Gambia; Oct. 30, 1963.

Alpha Khan, Sefu of Jokardu; the Gambia; Oct. 31, 1963.

Alpha M'Bodj, *conseiller coutumier*; Djilor, Senegal; Oct. 26, 1963.

Amadou M'Bodj, Kaolack, Senegal; Nov. 20, 1963.

Thierno Omar N'Dao; Kaolack, Senegal; Sept. 15, 1963.

Latgarand N'Diaye, *chef d'arrondissement*; Sokone, Senegal; Nov. 20, 1963.

Macoumba N'Diaye; N'Gatch, Senegal; Nov. 20, 1963.

Mansour Bouna N'Diaye; Kaolack, Senegal; Aug. 25, 1963.

Al Hajj Ibrahima Niasse; Kaolack, Senegal; Sept. 12, 1963.

Al Hajj N'Diack Samb, griot; Kaolack, Senegal; Aug. 23, 1963.

Alioune Sarr, President of the Regional Assembly of Sine-Saloum; Kaolack, Senegal; Aug. 24 and Sept. 11, 1964.

Masayer Sise; Yundum, the Gambia; Oct. 28, 1963.

Thierno Sire Sow; Kaolack, Senegal; Sept. 14, 1963.

Collective renditions of oral tradition by villagers: Diakhao, Senegal, Aug. 13, 1963; Djilas, Senegal, Dec. 29, 1963; Latmingué, Senegal, Jan. 12, 1964; Saba, the Gambia, Nov. 1, 1964; and Thiewandou, Senegal, Sept. 28, 1963.

INDEX